THE
ORIGINAL
CURSE

THE ORIGINAL CURSE

DID THE CUBS THROW THE 1918 WORLD SERIES TO BABE RUTH'S RED SOX AND INCITE THE BLACK SOX SCANDAL?

SEAN DEVENEY

FOREWORD BY KEN ROSENTHAL

New York Chicago San Francisco Lisbon London Madrid Mexico City
Milan New Delhi San Juan Seoul Singapore Sydney Toronto

Library of Congress Cataloging-in-Publication Data

Deveney, Sean.
        The Original Curse: Did the Cubs throw the 1918 World Series to Babe Ruth's Red
Sox and incite the Black Sox Scandal? / Sean Deveney.
                p.   cm.
        Includes bibliographical references.
        ISBN 978-0-07-162997-3 (alk. paper)
            1. Chicago Cubs (Baseball team)—History.   2. World Series (Baseball)
(1918).   3. Baseball—Corrupt practices—United States—History.   I. Title.
        GV877.5. D48   2009
        796.357'640977311—dc22   2009014090

2 3 4 5 6 7 8 9 10 11 12 13 14 15 16 17 18 19 20 21 22   DOC/DOC   0 9

ISBN 978-0-07-162997-3
MHID   0-07-162997-1

*For Robbie, who shaped and inspired my ideas for this book;
for Mom and Dad, who read eagerly and pushed me along;
and for Brice, who always kept the volume on the television low
when I was working*

CONTENTS

Contents

FOREWORD

Ken Rosenthal

I have known Sean Deveney for the better part of a decade, and I've always known him to be a thorough journalist and an entertaining storyteller. Of course, I've gotten accustomed to seeing that from Deveney in 2,000- or 3,000-word magazine features. Now he's written a book, and even in this much longer format my opinion hasn't changed. He's both thorough and entertaining.

In *The Original Curse*, Deveney artfully attacks one of baseball's most widely accepted notions—that the sport's gambling problem in the early part of the 20th century was restricted to the 1919 Black Sox, who conspired to fix the World Series.

Baseball, by banning eight members of the Black Sox, including Shoeless Joe Jackson, attempted to portray gambling as an isolated problem. History has generally accepted that view. Deveney does not, challenging that preconception with the drive and curiosity of a classic whistle-blower. The job of a great writer is to provoke thought, and here Deveney has created a veritable riot for the imagination.

Gambling in baseball was rampant in the early part of the 20th century, and the pages that follow make a convincing argument that the 1918 World Series also was fixed—maybe not the entire Series, but at least part of it. Whether Deveney's conclusion is accurate we will never know, because the game did such a thorough job of covering up its gambling problem. This notion of a cover-up should ring true for those who follow baseball now, because baseball's gambling culture in that era was not unlike the steroid culture that infiltrated the sport eight decades later. Clandestine. Widespread. A charade worthy of deep and intense investigation.

The Red Sox met the Cubs in the 1918 Series, back when they were considered merely baseball teams, not the two most famously cursed voodoo dolls of sports. History shows that the Sox won the series, four games to two. But look closer. After Game 3, the players learned their share of the Series receipts—usually around $3,700 for the winners—would be about $1,200.

That fact alone would make a fix understandable, if not quite forgivable. But, by detailing the social and economic forces triggered by World War I, *The Original Curse* goes further and sympathetically examines the social forces that explain the players' motivations. Contrast that with today's scandalized players, the steroid users. They are not viewed sympathetically but were motivated by outside forces as well. Owners and players used their own rationales in reacting slowly to the excesses of the era. Baseball needed to recover from the players' strike of 1994–95. The players wanted to capitalize fully on that recovery and on their growing celebrity in an entertainment-driven society.

By the end of this book—after the players' haunting stories are detailed and fresh insight is given into an age marked by rampant inflation, domestic terrorism, and, above all, fear of Germans—the corruption of the 1918 World Series seems not only plausible but also probable. Deveney does not pretend to offer certainty. He is, after all, writing about events that took place 91 years ago. While he vividly portrays players such as the Cubs' shortstop prodigy Charley Hollocher and their future Hall of Fame pitcher Grover Cleveland Alexander, Deveney obviously did not follow the Cubs and Red Sox in 1918 the way authors track professional sports franchises today.

But, like any good journalist, he challenges conventional wisdom, especially that stemming from the self-righteous judgment of Kenesaw Mountain Landis, baseball's first-ever commissioner. Landis banned the Black Sox's eight alleged fixers, tainting them forever, though they were acquitted by a grand jury. At the time, baseball wanted the public to believe that Landis's ruling was the final say on the matter, that the sport had addressed the threat of gambling once and for all. Sound familiar? In 2007, baseball issued a report by former senator George Mitchell detailing the excesses of the Steroid Era. The report, combined with the toughest steroid testing in professional sports, was intended to be the final word on the issue of performance-enhancing drugs (PED) in baseball. But check the headlines. Neither the report nor the testing has achieved its desired effect.

As prevalent as steroids were in the baseball culture from the mid-1990s to the early 2000s, gambling might have been just as ubiquitous in 1918; gamblers shadowed players as diligently as drug pushers did decades later. Not every player back then gambled. Not every player today uses performance-enhancing drugs. But enough engaged in illicit activity to shape the perceptions of their respective eras.

The beauty of *The Original Curse* is the empathy displayed toward players who are effectively being accused of dishonesty. Few men are born cheaters, but many find temptation difficult to resist, particularly when desperate. If you were outfielder Max Flack, say, with a young wife and a newborn son, or Phil Douglas, with money problems that went hand in hand with a drinking problem, surely you would have been tempted to accept gambling money. And surely anyone facing the prospect of a tour in World War I's trenches also would have been tempted.

The cheaters of today—the wealthier ones anyway—are less forgivable. Alex Rodriguez said he used steroids because he felt pressure to justify a new $252 million contract. Barry Bonds and Roger Clemens, if the allegations against them are true, seemingly wanted only to achieve a higher level of immortality. Such rationales elicit little sympathy from disgusted fans. Players with more to lose, though, warrant a different view. When two pitchers, one a PED user, one not, vie to be the 5th starter or 12th man on the staff, the nonuser no doubt experiences tremendous pressure to cheat, knowing his career otherwise might be in jeopardy. The same goes for two shortstops or two outfielders of similar ability—any players in competition, really.

Context is critical, and Deveney provides just the right perspective. *The Original Curse* is not just about baseball. It is a sweeping portrait of America at war in 1918, one that examines baseball's place in that unsettled society. The revelation of this book is not simply what might have happened but why. In the end, the proper question is not "How could a player from that era fix the World Series?" It's "How could he not?"

AUTHOR'S NOTE

So that readers can truly see things from the perspective of the players, officials, and citizens of 1918, many of the chapters that follow begin with words and thoughts attributed to the various characters involved. Though the bulk of the book is strictly historical, these opening interludes are, of course, not verifiable. They are based on the facts of the actual life histories of the characters, though, and in many cases their language and attitudes are borrowed directly from newspaper, magazine, and other accounts. The reader simply seeking entertainment may take the interludes on their face. The reader interested in the historical background and the research on which these interludes are based, however, is encouraged to find that information in the end notes.

Special thanks to Peter Alter of the Chicago History Museum and the staff of the research library at the Baseball Hall of Fame.

ONE

Fixes and Curses: Aboard a Train with the White Sox

Summer 1919

Picture it. A bunch of ballplayers, lounging in a Pullman car in the summer of 1919, speeding past Midwestern greenery, jackets unbuttoned, sleeves rolled, games of poker and whist in high pitch. These are members of the White Sox, and they're talking, increasingly hushed, squint-eyed, smiling slyly, as if not quite sure about the nature of the conversation, not sure if this is for real. Because if this is serious, it's the beginning of something very big. A conspiracy. A conspiracy to throw—take a dive, lose intentionally—the biggest event of the season, the game's crown jewel: the World Series.

Who would have to be involved? How much money could be made? And, most important, could an entire World Series really be fixed?

These players were not dumb. Game-fixing talk on team trains was nothing new. Sometimes it was idle chatter. Sometimes not. Gambling and baseball were already intricately linked, the sport being one of the nation's most popular outlets for both casual and serious bettors. Small-timers could get in on widely circulated pools for dimes and quarters, bets could be made easily in the stands of any ballpark—where gamblers would haggle and shout like traders in a Casablanca market—and for those who preferred higher stakes, there were back-room bookies who made their livings out of pool halls and cigar stores.

For the public, that's where the association between gambling and baseball ended. Players played. Gamblers gambled. Ne'er the twain did meet.

This was what the game's overlords wanted the public to think. In truth, ballplayers were never far from gamblers, but the perception of the game as pure and honest was well crafted and managed. In 1914, American League president Ban Johnson wrote an article called "The Greatest Game in the World" that typified this see-no-evil posture. "There is no place in baseball for the gambler; no room in the ball park for his evil presence," Johnson wrote. "The game, notwithstanding loose occasional charges, stands solely and honestly on its merits. In the heat of an exciting race for the pennant, with clockwork organizations in rivalry, imagination sometimes runs riot and assertions are made, under stress of excitement, that games are not played on the level. As a matter of fact, to fix a ball game, that is, to arrange in advance a scheme by which one team would be sure to win, would be harder than drawing water out of an empty well."[1]

This was tripe. Gamblers were all over baseball. They knew players intimately, and fixing a game was not difficult. While the 1919 White Sox held hushed conversations about the World Series, it may have been that members of the New York Giants were simultaneously conspiring to throw the entire *season* to the Cincinnati Reds.[2] Approach a player of the era with a notion of fixing a game or two, and you'd likely get a range of reactions. Some reveled in it, because the extra money was handy and over a 154-game season no one would notice if a few games were not played on the level. Other players might pucker their lips in disapproval and say, "No, thanks." Some might even tell the team's manager about their crooked teammates. Still others might answer a fix proposal with a punch to the jaw. Whichever reaction came forth, though, there would be no long-term consequences—few players squealed on teammates, and when they did, their complaints were ignored. Gambling was simply tolerated, and gamblers were just part of the bawdy off-field scenery that accompanied baseball teams, like high-stakes card games, hotel bars, and women who did not answer to "Mrs."

In a 1956 *Sports Illustrated* article, Chick Gandil—one of those members of the '19 White Sox—remembered the attitude toward gamblers at the time: "Where a baseball player would run a mile these days to avoid a gambler, we mixed freely. Players often bet. After the games, they would sit in lobbies and bars with gamblers, gabbing away. Most of the gamblers we knew were honorable Joes who would never think of fixing a game. They were happy just to be booking and betting."[3] Another player of that era, catcher Eddie Ainsmith, later told an interviewer, "Everybody bet in those days, because it was a way of making up for the little we were paid."[4]

So it wasn't unusual for the White Sox to be talking this way, about taking a fall for a cut of the gambling loot. Not just any loot—World Series loot. The 1919 White Sox were the best team in baseball, spending most of the season in first place. As likely American League champions, their spot in the World Series was almost assured. No matter who won the National League pennant, the White Sox would be favored to win the championship. Even modest bets made on the NL underdog would yield big payoffs. Which was why the White Sox's discussion of throwing that Series was so intriguing. It had the potential to be very big indeed.

Now picture this: While considering the World Series fix, one of the White Sox says, "Hey, why not? The Cubs did it last year."

Whoa.

We know what happened to the '19 White Sox. They did throw that year's World Series, to the Reds. A year later, in 1920, they got caught and forever became known as the Black Sox. Eight members of the team were indicted in a Chicago court, acquitted by a sympathetic jury, but then famously banned from baseball for life by Commissioner Kenesaw Mountain Landis despite the acquittal. Their story was retold in a popular book and movie, *Eight Men Out*, though the facts of the Black Sox case are still debated. The trial was poorly run, documents disappeared, and interference from baseball officials and gamblers left the truth forever obscured. What cannot be debated is that the Black Sox attempted the loosest, clumsiest, and most audacious gambling fix in American sports history. What also cannot be debated is that they were hardly the first, or the last, crooked players of their era. They're just the ones that history remembers best.

The conversation on the train, though, indicates that members of the Black Sox had heard rumors about another fix before plotting their own. At least that's how pitcher Eddie Cicotte remembered it. Cicotte was one of the chief conspirators in the Black Sox plan and the first to confess. He mentioned rumors about the Cubs matter-of-factly in a deposition, saying: "The way it started, we were going east

3

on the train. The ballplayers were talking about somebody trying to fix the National League ball players or something like that in the World's Series of 1918. Well anyway there was some talk about them offering $10,000 or something to throw the Cubs in the Boston Series. There was talk that somebody offered this player $10,000 or anyway the bunch of players were offered $10,000. This was on the train going over. Somebody made a crack about getting money, if we got into the Series."

This should have perked up the ears of investigators. But, though the investigation originally promised to tackle widespread aspects of baseball gambling, political struggles among the game's leaders (chiefly, White Sox owner Charles Comiskey and Ban Johnson) tightened the focus on the Black Sox. Cicotte's Cubs rumor—as well as significant other rumors about the Cubs—was discarded, and only the 1919 World Series fix was bared by the legal system. Still, if Cicotte is to be believed, there's reason to wonder whether, in putting together their series-fixing scheme, the 1919 Black Sox had immediate inspiration from their Cubs friends on the North Side, who had lost a chaotic 1918 World Series in six games to the American League's Red Sox.

There's virtually no chance that the Black Sox were the first team to play a crooked World Series. In the *SI* article, Gandil discusses the World Series proposal Boston gambler Sport Sullivan made to him in 1919. "I said to Sullivan it wouldn't work," Gandil said. "He answered, 'Don't be silly. It's been pulled before and it can be again.'"[5] But other than 1919, there's little hard evidence of fixed championship games. There is, however, a long list of World Series whose honesty remains dubious:

- As far back as 1903, when the Boston Americans (later the Red Sox) played the Pirates in the first World Series, catcher Lou Criger claimed he was offered $12,000 by gamblers to call bad pitches. Criger turned them down and caught the entire series.
- Ahead by a count of 3–1 (with one tie) over the Giants in the 1912 World Series, Red Sox manager Jake Stahl was ordered by owner Jimmy McAleer to start pitcher Buck O'Brien instead of ace Joe Wood, who had gone 34–5 and already had two wins in the series. Stahl and Red Sox players knew McAleer's motives—

he wanted a seventh game, because it would take place at Fenway Park, allowing McAleer to collect more gate-receipt money. Stahl begrudgingly started O'Brien, and the Red Sox lost. In the next game, Wood and his teammates probably laid down. Wood had an impossibly bad outing, allowing seven hits and six runs in the first inning, and Boston lost, 11–4. In *Red Sox Century*, Glenn Stout and Richard A. Johnson write, "It is not inconceivable that the Red Sox, already upset with management, threw the game in order to recoup their losses by laying money on the Giants in game seven at favorable odds. In the days that followed, Boston newspapers intimated precisely that."[6] The Red Sox did go on to win the series.

- When Sullivan told Gandil that the World Series had been fixed before, he may have been talking about the greatest upset in series history to date, the sweep of Connie Mack's mighty, 99-win Athletics by the 1914 "Miracle" Braves. Rumors held that Sullivan had been involved in the fixing of that series. Songwriter George M. Cohan supposedly cleaned up on the Braves—and Sullivan was Cohan's betting broker.[7] Mack never accused his team of throwing the series, but after the series he dumped half his regulars and half his starting pitchers. The A's sank to 44–108 the next season.
- In the 1917 World Series, in which the White Sox beat the Giants, New York manager John McGraw suspected something was off about his second baseman, Buck Herzog. McGraw later told writer Fred Lieb that Herzog had played out of position throughout the series and that Herzog had "sold him out."[8] Herzog would later be accused of fixing games with the 1919 Giants—and the 1920 Cubs.
- Before the 1920 World Series between Brooklyn and Cleveland—while the Black Sox investigation was barreling through baseball—Illinois State's Attorney Maclay Hoyne declared that he had evidence showing that the upcoming series was fixed too. "It appeared that the gamblers had met with such success that they were brazen in their plan to ruin the national sport," Hoyne said. "What will be the result? I will not say at this time, but I will venture the assertion that there is more and a bigger scandal coming in the baseball world."[9] Hoyne's evidence, though, never materialized. The Indians won, 5–2.

5

- During the 1921 World Series, Lieb heard a story about Yankees pitcher Carl Mays pitching less than his best because he had been paid off by gamblers. Lieb reported the story to Landis, who took no action against Mays. Years later, Lieb sat with Yankees owner T. L. Huston, who had been drinking. Lieb recalled the conversation: "'I wanted to tell you that some of our pitchers threw the World Series games on us in both 1921 and 1922,' he mumbled. 'You mean that Mays matter of the 1921 World Series?' I asked. He said, 'Yes, but there were others—other times, other pitchers.' By now he was almost in a stupor and stumbled off to bed."[10] The Yankees lost both the '21 and '22 World Series. Mays lost three of the four games he started in the two series.

The Black Sox have *Eight Men Out* to commemorate their role in baseball's gambling era, but the Cubs were nearly as deep in betting associations of the day as the South Siders. Even most Chicagoans do not know that the Black Sox scandal might never have become public knowledge if not for a smaller-scale Cubs gambling scandal. Only after word spread that some Cubs had thrown a game on August 31, 1920, did the state of Illinois convene a grand jury to investigate baseball gambling. That grand jury, brought together because of the Cubs, eventually uncovered the 1919 plot. (Thus White Sox fans who are harassed by Cubs fans over the Black Sox should be quick to point out that it was crooked Cubs who started it all.) And just before the start of the 1920 season, the Cubs released a player—Lee Magee—who admitted to club officials that he had wagered on ball games.

The Cubs had gambling ties at all levels. One of the odd features of the Black Sox trial was the calling of Cubs ex-president Charley Weeghman as a witness. Under oath, Weeghman testified to his close relationship with Chicago gambler Mont Tennes. According to Weeghman, Tennes told him as early as August 1919 that the upcoming World Series would be fixed. Weeghman claimed he didn't give the notion much credence and thus could not remember whether he had reported it to baseball officials. Of course, why Weeghman associated with the likes of Tennes, the biggest (and baddest) Chicago gambling figure of his day, is a mystery.

This does not mean the Cubs of the time were completely tainted or that the World Series of 1903, '12, '17, '19, '20, and '21 were *all* fixed. But there's an awful lot of smoke for there to have been just one fire. No series-fixing evidence remains, which should not be surprising. It was by design. One of the primary aims of Ban Johnson and his friends who ruled "the greatest game in the world" was to push the view that baseball stood honestly on its merits, and to do that they snuffed out rumors about crooked players and kept whatever they knew about gamblers in baseball safely out of public view.

But Cicotte's deposition—part of a series of Black Sox documents purchased by the Chicago History Museum and shared for direct quotation for the first time in this book—provides a voice from the grave, raising a rumor and, at the same time, some questions. What if the '19 White Sox had a very recent and close-to-home inspiration for their bungled fix? What if the World Series of 1918, baseball's most tumultuous season, was thrown? What if the Cubs and Red Sox, in their only on-field meeting of the 20th century, played in a World Series tainted by gambling interests?

Considering what would become of the two franchises after the 1918 World Series, that would be fitting. Entering '18, few teams were more successful in the brief history of modern baseball than the Red Sox in the American League and the Cubs in the National League. In the first 14 World Series, each team made four appearances—the Red Sox won four times, and the Cubs won two. Boston was an unstable franchise, having undergone six ownership changes in 15 years, but fan support was strong and the team was a consistent contender. The Cubs excelled in the early 1900s behind their famed infield trio of Joe Tinker, John Evers, and Frank Chance and put on some of the best pennant races in history, against archrival McGraw and his powerful New York Giants. From 1904 to 1913, either the Cubs or the Giants won every NL pennant except one, and their '08 chase was a classic.

But the Red Sox and Cubs never met in a World Series until '18, and a funny thing happened after they did. Both teams took epic downward turns, their brief histories as dominant franchises forever replaced with a different kind of history altogether. The Red Sox and Cubs spent the rest of the 20th century, and into the 21st century, as baseball's two most star-crossed franchises. For the next 85 years the Red Sox would not win a World Series and would make just 10 play-off appearances. The Cubs would not win a World Series at all and would also make just 10 play-off appearances. The way the teams lost—blowing huge leads, making confounding mental errors, falling apart at the worst possible moment—left their devoted fan bases pained and desperate for explanation. To this day the mere mention of certain players and phenomena can induce psychosis among fans in both the Hub and the Windy City.

The black cat. Tim Flannery. Steve Bartman.

Bucky Dent. Bill Buckner. Aaron Boone.

Under those circumstances, it's natural for fans to turn to the supernatural. Surely there must have been something beyond human understanding intervening at Wrigley Field and Fenway Park. Surely, somewhere, baseball gods were angry, and for decades it was the Red Sox and Cubs who would pay. Thus the teams share both a sad-sack history and the distinction of the two most famous curses in sports. For the Red Sox, the curse was traced to the regrettable decision of team owner Harry Frazee to sell the greatest player in history, Babe Ruth, to the Yankees in 1920. That move was christened "The Curse of the Bambino," which was finally broken in 2004. For the Cubs, the curse source is William Sianis, owner of the famous Billy Goat Tavern under Michigan Avenue. As the story goes, when ushers asked Sianis to remove his pet goat from Wrigley Field (Sianis had bought a ticket for it) during the 1945 World Series, the angered barman cursed the team. The Cubs lost that series and have not played in another since.

But maybe those curses are entirely misplaced. What if the gods were not angry about Ruth or Sianis? What if the karmic problems of the Red Sox and Cubs started with their participation in a fixed World Series played at the end of a wartime season that probably never should have happened in the first place? Wouldn't that be cause for a curse if ever there was one? Two dominant teams, a fixed World Series, and decades of doom. Makes as much sense as a couple of curses imposed on behalf of a sold player and a malodorous goat, right?

8

Curses are, of course, silly. They're irrational ways to answer this perfectly rational question: "Why doesn't my team win?" In the cases of the Cubs and Red Sox, that question was asked so many times and over such a long period that a curse came to look like just as logical an answer as any other. Reasonable fans don't take the notion of curses seriously, and there are ways to explain the years of failure that defined both the Cubs and the Red Sox. For example, the teams play in relatively small parks that should favor power hitters, and for years neither paid proper attention to pitching and defense.

There are other explanations. Even after the sale of Ruth (which was accompanied by the sale of several other Red Sox stars to the Yankees), Boston didn't have the resources or the executive know-how to keep up with the dominant Yankees. Beyond that, the franchise's resistance to accepting African-American players put it at a competitive disadvantage. The Cubs, meanwhile, have a history of indifferent ownership, with lucrative national television and radio networks that have bolstered the franchise's bottom line. On-the-field performance was almost irrelevant to profits, and the team had little incentive to spend big money on top free agents. These are far more credible explanations for failure than voodoo and curses.

Still, most of us take curses for what they are: fun, offbeat ways to imagine that baseball is at the center of the universe and that, somewhere, higher powers dictate the success and failure we see on the field. And we like to think that higher power has a solid sense of right and wrong, as well as a long memory—100 years, even. If we can, with a wink and a smile, agree that baseball gods are meting out curses, the throwing of baseball's annual grand finale would have to get their attention.

As for 1918, there is nothing that can definitively prove a fix, and we should be mindful that evidence of a fix in that World Series is circumstantial. It's rumors and vague suspicions. It's dead men talking, like Cicotte, with no opportunity to press them for details. It's a skeptical reading of box scores and play-by-plays. It's questionable connections and questionable characters, within the teams themselves and lurking on the periphery.

Cicotte's deposition is not the only instance in which the possibility of a crooked 1918 World Series was raised. Henry "Kid" Becker, an associate of some of the St. Louis gamblers who were involved in the fixing of the 1919 World Series, had planned to fix the '18 series but came up short on cash and was murdered seven months later.[11] In his 1965 book, *The Hustler's Handbook*, baseball executive Bill Veeck transcribed parts of the lost writings of Harry Grabiner, longtime secretary to White Sox owner Charles Comiskey. Grabiner and Comiskey were wise to the Black Sox and hired a private investigator to look into the '19 series. Grabiner's diary chronicled the investigator's findings all over baseball. (It's important to note that Comiskey and Grabiner had no intention of going on a public crusade with the information their investigator gathered—their goal was to cover up whatever gambling they found, not expose it.) Among the notes Grabiner made was the name of Gene Packard, a pitcher for the Cubs in '16 and part of '17. Next to Packard's name, Grabiner wrote: "1918 Series fixer."

Veeck's reaction: "Oh boy."[12]

Whether or why the Cubs and Red Sox, as franchises, have been cursed can be debated, as can the possibility of a 1918 fix. But there's something strange about those teams that goes beyond franchise futility. There's a bizarre level of *personal* futility too. Scan the rosters of those who played and worked for the Cubs and Red Sox (especially the Cubs, the supposed fixers) and look at what happened to them after the 1918 World Series. You'll find an inordinate number of tragic endings, disturbing downturns, and sullied reputations—especially sullied by gambling scandals. You'll find that, not only did the 1918 World Series seem to leave what had been two very successful franchises dragging the ball-and-chain of stubborn curses, but a high number of individuals involved with those franchises suffered cursed fates too.

Weeghman, the team president and one of the city's best-known businessmen, went broke 16 months after the World Series. Red Sox owner Harry Frazee would die young, at age 48, and his lasting legacy would be pariahdom in Boston decades later. The Cubs' ace pitcher left to fight in World War I and came back an alcoholic and epileptic, later tainted as "crooked" in Grabiner's diary. One star Red Sox pitcher would get caught up in a gambling scandal of his own making, and another would become the only pitcher to kill a man during a game. Two reserve Cubs who left for war in '18 died young, one during an appendicitis operation and the other after a fall from a building. One star Cubs pitcher was forced out of baseball for contract jumping, and another suffered an arm injury from which he never recovered. A fourth Cubs pitcher, an alcoholic, was banished in 1922 after writing a suspicious letter to an opposing player (who had been his teammate with the '18 Cubs). Chicago's star shortstop mysteriously quit baseball at the peak of his career and later committed suicide. One Red Sox player, three Cubs players, and a Cubs secretary wound up entangled in the Black Sox scandal.

How's that for cursed?

But the story of these two teams is about more than curses, more than baseball, more than gambling. It's about the lives of those involved in baseball that year. The 1918 season presented unique pressures, which altered attitudes toward the game, toward gambling, toward salaries, and toward prospects for the future, not just as players but as men and citizens in a very turbulent United States. There was a constant threat of domestic terrorism. The drive toward prohibition was on, and there was a moral tug-of-war over vice—including gambling, which was as strong in Chicago and Boston as anywhere in the nation. Inflation was near its worst in history, making whatever money Americans had on hand increasingly worthless. And there was the Great War, the most brutal conflict in history, which was thrashing Europe with mechanized warfare, introducing the world to battles fought with submarines, airplanes, poisonous gas, long-range guns, tanks, and trench warfare. In 1918 the war was being joined by waves of just-drafted young American soldiers, ballplayers included.

This was a set of circumstances ripe for crookedness in baseball. Indeed, it was in 1918 that baseball's gambling problem finally pushed through to the surface, as actual allegations of game fixing, backed by evidence, were publicly brought before a league president with the press watching. It was due to happen, and with all of the '18 season played under the threat of early closure (and the probable shutting down of the game for 1919), it should be no surprise that this was the year when the baseball-gambling link began to unravel. It was in the 1918 season—not in the fixed 1919 World Series—we can say, for the first time with utter certainty, that there was game fixing in baseball.

That fixing might have spilled into the World Series. But, before judging the alleged fixers, we should get to know them, to know how the world looked at the time. It's not hard to muster empathy—those times were similar to our own. There was war abroad and fear at home, a stumbling economy and rampant corruption. There wasn't Brad Pitt and Angelina Jolie, but there was Doug Fairbanks and Mary Pickford. In baseball, writers of that time, as in our time, pined for the good old days, when players were not overpaid, when the game wasn't dependent on specialists and dominated by commercialism, when wealthier teams could not simply buy pennants. And in 1918, baseball was seeing problems crop up from the gambling issue it had ignored and covered up for the previous 15 years or so—the same pattern of

11

denial that has defined baseball's approach to today's problems with performance-enhancing drugs.

We can't prove that the Cubs threw all or even part of the '18 series, but we can wonder—if they did, would reasonable, moral people have done the same in their situation? If participation in that World Series left both the Red Sox and Cubs franchises with curses to carry into the following century, if the baseball gods can't find them worthy of forgiveness, at least, maybe, we mortals can.

TWO

Luck: Charley Weeghman

CHICAGO, SUNDAY, DECEMBER 9, 1917

It was still dark. Lucky Charley cinched the buttons of his waistcoat. He smoothed the bottom of the waistcoat with both hands, dropped his watch into his pocket, squeezing the fob into the opposite pocket. He slid into his overcoat, pressed his derby over his forehead, and grabbed his kit and bag. He took a deep breath and looked in the mirror. Natty, he thought, smiling. They'd called him a natty dresser as far back as his days at King's diner down in the Loop, where he was a $10-a-week waiter hustling eggs and doughnuts and mugs of Postum to the midnight crowds, mostly newsmen. But that was 20 years ago. Gray hairs had presented themselves in the interim. Charley patted his waistcoat again. Still thin. Now he was one of the best-known businessmen in the city, owner of a chain of lunchrooms, a movie theater, a billiard parlor. Lucky Charley was a millionaire, president of the Chicago Cubs.

Millionaire? Charley knew better. He was no millionaire, but the papers liked to speculate that he was, and he'd done little to discourage them. He hadn't really been a waiter at King's either—more like a night manager—but Charley had spent enough time around Chicago's newsmen to know that what they wanted was a good and splashy story, details be damned. So he'd let them believe he was a waiter-turned-millionaire.

Charley knew how to work newsmen, and he was planning to do it again this week. When he got to New York, he was going to give Chicago a story, a big story. A Cubs story. He'd give them the greatest pitcher and catcher in baseball today. Perhaps, too, the greatest young hitter. Yes, there was a corker of a story in New York.

Charley stopped in to kiss his daughter, Dorothy, on the forehead before he left. He did not kiss his wife, Bessie. He took the elevator to the lobby of the Edgewater,[1] and when he got there he gave a wink and a thank-you to the deskmen who had, with alacrity, brought him the telegram hurrying him to New York today, Sunday, rather than tomorrow.[2] The boys gave Charley goofy smiles. Charley loved playing the part of baseball magnate. The lobby boys did not care a whit when the well-to-do lumberyard owners and doctors and auto parts suppliers who lived here at the Edgewater Beach Hotel received messages. But when Charley got a telegram, it was different. The boys fought to deliver it, because they just knew it had something to do with the North Side ball club, and each wanted some part, however small, in putting over the Cubs' latest transaction. They looked at Charley with admiration. Charley liked being admired.

This morning the telegram told him there was a change of schedule and he should get to New York early for the league meetings. Charley stepped out of the lobby, into a blast of morning cold, to the waiting car. As he slid into the backseat, Charley looked up at the Edgewater Beach Hotel, with its stucco facade and red terra-cotta roof. It looked ridiculous, a luxury resort plucked off the Riviera and placed on Sheridan Road, along the icy shore of Lake Michigan. But the Edgewater's mere existence, let alone the fact that he lived there, helped to assure Charley that he was as lucky as everyone thought him. These days he needed that assurance.

Coincidences always seemed to fall in Charley's favor. For example, back in 1914, John T. Connery's syndicate had attempted to buy the Cubs from Charles Taft for $750,000, promising another $500,000 to upgrade the Cubs' West Side park. Taft turned down Connery. Charley wanted the Cubs too, but he couldn't afford them. Instead he bought into the Chicago Whales of the upstart Federal League, which was challenging the dominance of the American and National leagues. By 1915 the Federal League had failed but had done enough financial damage to the other leagues that Taft now wanted out. As part of baseball's peace deal with the Feds, Charley was allowed to

Charley Weeghman, ever the sharp dresser, broke into Chicago's baseball scene as owner of the Federal League's Whales in 1914. (NATIONAL BASEBALL HALL OF FAME LIBRARY, COOPERSTOWN, N.Y.)

15

put together a group to buy the Cubs. *For $500,000.* And Charley, naturally, moved the team to the Whales' new park at Addison and Sheffield.[3] Connery, having missed out on his chance at the Cubs, tried his hand at the hotel game instead. He built the Edgewater. How about that? Charley wound up with the Cubs for one-third less than what Connery offered, and Connery wound up building Charley a place to live.

See? Lucky him.

But lately Charley's reservoir of luck had been draining, thanks to the damned war in Europe. It was difficult enough to watch America mobilize against Germany, his parents' birthplace (the family name was actually Veichman but had been Americanized after the family settled in Richmond, Indiana).[4] For Charley, though, the war was primarily a financial matter. Food rationing had sapped his quick-serve restaurants, which had once seen lines snake around corners in the downtown Loop district. Charley was Chicago's Lunchroom King, and, at its peak his flagship spot at Madison just west of Dearborn served 5,000 customers daily.[5]

With the war on, though, the government was conserving resources, and Herbert Hoover (head of the Food Administration) was single-handedly crushing the restaurant business. Hoover pushed the population to cut out certain food groups on certain days—wheatless Mondays and Wednesdays, meatless Tuesdays, porkless Thursdays and Saturdays. Flour was in short supply. Sugar and milk too. Hoover tried to get Americans to eat fish, which was fine in the East but no easy chore in the Midwest, especially for a hurry-up lunchroom like the Weeghman chain. Chicagoans were not eaters of fish, and most fish caught in Illinois rivers was sent to New York. Hoover also asked consumers to cut back on grains, making the bread for sandwiches—that staple of the lunchroom—harder to come by. In September 1917, to conserve the supply of grains, whiskey production was banned, which did not affect Charley's restaurants but surely affected his ability to cope with his losses. (Beer production, too, would be banned later—the path to prohibition in America was rooted as much in patriotism as in morality.)

Charley's restaurants were his income. Truthfully, he was a financial lightweight in baseball. He valued his position and his stock holdings in the team, but the Cubs' real clout was in the investors he had assembled when he bought the club. These were Chicago's wealthiest businessmen, like meatpacker J. Ogden Armour, Sears-Roebuck head Julius Rosenwald, and chewing gum magnate William Wrigley Jr. The group was so flush with cash that, when the sale was first announced, one newspaper giddily estimated that the Cubs were a "$100,000,000 ball club."[6] That was a stretch. Either way, Charley's bank account was not nearly on a par with those of the Cubs' other owners. He was much better at being around wealthy men than being a wealthy man himself.

He also wasn't very good, it seemed, at assembling baseball teams. In two years at the helm, success on the field was elusive for Charley, and 1917 had been a particular nightmare. The United States officially entered the war in April, and baseball attendance plummeted. Chicago was still baseball crazy, but for the second year in a row the Cubs struggled to a fifth-place finish with a young, no-name roster. Meanwhile, on the South Side, the White Sox rolled to the AL pennant and led the league in attendance by a wide margin—684,521 fans, well ahead of the Cubs' 360,218. This greatly displeased the Cubs' backers. At least they could afford the financial hit. Charley couldn't. With his restaurants strangled by rationing, if he wasn't making money on his Cubs holdings, he wasn't making money. To stay afloat financially, Charley took the painful step of selling shares of Cubs stock to his friend Wrigley. Publicly he was still the face of the Cubs, but privately he was ceding more and more power to Wrigley.

This wasn't how it was supposed to be. When he had gained control of the team, Charley spent lavishly to publicize and aggrandize the Cubs. He employed endless parades and brass bands and dancing girls (there were always dancing girls at Weeghman events, which might help explain his impending divorce). On the spring training trip of '16, Charley chartered a special Cubs train to camp in Tampa, outfitted with electric pianos, record players, canaries, fine foods, and a singing group called the Florida Troubadors. There was even a billiard table. *Baseball Magazine* reported, "These gorgeous accommodations were really for ballplayers and not for millionaires."[7]

The pool table on the train, it turns out, was a good metaphor for Charley's finances—impressive looking from the outside but not reflecting the reality inside. The pool table was a beauty, a Brunswick, and as the train stopped along the way to Florida in March 1916, those who saw folks calmly shooting pool most likely whistled in amazement at the decadence. That's because it was easy to play pool on a train when the train was stopped. For most of the trip, the train was speeding and bumping along. As *Tribune* writer James Crusinberry noted: "Playing billiards [on a moving train] was like trying to spear goldfish with a table fork. A few of the downstate boys were fooled, however, because whenever the train stopped someone grabbed a cue and started playing, while the fellows outside gazed in wonder."[8]

17

From the outside, folks gazed in wonder at Lucky Charley Weegh-man, the $10-a-week-waiter-turned-millionaire-magnate. From the inside, it was a different story.

In the winter before the 1918 season, Charley still had hope. He just needed a quick end to the war, and some felt that could happen by the spring. It wasn't hard to project how things would go from there: mass celebration at home, the end of rationing, lines of diners back at his restaurants, Americans flocking to their favorite diversions. Like baseball. Charley's task this winter was to land top players for the Cubs so that when fans came back they'd come to the North Side. Cubs owners, tired of losing while the White Sox were winning, had authorized Weeghman to spend $250,000 to acquire players. It was an absurd amount. The biggest purchase price one team had given another for a player to that point was $55,000, paid by Cleveland to the Red Sox for Tris Speaker in 1916. Theoretically, $250,000 would buy four Speakers, and there weren't four for sale. But Charley made a splash with fans and press wags by very publicly announcing his bankroll. *The Sporting News* labeled him "The Mad Spendthrift."[9]

Few shared Charley's optimism. Overall, baseball's 1917 attendance was 1,283,525, a staggering 19.7 percent drop from the '16 season. That, in a way, made that winter the perfect time for player shopping. Some of the game's magnates, concerned about the war and facing continued attendance problems, were eager to cut salaries by selling players, hoping to make up for the previous year's losses and gird the bottom line for the coming season.

It was this business—plucking players and building a sure pen-nant winner at the National League meetings—that called Charley to New York a day early on that frigid day in December. It was only four degrees outside, and Charley's early-morning hurrying was prob-ably unnecessary. His train left at noon. At the LaSalle Street station, Charley met Walter Craighead, the Cubs' 31-year-old business man-ager. Craighead and Weeghman boarded the 20th Century Limited, a businessman's special that could zip to New York in less than 18 hours, and Charley had no worries about keeping himself natty over the trip. The 20th Century had a tailor, a manicurist, saltwater baths, and a barber to ensure that businessmen aboard would not arrive in the East a stubbled mess.

Craighead was Charley's brother-in-law, married to his younger sister, Myral. Charley had been criticized that winter for dumping well-respected team secretary Charley Williams, who had been in Chicago baseball for 33 years, longer than Craighead had been alive. But, for Weeghman, family trumped all. His clan was from conservative German stock and did not necessarily approve of his showmanship and man-about-town bearing, but that did not seem to affect the family bond. He had given his two younger brothers jobs running his restaurants. He had moved his parents to Chicago from Indiana and taught his father baseball. Craighead had no real experience in business or baseball, but Charley still pushed out Williams for his brother-in-law.

In New York, Craighead and Charley were to meet Cubs manager Fred Mitchell, who would be coming down from his farm in Massachusetts, to settle on a strategy for adding players. Already the Cubs had one big deal all but complete. Back in November, Weeghman had agreed to a blockbuster deal with Phillies owner William F. Baker. The Cubs would send two low-level players and a large sum of money to Philadelphia for ace Grover Cleveland Alexander and catcher Bill Killefer. Baker had sworn Charley to secrecy. He wanted to wait before announcing the deal, because he knew the trade would not play well with fans or the press.

That's because Alexander was, by far, the best pitcher in baseball. Off the mound, he looked like a typical Nebraska farm boy, with a slow, loping gait and a cap that never quite fit his head. But on the mound, he was devastating, with a fastball that zipped in from his three-quarters delivery and pinpoint control with his breaking ball. He was still only 30 and had been incredibly durable, leading the league in innings pitched and complete games for the previous four years straight. Those four years—leading up to the trade to the Cubs—might be the greatest four-season span any pitcher has ever had. Alexander led the NL in wins (121 total) and strikeouts all four seasons and won the ERA title three of the four years.

Killefer, Alexander's best friend and batterymate, wasn't bad either. Though not a great hitter, he was considered the best in the league at working with pitchers and calling a game. That Charley was willing to trade for him shows just how determined he was to build a winner. In 1914, Killefer had signed a contract to jump to Weeghman's Federal

19

League Whales but jumped back to Philadelphia when Baker upped his contract offer. Charley sued Killefer (challenging baseball's treasured reserve clause) and lost, but still, the judge in the case scolded Killefer, calling him, "a person upon whose pledged word little or no reliance can be placed."[10]

The Cubs needed players, though, and this was no time for Charley to hold a grudge. The deal for Alexander and Killefer was set, and if all went well, Charley would add a third feather to the Cubs' cap. Mitchell had been pushing the team to buy the best young infielder in the game, Rogers Hornsby, from St. Louis. That would be trickier, because the Cardinals' new executive, Branch Rickey, already had been giving the Cubs pains on a Hornsby deal. Charley wasn't sure how to handle Rickey, who was different from most of the game's magnates because he could not be plied with good scotch or a bawdy story about some dancing girl. To Charley, Rickey must have seemed so strict a Methodist that he felt a tall glass of lemonade was a sin. But still, Charley had an endless supply of cash, and surely Rickey could not turn down cash.

Aboard the 20th Century, Charley and Craighead could daydream about the 1918 Cubs roster, complete with Alexander, Killefer, and, maybe, Hornsby on board. Mad Spendthrift, indeed.

By 5:00 P.M. on Tuesday, the second day of the NL meetings, word of the Killefer-Alexander deal spread through the Waldorf-Astoria Hotel, the site of the meetings. Weeghman stepped into the lobby to a pack of reporters and well-wishers. (Today's baseball scribes who chase general managers around hotel lobbies at league meetings can take comfort: it's an old tradition.) Weeghman ratcheted up the charm. He claimed he had paid Baker $80,000 for Killefer and Alexander, plus two players—Pickles Dillhoefer and Mike Prendergast. Weeghman said the total value going to the Phillies was $100,000. The *Chicago Daily News* took Weeghman at his word, and the headline in that evening's paper read, in large type: "CUBS PAY $100,000 FOR ALEXANDER AND KILLEFER."[11] That wasn't quite true. The Cubs paid closer to $55,000, and whatever creative math Weeghman used to value Dillhoefer and Prendergast remains a mystery. But bigger numbers made for a bigger splash. In an aw-shucks style befitting his rags-to-riches, former-waiter persona, Weeghman claimed that his heart nearly stopped beating when he signed the check. "This is the biggest transaction ever completed in the history of baseball," he declared.[12]

Things were less joyful for Baker and the Phillies. In selling two stars, Baker had ensured 1918 would be a disaster, but he was betting that, with the war, it would be a less expensive disaster this way. Baker knew, too, that Alexander, as an unmarried man with no dependents, was a prime target to be drafted. Still, the deal was not well received. Baker hadn't even told manager Pat Moran. "It was pathetic to see Moran after the announcement," the *Daily News* reported. "He actually wept when asked to discuss the deal and what it meant to him. He looked as if he had lost his entire family."[13] Baker called local beat writers into his room for a quiet dinner at the Waldorf and explained his side of things. One *Philadelphia Inquirer* reporter wrote: "President Baker . . . has deliberately chased the Quaker city off the baseball map. In parting with Alexander and Killefer, he has not only obliterated any chance the Phillies had of coming back next season, but he has given to Chicago the players who will doubtless make the Cubs the only rival of the Giants."[14]

There was more behind the deal, which Baker apparently kept to himself. According to excerpts from Harry Grabiner's diary, Baker thought Killefer and Alexander were involved with gamblers. Grabiner's private investigator later reported, "Baker said Killefer and Alexander [were] traded after they were crooked."[15] On the day after the deal with the Cubs was announced, an article in the *Philadelphia Inquirer* reported, "In justifying the trade, Mr. Baker said today that if one-half the things about the Philadelphia club were known to the fans, he would not be blamed for practically breaking up his team."[16] It is not difficult to piece together what Baker meant. If fans knew Alexander and Killefer were "crooked," he would not be blamed for trading them. It's likely that Baker, a former New York police commissioner, would have had a pretty good sense of when someone was being less than honest with him. It's also important to note that, if Baker really did think Alexander and Killefer were crooked, he did not try to bring them to justice. Instead he simply traded them. That pattern—moving players suspected of gambling rather than exposing them—seems to have repeated itself endlessly in the 1910s.

Even after the big buy from Philadelphia, Weeghman had plenty of kale (that's 1918-speak for money) remaining, and Hornsby was next. Alexander gave the Cubs the pitching staff of a contender. But the

21

team was far too light on hitting, and though there were high hopes for young second baseman Pete Kilduff and even younger shortstop Charley Hollocher, the Cubs needed an infielder who could hit in the middle of the lineup. They wanted Hornsby, who had just finished his third season. He was a talented but very cocky 21-year-old Texan whose attitude didn't play well in St. Louis, especially not with Rickey. After 1917, Hornsby demanded a salary of $10,000, a ridiculous amount for a player of such little experience. (Alexander, by way of example, was being paid $12,000 per year and had been in the majors for seven years.) The cash-strapped Cardinals offered $5,400, and the irascible Hornsby threatened to retire rather than sign—a threat that, with no system of free agency, was commonly made by players but rarely acted on. Still, Hornsby's threat created a window for the Cubs. Hornsby would later become the greatest right-handed hitter in history, winner of seven batting championships and two triple crowns. But, as of that winter, no one knew Hornsby would be *that* good. He was just a young player with big potential and a bigger ego.

Weeghman and Rickey had been dueling publicly over Hornsby. Without being quoted directly, Weeghman showed a letter to *Daily News* reporter Oscar Reichow in which he wrote, "What are you going to do about players? The offer for Rogers Hornsby still goes. There is $50,000 in the bank, you can take it or leave it."[17] The letter was addressed to Rickey. Two days later, Rickey blasted Weeghman, denying that any offer had been made and asserting that Hornsby could not be bought. Weeghman responded with feigned surprise. He was shocked—*shocked!*—by Rickey's accusation, apparently forgetting the letter he'd shown Reichow. "In my talk about players needed I have not mentioned St. Louis or any other club by name," he said. "As for Horsnby, I have not tried to get him."[18]

This is how the Hornsby negotiations went all winter. Weeghman and Rickey poked each other publicly and made angry statements but continually held secret talks. Weeghman and Rickey met during the NL meetings and again later that week. On December 21, the *Daily News* reported that Weeghman "padded his feet and tiptoed out of town last night to attempt to close a deal" in St. Louis for Hornsby, estimating that Weeghman would offer $75,000.[19] But Rickey put out word that he would not give up Hornsby for cash alone. At another meeting in Cincinnati in January, Weeghman was so confident he'd land Hornsby that he brought a contingent of Chicago writers. The

Tribune reported, "Diligent scribes had Hornsby sold to the Cubs today. In exchange, they allowed the Cards pitchers [Claude] Hendrix, [Paul] Carter and [Vic] Aldridge, shortstop [Chuck] Wortman and a bale of cash."[20] But the Hornsby deal—discussed into March—never happened, and the scribes' diligence was misplaced.

Missing out on Hornsby was a personal defeat for Charley, on two fronts. First, by focusing so intently on Hornsby, the Cubs missed other opportunities to upgrade their offense, by adding either a different infielder or an outfielder. The Cubs did get 36-year-old Dode Paskert from Philadelphia, swapping talented hitter Cy Williams. They also landed pitcher Lefty Tyler, a protégé of Mitchell's when he was coaching for the Braves, for two players and $15,000. But, as the winter went on, it became clear that other owners were embittered toward Weeghman. He was too public about his $250,000 bankroll, and his offers for Hornsby only further swelled Hornsby's ego and made him firmer in his contract negotiation with St. Louis. Rickey made a strong anti-Weeghman speech at one NL meeting, and Pittsburgh owner Barney Dreyfuss accused Weeghman of tampering.

That bitter cold of December was a harbinger of one of the worst Chicago winters on record. By the middle of January, Chicago was brought to a standstill by snow, keeping residents homebound for much of the month—in all, a record 42.5 inches of snow fell that January, which did not help Weeghman's restaurants. Nor his mood. Charley was, according to *The Sporting News*, "somewhat depressed and out of humor."[21] He'd already indicated a desire to get out of the Cubs presidency, which probably had more to do with his sliding financial condition than with a desire to leave. But the Rickey mess further soured him. The Alexander-Killefer trade was great, but Weeghman had been foiled and humiliated in his attempt to decorate the Cubs roster with star players. The Mad Spendthrift hadn't come close to using all of his $250,000, and the Cubs eventually saved face by putting $100,000 of the bankroll into a Liberty Bond.

Weeghman had been suckered. "There is good reason to believe that Branch Rickey of the St. Louis Cardinals did rather encourage Weeghman in the idea that the Cubs could land Rogers Hornsby," *The Sporting News* reported, "but when it came to a showdown, Rickey changed front."[22]

The Cubs would enter the 1918 season with a revamped pitching staff but with a questionable offense. It seemed to Weeghman

23

that there was a conspiracy against him on the part of other owners. Maybe it was payback for his Federal League involvement or, more likely, payback for his parading about with an enormous bankroll. Or maybe the conspiracy was all in Weeghman's head. Maybe, for once, he was just unlucky.

THE ORIGINAL CURSE: CHARLEY WEEGHMAN

The 1918 season was the last time anyone would, without irony, call Charley Weeghman "Lucky Charley." By December, Weeghman had sold all his stock to Wrigley and was out of baseball. Just over a year later his wife, Bessie, filed for divorce, citing infidelity—she was awarded $400 per month, a good indication that Charley was no millionaire. On August 9, 1920, Charley's business interests were placed in receivership for failure to pay bills. As Wrigley put it, Charley had tried to "butter his bread too thin."[23]

Weeghman left Chicago but failed in three separate efforts to start restaurants in Manhattan. Far from matching his former wealth (real or imaginary), Lucky Charley was employed as an associate manager at the Riviera club and restaurant at the Palisades in New Jersey when he died in 1938.

THREE

Preparedness: Harry Frazee and Ed Barrow

NEW YORK, MONDAY, FEBRUARY 11, 1918

It should have been a momentous announcement, a decision made after much wrangling, after interviews, after careful consideration of a parade of candidates. But Ed was not going to argue. He wasn't going to sneeze at a job like this one—not in these times. His resignation was official, to no one's surprise—his near fistfight with Buffalo owner Joseph Lannin had been the talk of baseball back in December, and there was no way he was coming back after that. Now he was no longer Ed Barrow, president of the International League. The whole thing could go to smash for all he cared, and it probably would with the war on. He had worked hard for the IL. It was an exhausting job. His reward: they cut his salary from $7,500 to $2,500. Ed was through with minor-league ball. For more than two months, Barrow had been advising Red Sox owner Harry Frazee on transactions, and now he officially would be given a job with Boston.

The job itself was a surprise. Manager. It had been 14 years since Barrow had been a field man in the big leagues, those two miserable years with the Tigers in 1903 and '04. Ed knew he was not the first choice. Frazee had hoped that the previous year's manager, Jack Barry, might get exempted from the war, or that Bill Carrigan, hero of Red Sox champs past, might be sweet-talked out of the Maine banking game into a return. Barrow, in that case, would have gone to Boston as team secretary. But now it was manager. Ed was not well versed on inside strategy, but he'd get help with that. If there was one thing Ed was sure he could do, it was keep the boys in line, get 'em to bed early, and keep 'em in condition. Barrow had been cast aside by the major leagues after his poor showing in Detroit, which wasn't particularly fair. A bunch of pikers, that Tigers team. But the Red Sox were not pikers. Ed thought he might do something big with Boston.

Almost as soon as he turned in his official resignation to the heads of the IL, Ed got the call from Frazee. He answered the telephone to Frazee's voice saying this: "Say, Ed, I have just selected you as manager of the 1918 Red Sox. Want the job?"

Ed replied: "Well, Harry, I wanted that job ever since I knew Jack Barry couldn't return. But I was afraid that if I asked for it, you might say, 'Get out of this opera house.'"[1]

So that was it. Anticlimactic, sure. But he was now Ed Barrow, manager of the Red Sox. He walked out of the lobby of the Hotel Imperial and out of minor-league ball forever. There was a gray chill on Broadway, and Ed looked up 32nd Street to Penn Station. He hoped he was prepared for this.

This is how the devil—or, at least, the greatest boogeyman in the history of baseball curses—once described himself:

Stature: 5 feet, 7 inches
Forehead: High
Eyes: Gray
Nose: Grecian
Mouth: Medium
Chin: Firm
Hair: Black
Complexion: Ruddy
Face: Full, clean shaven

When it comes to Harry Frazee, much is misunderstood, exaggerated, debated, or just plain false. He was wealthy, or he was broke. He was desperate for money to produce a failed musical called *No, No, Nanette*, or *No, No, Nanette* was a hit and came well after the sale of Ruth. He greedily sold players for money, or he made shrewd transactions that just didn't work out in the end. And maybe his contemporaries thought he was Jewish and disliked him for it. Maybe not. At least when Frazee filled out an application for a U.S. passport on June 8, 1911, just three weeks shy of his 31st birthday (he is often listed as having been born in 1881, though he wrote 1880 on official documents), there were some definite truths on the record. He was five-foot-seven, with black hair, for example. His nose was, um, Grecian.

Today's fan knows Frazee as the Red Sox owner who sold Babe Ruth to the Yankees in 1920. That's true. But he did not, as suggested by popular lore, sell Ruth to support a musical called, *No, No, Nanette*, which came well after the sale of Ruth. Closer timing-wise was the play on which *No, No, Nanette* was based, called *My Lady Friends*, but even in that case there is scant evidence that the sale of Ruth was directly related to the financing of the production. Ironically, *No, No, Nanette*, so despised by Red Sox fans, was a hit more than a year before it reached Broadway—a 1925 review in the *New York Times* said, "It was not difficult last night at the Globe Theatre to understand why 'No, No, Nanette' for the last twelve and more months has proved so popular with the natives of Chicago and points West, East, North, South."[2] Hits were not uncommon for Frazee, a self-made giant of the theater world. Many of his productions were hits, and he owned theaters in Boston, New York, and Chicago. Frazee did sell Ruth. He sold a slew of stars, mostly to the Yankees, and his ownership of the Red Sox undoubtedly caused him financial distress. But there's no evidence that his motives for selling Ruth were *Nanette*-related, as legend holds.

Frazee liked to spend and wasn't very responsible with his money. But just how irresponsible he was, and what condition his bank account was in when he sold Ruth in 1920, is a subject of testy debate among baseball historians. Frazee owed money to Joseph Lannin, the team's previous owner, and Ruth had become a headache who was disruptive to the team and to Frazee's bottom line—Ruth had gotten into the habit of making exorbitant contract demands. When the Yankees made a reported $125,000 offer to Frazee (some historians say it was actually $100,000), it proved too much to pass up. But was Frazee selling because he thought he could make the team better? Or because he was making a cash grab? If he wanted to make the team better, he could have accepted an offer from the White Sox, who would have given up $60,000 and outfielder Joe Jackson. There are

27

tax filings showing Frazee was so down on his luck that he reported negative income in 1918,[3] but there is a counterargument that Frazee and other well-heeled men of the day easily found loopholes in the nation's fledgling income tax system.

Either way, Frazee's sell-off—though not universally panned by the press—was labeled "the rape of the Red Sox" by writer Burt Whitman, a phrase perpetuated by Fred Lieb's oft-cited book, *Baseball as I Have Known It*.[4] But Whitman and Lieb weren't the only ones with a negative view of Frazee. "He was money-mad," Red Sox outfielder Harry Hooper said. "He soon sold most of our best players and ruined the team."[5] Hooper told another interviewer, "I was disgusted. The Yankees dynasty of the twenties was three-quarters the Red Sox of a few years before. . . . [Frazee] was short of cash and he sold the whole team down the river to keep his dirty nose above water."[6]

That view persists. But go back to 1918 and remember that Frazee was seen as well liked (by most), wealthy, and powerful. His passport application is a reminder that Frazee was just a guy—imperfect, but not the embodiment of evil a generation of Red Sox fans would later imagine. Frazee was heading into his second season as owner, a bit stockier than when he had applied for a passport in 1911, and the stress of his business interests no doubt made his face ruddier. Alcohol added to the ruddiness. Irving Caesar, a lyricist, once said, "Harry Frazee never drew a sober breath in his life, but he was a hell of a producer. He made more sense drunk than most men do sober."[7] In a *Baseball Magazine* article, Frazee was described as being, "short, stocky, heavy set . . . his head is enormous."[8] He was a bundle of energy, always talking, shifting from one task to the next. In the clichéd language of the day, *Baseball Magazine* called Frazee "a sizzling, scintillating live wire." With an enormous head.

28   With few other options, Harry matter-of-factly hired Ed to be his manager in February 1918. There was some question about whether Barrow, accustomed to the front office, could handle the job. From Frazee's perspective, Barrow's personnel experience was an added benefit. After his first year in the owner's chair, Frazee decided that, however much fun it was to own a team, he'd prefer to have someone else make player decisions. Someone like Barrow.

It was an odd match. Barrow was a favorite of AL president Ban Johnson, and after Barrow quit the International League that winter it was Johnson who helped place Barrow with the Red Sox. Frazee wasn't a likely candidate to be offered—or to accept—favors from Johnson. Though he had been the owner of the Red Sox for only one full season, Frazee already knew that if there was one aspect of owning a baseball team he most disliked, it was dealing with Ban Johnson. The feeling was mutual.

If Frazee remains a controversial figure these days, it's only fitting, because in his 1918 heyday he was the AL's most controversial owner—which is to say, simply, that Johnson hated him. As the father of the AL, Johnson ruled his league like a benevolent dictator, though in 1918 his dictatorial grip would begin to weaken. Johnson's domineering personality helped sustain the AL through hard times, and elder magnates tended to put up with Johnson's quirks in deference to his past leadership. But Frazee was not an elder magnate. He was young and brash, just 38. When he bought the Red Sox in November 1916, the deal was done strictly between Frazee and Joseph Lannin (the same man who later owned an International League team and nearly came to blows with Barrow). There had been no consultation with Johnson on the sale. That's just not how things were done in the AL. Everything went through Johnson. Within two days of the sale to Frazee, an article in the *Boston Globe* said Johnson was already wondering if the deal should be undone. The tone was set for a contentious relationship.

It was contentious, and eventually Johnson and Frazee became the bitterest of enemies. But they weren't yet enemies in 1918, and Johnson's fondness for Barrow outweighed his disdain for Frazee. Johnson even manipulated his league's rosters to benefit Frazee's club—which, Johnson already knew, would be Barrow's club too. Frazee, like Weeghman, saw the 1918 season as an opportunity and was a buyer. That winter word spread that Frazee had wagered $2,000 against $12,000 that the war would be over by the time baseball began its season in the spring.[9] Even if the war persisted, Frazee thought Americans would attend ball games. "People must be amused," Frazee said. "They must have their recreation despite the grim horrors of war."[10]

Connie Mack, manager of the Athletics, was a seller. The day after Weeghman traded for Alexander and Killefer, the Red Sox made a blockbuster purchase at the AL meetings in Chicago, facilitated by Johnson. Frazee laid out $60,000 and sent off three players for speedy outfielder Amos Strunk, catcher Wally Schang, and pitcher "Bullet

After being traded from the A's, Stuffy McInnis (left) prepares to sign his contract, with Red Sox owner Harry Frazee (middle) and former manager Jack Barry seated with him. (NATIONAL BASEBALL HALL OF FAME LIBRARY, COOPERSTOWN, N.Y.)

Joe" Bush. At the same time, Mack and Frazee arranged for the trade of another star, first baseman Stuffy McInnis—the pride of Gloucester High, just 35 miles north of Boston—for cash and players to be named, though that trade did not become official until the middle of January. Mack's once-proud A's were gutted. The demolition job done on Philadelphia's AL team ranked only with Baker's crushing of the NL's Phillies.

Writing about the deal in the *Daily News*, Reichow speculated, two months in advance, "This may sound odd to those who know the wrangle that Johnson and Frazee have had for several months, but . . . this deal, it is said, was engineered by Johnson, who wanted to help Mack out financially and make it possible for him to find a place for Barrow in Boston."[11] Reichow was right about Barrow. Other AL clubs grumbled. Yankees owner Colonel Jake Ruppert claimed he would have outbid Frazee for Strunk, Schang, and Bush, but he hadn't been told the players were for sale. White Sox owner Charles Comiskey was "not overjoyed" when the announcement was made and "intimated that he should have at least been given a chance to bid for the services of the three players."[12]

Both Frazee and Weeghman believed that boosting their rosters made sense because the war in Europe would soon end. But there were significant differences in their motivation to stock their teams for the 1918 season. The Cubs were buyers because the team was coming off two disappointing seasons. Boston, though, was a very good team in 1917, finishing with 90 wins, second only to the White Sox. Before that, Boston had won back-to-back championships. But where the Cubs had been virtually untouched by the war, the Red Sox roster had been slashed. Barry, manager and second baseman, took a soft job with the naval reserves. Star outfielder Duffy Lewis, a .302 hitter, and pitcher Ernie Shore, who had gone 13–10 in 1917, were gone to naval jobs too. In all, 11 Red Sox were in some branch of the military. Frazee added players thinking he would get Barry, Duffy, Shore, and the rest back when the war ended, possibly before the season started, leaving the Red Sox with one of the greatest rosters in baseball history.

The off-season was baseball's busiest on record, but Frazee and Weeghman made the biggest splashes—for better or worse. Weeghman was given harsh public scoldings by NL owners that winter, and Frazee, too, was criticized. A *New York Times* editorial stated: "[Weeghman and Frazee] have stirred up no end of commotion in the two major leagues by starting out to monopolize the two pennants next season. Baseball club owners of the past never knew the methods in accord with which these two owners have started out to buy players who can land them a pennant at any cost."[13]

They were buying at any cost, but for what were they buying? No one could even say for sure whether there would be a 1918 season. Since the United States declared war on Germany in April 1917, baseball had struggled to find its place in a mobilized nation. The game attempted to ingratiate itself to the public with patriotic displays. Johnson had players spend their pregames conducting military drills, using bats instead of Springfield rifles. Magnates bought Liberty Bonds, making sure the papers knew about it. Teams hosted endless military parades and Red Cross benefits. From the war's outset, America frowned on slackers, and baseball did its best to avoid the label.

But the game's magnates got mixed signals from the government. In May 1917, Congress passed the Selective Service Act, making all single men between the ages of 21 and 30 (inclusive, which is why the draft age is sometimes listed as 21 to 31) first in line to be drafted.

31

That made players prime targets. It was a tenuous situation. Nobody wanted to see baseball shut down, but how could a league be run when its best players could be called to war at any moment? And how could the frivolity of sport be reconciled with the reality of war? The *Tribune* soberly summed up the situation in May 1917: "An American newspaper will sacrifice a great deal of self-respect if it has to print, or does print, box scores and casualty lists in the same issue."[14]

Baseball pushed forward. Ban Johnson tried to get answers from the government on behalf of the National Commission, the game's governing body, which was made up of three members: Johnson, representing the AL; John Tener, the former governor of Pennsylvania and now head of the National League; and Garry Herrmann, the owner of the Cincinnati Reds, who was supposed to serve as the neutral head of the commission (though, since the two were old friends and drinking buddies, Johnson held sway over Herrmann). Johnson has been treated harshly by historians for his handling of the war, and that's reasonable, because he was treated harshly by the public and press at the time. But the circumstances were extraordinary, and what rarely is mentioned is that Johnson's positions proved right in the end. In July 1917, Johnson offered to shut down baseball to support the war effort, but the public protested, and one week later President Woodrow Wilson put out assurances that he wanted baseball to continue. Johnson was accused of being a calamity howler, and the *Chicago Daily News* said, "All the leader of the American League has done for a year is take a pessimistic view of the situation and has done almost everything possible to create the idea that the sport is gasping its last."[15] Within months, newspapers would be reporting that the sport was, in fact, gasping its last.

Johnson knew that running baseball during the war was a losing proposition. He pressed authorities to define baseball's status, and when he was ignored he came up with a plan on his own. In late November, he made public a suggestion that each team be allowed to exempt 18 players from the draft, 288 players total, making everyone else fair game for the military—the logic being that, if the government wanted baseball to keep going, then leaving 288 men out of the war was a small sacrifice in the context of an army that would eventually top 3.6 million fighting soldiers. But Johnson's suggestion was a disaster. General Enoch Crowder, who, as provost marshal, was in charge of running the selective-service draft, was outraged. "That

Throughout 1917, baseball did its best to dodge the "slacker" label by, among other things, inviting elaborate pregame military demonstrations, such as this one given at Weeghman Park on Opening Day. (NATIONAL BASEBALL HALL OF FAME LIBRARY, COOPERSTOWN, N.Y.)

must be a pipe dream," he said. "There is nothing in the regulations to warrant making exceptional rulings for men liable to service who make baseball their means of livelihood. It is absurd."[16] John Tener agreed. "I would not go an inch toward Washington to ask President Wilson or the Secretary of War for special favors for baseball," Tener said. "I think it most unpatriotic to suggest that baseball should even appear to shirk a duty at this time, when so many parents are giving their sons and when other business interests are giving their best men to the service."[17]

Exasperated, Johnson issued a 10-paragraph statement. He had offered to shut down the game, but Wilson and the public disapproved. He floated the 18-player exemption but was slammed for it. Most magnates seemed resigned to simply pressing forward with a stiff upper lip, even with their best players subject to the draft. That was a sure failure. Johnson simply wanted the government to say where the

33

game stood. Not only would this inform players and magnates how to proceed, but it would let the public know that supporting baseball during the war was acceptable. Without word from the government, there were no good options. "Such conditions will arise in 1918 and must result in endless confusion in the great baseball family," Johnson wrote in his statement. "The matter of maintaining a contest of keen interest that would appeal to the public seems impossible of accomplishment. We ask for nothing but an interest that represents millions of dollars seeks wholesome advice on the subject."[18]

Alas, it would be eight months—well into the season—before the government was prepared to give baseball its wholesome advice. By then it would be too late.

The press disapproved of the methods employed by Weeghman and Frazee, but the results were undeniable—the Red Sox and Cubs were well prepared for 1918 and were instant pennant contenders. Start with the Cubs. There was no Hornsby, but they had assembled baseball's best pitching staff. Alexander and lefty Hippo Vaughn made a fearsome front two. Lefty Tyler and Claude Hendrix added lefty-righty depth, and Phil Douglas would bolster the slabmen when he recuperated from an appendectomy.

Offense was lacking. The infield was young. In the outfield the Cubs had only slap hitters. Center fielder Dode Paskert hit eight home runs in 1916, but no other Cub had hit more than four in a season. Left fielder Les Mann hit for power in the minors but not in the big leagues. In right field would be ex–Fed Leaguer Max Flack or youngster Turner Barber, for whom Weeghman had paid $15,000 the previous year. A Tennessee native and a bit of a rube, Barber hurt his toe on his arrival in Chicago before spring training when, confused by the bustle of traffic, he, "forgot himself in crossing a downtown street when he should have been waiting for the cop's whistle. A taxi whizzed past him and ran over one foot."[19] Injured, Barber sat for most of spring training and struggled throughout 1918.

(Perhaps the tragedy of the 1918 Cubs was foreshadowed when, just before the season, a player named King Lear vowed to Mitchell that he would win the third-base job. He did not. How sharper than a serpent's tooth it is to have a thankless manager!)

The Red Sox were impressive on the mound too. Left-hander Babe Ruth—whose hitting was still a sidelight to his pitching—was just 23 and coming off a 24–13 season. Submariner Carl Mays was 22–9 in '17. Dutch Leonard and ex-A's righty Joe Bush were inconsistent but had star qualities. Offensively, the Red Sox figured to be strong, with Harry Hooper in right, joined in center by Strunk, one of the league's fastest players. In left field, Barrow drew on his knowledge of the minors to sign 35-year-old journeyman George Whiteman from the International League for $750. Everett Scott was a mainstay at short, with Schang behind the plate and team captain Dick Hoblitzell at first base—McInnis's primary position. The Red Sox wanted to try McInnis, a slick fielder, at third base, with new coach and ex-Cubs star Johnny Evers (who was to assist Barrow with strategy as a coach too) taking a crack at second base.

But baseball as a whole had not done a good job preparing for 1918. Captain T. L. Huston, part owner of the Yankees and a member of the army's engineering corps, wrote a letter from France that was printed all over the country. In it, Huston said: "Baseball must watch closer the signs of the times. The Alexander-Killefer deal, as well as that of Bush, Strunk and Schang, indicated that it is strangely out of step with national events. The loud publicity given the purchase of players for the large sums of $60,000 to $80,000 will be a harsh, discordant note in the existing worldwide atmosphere of economy, retrenchment and sacrifice, and tend to shock the fan public and make it pause and ask, 'Is baseball still stark crazy?'"[20]

Huston ripped the small portion of 1917 World Series money that was given to war charities and criticized the magnates on baseball's business end—he was the only one who enlisted. "Ye gods, what a mortifying and shameful spectacle," Huston wrote of his cohorts. He went on: "Men of baseball, reveille sounded for you long ago. If you are deaf to that call, the nation will sound taps for you, and you will hear it."

The winter slipped by without baseball making significant war-time adjustments. As teams prepared for spring training in 1918, the country was squeezed by food rationing, gas rationing, and limits on rail use. But, despite wise proposals to shorten the schedule, baseball kept the same 154-game marathon. Players, too, seemed clueless. Men were being drafted and paid $30 per month in the army, and yet many players held out for big contracts and bonuses. The government enforced a war tax of 10 percent on tickets, and the magnates responded by bumping up prices more than necessary—grandstand tickets that were 75 cents, for example, technically should have been 83 cents with the tax, but the magnates decided to just make it 85 cents. A proposal that the extra pennies go into a Red Cross fund was made but not mandated.

The game made one change of note, altering the player payout system for the World Series, so that the top four teams in each league, rather than just the top team, would get some kind of share of Series receipts. This would wind up being a regrettable decision—though, it should be pointed out, players protested because they wanted a *deeper* division of the shares, so that even last-place teams got World Series money. They'd change their tune later.

Against this backdrop, teams headed to spring training, the Cubs to Pasadena and the Red Sox to Hot Springs, Arkansas. Both trips were marked by bad omens. The Red Sox were stranded by a snowstorm in Buffalo. The Cubs found, when they arrived in California, the trunk containing their uniforms had gone missing. Otherwise, the trips were notable only for their frugality. The Cubs, with a meager 27-man traveling party, made the 2,000-mile journey riding on the back two cars of a mail train. The special Cubs train that had been a point of pride in 1916 and '17 was but a memory. "There was no de luxe special train for wealthy stockholders and their wives," the *Tribune* reported. "There were no compartments and drawing rooms. There was no phonograph for entertainment during the long journey. There was no dining car, and there were no women."[21]

And no Weeghman. He stayed in Chicago, tending to his restaurants.

THE ORIGINAL CURSE: HARRY FRAZEE

Poor Harry. If he hadn't dropped $60,000, Boston would not have won the 1918 World Series. But no one remembers that. They only remember the "rape."

Frazee, especially when it comes to finances, is a fuzzy character. But we can say for sure that, sometime between the 1918 World Series and his death in 1929, Frazee fell on hard times. His drinking caught up with him—he contracted Bright's disease, a kidney ailment linked to alcoholism, and was only 48 when he passed away. In his obituary, the *New York Times* reported, "For years, he seemed to possess the golden touch, but recently, it was reported among his associates that his fortune had dwindled. His more recent ventures were less fortunate and he always was a generous spender."[22]

Though Frazee is doomed to eternal demonization as a greedy bungler in Boston, we should remember that he was a real guy and that for too long we were given a cartoon villain caricature of Frazee. His story runs deeper than that. New York mayor Jimmy Walker, a close friend who was at his bedside when Frazee died, was quoted in his obituary: "Harry Frazee was one of the most popular figures in the theatrical and baseball worlds. I have known him a great many years. His was a unique character—unique in his friendship for others—and he was immensely popular with every one who knew him. He was a man of great energy, great mental ability and was greatly respected in the business and baseball world."

FOUR

Discipline: Five Days in Spring Training with Ed Barrow

MAJESTIC PARK, HOT SPRINGS, ARKANSAS, MARCH 22–26, 1918

Friday

Barrow removed a handkerchief, pushing up the brim of his straw hat, a sheet of sweat on his brow. He wiped it off, futile though that was, and retucked the handkerchief into the pocket of his suit coat—Ed had never really been a ballplayer, so he did not like wearing a player's uniform. Morning rain had been replaced by a brutal afternoon sun. Barrow leaned against Majestic Park's wooden bleachers. He had canceled the scrimmage against the Yannigans—that bunch of rookies and longshots that are the staple of spring training—that day, because the weather was too odd, there was no pitching on hand, and illnesses were depleting an already short supply of players. Sam Agnew had the grippe. John Evers was back at the hotel with tonsillitis,[1] probably contracted while loudly urging on a nag over at the Oaklawn track. No matter. Evers wasn't well liked by the men, or by Barrow for that matter. Just a few days into camp Barrow already wondered if taking on Evers as player/coach had been a mistake.

Barrow looked up. Dutch Leonard. He was not Barrow's kind of man. He was out of shape. Undisciplined. Barrow again removed the handkerchief, again dabbed his brow.

Ed Barrow in a rare relaxed moment in 1918. (Boston Public Library)

"Hubert, you've decided to join us," Barrow said as Leonard, draped in rubber, awkwardly jogged past. "You look smashing in that rubber shirt."

"I don't see why I need to wear this thing," Leonard said. "I am skinny as a schoolboy."

39

"Leonard," Barrow said, "you would not have to wear the rubber shirt if you had not arrived wearing the suit of flab you call your body. You have some poundage to leave behind. Out-of-shape ball players have always donned the rubber shirt. Melts fat."

"Like hell it does," Leonard said.

"This is the way things have been done since before you were born," Barrow said. "Rubber shirts drop weight. Red flannel shirts—

not white, mind you, red—keep pitchers from rheumatism. Everyone knows these things. It's baseball tradition."[2]

Leonard grumbled about tradition and his arse.

Saturday

Rain. The Red Sox had left Hot Springs and spent three miserable hours on a train just to get 53 miles south—Barrow could have gotten his team that far jogging at a steady trot—to play the Brooklyners in Little Rock, in front of the Camp Pike soldiers. Blue skies and sun, the entire ride from Hot Springs. Off the train and, goddammit, rain. No game. But Barrow told his hitters to get in some batting practice, rain and all.

Ruth was preparing for practice, stretching. Barrow sang, in his head:

> Molly, my Molly—Molly, my dear
> If it wasn't for Molly, I wouldn't be here
> Write me a letter, send it by mail
> shoot it to me at the old city jail.

Ruth had sung the tune on the train. Now Barrow could not get rid of it.[3]

Ruth stepped to the dish. He reared back and swung into his fierce uppercut motion, clubbing a pitch over the right-field fence. The soldiers cheered. Barrow stared.

Ruth hit another. More cheering. And another. Cheering, louder. And another. Louder. And another. Louder. Barrow still stared. No one hit them like that. Five apples knocked out of the park in batting practice.

Ruth was part blessing, part curse. He wasn't quite square in the head—he'd eat five, six times a day, drink enough for five men, and, Barrow was quite sure, had already done business at every brothel in Hot Springs. But Barrow needed him. Ruth was his ace pitcher. And a hell of a hitter. If only he could split Ruth in two, one on the mound, one at bat. That's what Barrow needed. Two Ruths.

But now Ed had another problem. The Red Sox would have to pay for all those balls sailing over the fence.

"That's enough of that," Barrow announced.

Ruth shrugged, turned, and walked back to the dugout. He smiled at Barrow and belched vigorously.

40

Sunday

Back in Hot Springs. Scrimmage against Brooklyn. Carl Mays—sneering, Mays was always sneering—on the pitching mound, getting ready to throw to Zack Wheat at bat. Barrow leaned in to watch.

"No hooks, Mays," Barrow said loudly. "Save that arm."

Mays nodded. Barrow glanced beyond the fence, out to Baptist Hill and beyond, where the Ozarks wrinkled the horizon. Ruth was in right field. Barrow had done some pitching when he was a young man back in Des Moines, and he knew the value of a pitcher. Ruth would remain a pitcher. But Barrow stuck him in the outfield because the Red Sox were so short on material and Harry Hooper had been suggesting getting Ruth into the lineup. Now Barrow had his eye on Ruth, just to see how the kid looked. Not good. He could hardly keep still, fidgeting, bouncing, examining curiosities in the grass. Look at him out there. He's bored. He's a pitcher; he needs the every-pitch action. But he sure did whack that grand slam back in the third inning. Cleared the fence by, what, 200 feet? Into the alligator pond past the right-field fence.[4]

After Ruth hit the grand slam, Dan Howley, Barrow's pitching coach, turned and said, "Never saw one quite like that."[5] Neither had Barrow.

Ed turned back to the mound. Mays was rocking into his submarine delivery. Ed could see Mays's grip on the ball. *Sonovabitch!* Barrow's face flushed. Mays was throwing a curve. "Mays, you bastard!" Barrow shouted. "I said no hooks!"[6]

Monday

Finally, Leonard was throwing. Ed had been working with six pitchers—just six!—and he needed all the boxmen he could get. Dutch looked to be in good form, tossing for 30 minutes. Coming off the mound, Leonard approached Barrow, wearing that irritating crooked smile. Barrow needed Leonard. He needed pitching. Leonard did not need Barrow. He was said to be making a killing in raisin farming. This annoyed Barrow. In his younger days, Barrow would have knocked Leonard's smile clear to Little Rock.

"So, when is the Duke coming back?" Leonard asked.

"What Duke?" Barrow said.

"The big gun, the head gizzazzer," Leonard said. Barrow stared blankly.

41

"Frazee." Leonard continued, "You know, we are close, me and him. He and I are just like that," holding up two crossed fingers. He then reached down and cupped his crotch. "Yup, me and Frazee are closer than my raisins are packed."[7]

Barrow did not like this Dutch Leonard.

Tuesday

Discipline was Ed's strength. And so there were rules that spring. No wives. No poker wagers bigger than 10 cents, and all games were to end by 11:00 P.M. Wake-up call: 8:30, and no one was to be in the breakfast room past 9:30. The team would practice straight through the afternoon, with no lunch. It was two miles between the hotel and the stadium. Players were required to walk or run the two miles each day.[8]

Ed was clear on the rules.

Barrow himself was huffing and sweating his way to Majestic Park this morning. A few yards from the entrance he heard applause, followed by a shout from a taxi: "Hey, Ed, you are good for a few more blocks!" He turned and looked, and there they were—what looked like half his players, stuffed into a cab, hooting at him. So much for the required two-mile walk. Ed's neck burned, and his face reddened.[9]

Of the 16 major-league teams limbering up for the '18 season, only the Cubs traveled all the way to California for spring training, and that was mainly because stockholder William Wrigley owned land near Pasadena. In deference to the war, spring training was limited to 30 days, and though no one went quite as far as the Cubs, other teams traveled long distances to hold their camps. Four teams were in Florida. Four others were in Texas. Two were in Louisiana, two were in Georgia, and one was in Alabama. The Red Sox and Dodgers were both in Hot Springs, arguably the birthplace of spring training. As the story goes, the 1886 White Stockings (who later became the Cubs) stopped there on their way back to Chicago after a winter of barnstorming and found the area's mineral baths useful for melting flab and sobering up. Spring training at the time was similar to modern spring ball—teams brought large groups of players, many of whom had no chance to make the club, for weeks of workouts. They played exhibition games against minor-league teams, against nearby big-league teams, or against their own teammates.

But railroad travel had been restricted because of the war, and the Red Sox took a skeleton crew on their 1918 trip. Barrow was short on players, especially pitchers. That limited his opportunities to have regulars vs. Yannigans games, a problem for Barrow (and all big-league managers) throughout the spring. Another issue was that, though he was strong on discipline, Barrow had never been much of a field manager. The team brought in Evers, after firing the popular Heinie Wagner, to help Barrow with his bench coaching and to play some second base. Nicknamed "the Crab," Evers was baseball's top "goat-getter," a role defined by *The Sporting News* as "loud-mouthed persons who, in uniforms, sit on the benches and attempt to 'ride' the enemy with foul abuse of a personal nature . . . [using] alleged wit and humor of the coarsest kind."[10] Evers, it turned out, also liked getting the goats of his teammates and would soon be let go because he was too sharp-tongued and combative for Red Sox players.

Barrow had other serious problems to solve, especially difficult for a new manager with a limited knowledge of the day-to-day workings of a big-league team. The Red Sox were an almost entirely new mix, with Scott and Hooper the only everyday players returning from the '17 team. Converting McInnis into a third baseman was a top priority. Left field was the other major question. Boston had signed George Whiteman, but he was out of his league. Barrow, testing all of his options, even tried catcher Wally Schang at third and in the outfield. Asked, at one point, what ground he was covering, Schang shrugged and replied, "Siberia, I guess."[11]

Barrow wanted to put his mark on the team with toughness and discipline. About the Red Sox's first practice on March 13, the *Boston Post* reported, "It is evident that the men are a little in awe of their new boss."[12] But for all Barrow's focus on discipline—he had a notoriously quick trigger when it came to fining players—these were still ballplayers, and they were going to have typical ballplayer entertainment. Throughout the spring, the Red Sox bolted from practice as quickly as possible in order to get to the horse races at Oaklawn (Barrow often went too). They hung out at the vaudeville shows in Hot Springs' Calamity Alley. The players were not so awed by Barrow that they could not poke fun at him, either defying him by hiring a car to the park instead of jogging or by nudging his short temper. Pitcher Sam Jones, speaking years later to Lawrence Ritter in *The Glory of*

Their Times, recalled an exchange with Barrow during 1918. Having pitched the day before, Jones was playing checkers in the clubhouse when the batboy told Jones that Barrow wanted him outside for a photo. Jones ignored the request and, as he told Ritter:

"In comes Mr. Barrow himself. As you might know, he was a pretty rough talker. Huge man, with these fantastic bushy eyebrows. They always fascinated me. Couldn't take my eyes off them. Well, he gave me a good going over for sitting in the clubhouse playing checkers when he'd asked for me outside. . . .

"'This newspaper photographer came all the way from Providence to take your picture,' he says.

"'Is that so?' I said. 'Well, he can go all the way back to Providence without it.'

"Oh, did that get him! . . . I thought he was going to take a sock at me. He'd been known to do that on occasion, you know. 'This will cost you $100,' he shouts. His face was so red he could hardly talk. And you should have seen those eyebrows!

"'Make it $200,' I said, still sitting there.

"'It's $200 all right.'

"'Make it $300,' I said, 'and then go straight to hell.'

"'It's $300,' he roars, and slams the door.

"Finally, I went out on the field and the photographer posed me and Mr. Barrow together. Arms around each other's shoulders, both smiling, best friends ever. But as soon as the shutter clicked we both walked real fast in opposite directions."[13]

More than Barrow's temper, though, Boston's spring foreshadowed what 1918 would become: the Babe Ruth Show. Ruth was a popular left-handed pitcher who had gone 47–25 in the previous two seasons. He was immature on and off the field. He had received a 10-game suspension for punching umpire Brick Owens the previous year and in 1916 missed two weeks with a broken toe suffered when he kicked the bench in anger after an intentional walk. He had well-known appetites for food, drink, and women, but there was an appealing innocence about him. Hooper described him as "a big, overgrown green pea."[14] After four years as a pitcher in the majors, Ruth had just nine career home runs, but his swing-for-the-fences approach was unique. He tried for a home run every at bat. That just wasn't how things were done. The focus of hitters was on making contact, not busting home runs. The fact that Ruth was a pitcher early in his career probably enabled him to become a power hitter later—had he been an everyday player, some manager surely would have forced him to cut down his swing and focus on contact.

Ruth's spring success with the bat made an impression—with Barrow, with Hooper, and, most important, with Ruth himself. He was a pitcher, but he liked hitting. His home runs riled the fans. In the Red Sox's 14 games with Brooklyn that spring, Ruth hit .429 with four homers in 21 at bats. No other Red Sox player hit more than one home run. The *Globe's* Edward Martin described the home run Ruth hit on March 24: "The ball not only cleared the right field wall, but stayed up, soaring over the street and a wide duck pond, finally finding a resting place for itself in a nook of the Ozark hills."

Ruth joked, "I would have liked to have got a better hold on that one."[15]

On April 3, the Cubs arrived in Bakersfield, California, from Fresno, prepared to wrap up 17 days of training on the West Coast and begin the trek back to the Midwest. It hadn't been a good trip. Mitchell was having the same trouble in California that Barrow was having in Arkansas. Conditions were bad, and not enough players were on hand. A weeklong holdout by Grover Cleveland Alexander hadn't helped. Now there was one last game before the team would begin heading east, a trip that promised to be a slow crawl, because the Cubs were scheduled for a packed slate of games against minor-leaguers throughout the Southwest. The final game before they left California was in Taft, 46 miles west of Bakersfield, and—this was fitting, given the Cubs' spring travel woes—the only way to get to Taft was by stagecoach. This helps explain why, over the course of the California misadventure, the Cubs called themselves "Weeghman's trained seals."[16]

Still, the Taft game drew 3,000 fans. Before it started, a band began to play "The Star-Spangled Banner," a practice that was becoming more common during the war. Most of the Cubs were not quite sure what to do. Outfielder Les Mann, who had served in a quasi-military position in the off-season, training soldiers for the YMCA at Camp Logan in Houston, instructed them—*take off your caps, put them over your hearts, face the band, and, for Pete's sake, shut up!*

Miserable travel conditions notwithstanding, there were some positive aspects to the Cubs' stint in California. Already, it appeared that 21-year-old shortstop Charley Hollocher—who stood just five-foot-seven and weighed about 150 pounds—would make good. Hollocher showed terrific bat control and plate discipline, nearly impossible to strike out. He was also quick, with good footwork in the field. This was a relief for Mitchell, who worried about his infield. *The Sporting News* wrote, "Too much boosting has been the handicap that many a likely youngster coming up to the majors has found his undoing, but Charley Hollocher, the new shortstop of the Chicago Cubs, gamely faces the barrier and believes he can make the jump, however high the bar has been set. . . . He is a mite of a fellow physically, but bold with the bat and shifty as a rabbit in the field."[17] In the course of spring training alone, the *Daily News* ran two feature stories on Hollocher and his St. Louis background. By the second week in April, James Crusinberry wrote that it was "Little Charley Hollocher, the boy shortstop of the Cubs, upon whom hinges the success or failure for the Chicago team this year."[18]

Another travel problem struck the Cubs on their way back to Chicago. On April 4, they were late leaving California on their way to Deming, New Mexico, and were delayed further when their train died because the engine ran out of water outside Yuma, Arizona. By the time they finally got to Deming, near the Mexican border, they still had to head about 40 miles north to the copper mine at Santa Rita (a town so small it no longer exists) in cars. The ride took two hours. According to the *Daily News*, "Traveling Secretary John Seys has a few more gray hairs trying to get the club to its destination."[19] Once in Santa Rita, the Cubs were slated to play the mining company team, headed by former journeyman pitcher "Sleepy" Bill Burns. Because the Cubs arrived late, they could not get back to Deming and spent the night at the mining companies' dormitories. It wasn't all bad. Burns was pleased to be among big-league friends. The Cubs "were given an excellent wild turkey dinner, at which Bill Burns . . . was the host. Burns killed the birds himself."[20]

46

Let's pause to remember exactly who Bill Burns would become— one of the central characters in the World Series scandal that turned the 1919 White Sox into the Black Sox. Burns and his partner, Billy Maharg, helped orchestrate the plot to throw the series and attempted to have the venture backed by gambling kingpin Arnold Rothstein. After Rothstein ostensibly turned him down, Burns was approached by Rothstein's right-hand man, ex-boxer Abe Attell, who promised he'd get Rothstein to finance the fix after all. Burns and the Sox players proceeded with the scam. When the grand jury began investigating the 1919 World Series, Burns turned state's evidence.

But here was Burns, 18 months ahead of the Black Sox plot, hosting dinner for one of the favorites to represent the National League in the 1918 World Series. That's no crime, of course, but there are Burns-related dots that are interesting to connect. In an interview given to *Eight Men Out* author Eliot Asinof, Abe Attell pointed out that Burns was no stranger to fixes. Before Game 3 of the 1919 World Series, Attell said he was visited by Burns, who warned him about Dickie Kerr, that day's starting pitcher. Kerr was not part of the Black Sox fix. Here's what Attell (who, it should be noted, had only a loose association with the truth) said Burns advised when it came to betting against Kerr: "I'm an old-time ballplayer and we've been behind pitchers and tried to lose a game and he pitched such a good game, the players couldn't toss it off."[21]

Burns himself claimed to have bet heavily against Kerr and lost. Either way, we can assume Burns had been involved in game fixing during his career. And we know he played with several members of the Cubs, including Alexander and Bill Killefer in Philadelphia in 1911. Those two were dubbed "crooked" by Phillies owner William Baker, according to Grabiner's diary, and were sold because of it. (Maharg, too, had connections here. It appears he was sort of an honorary Phillie. In 1916, at age 35, he played one game for the Phillies and was photographed as the team's assistant trainer.[22]) Burns played with Cubs coach Otto Knabe in Philadelphia, too, and according to Grabiner's diary Knabe was no stranger to baseball gambling either.

All of this is not to say that the Cubs and Burns sat down to plot a throwing of the 1918 World Series then and there, while chomping on drumsticks and white meat. But it's a lot of dots. Gamblers were never far from players. If some Cubs got a notion to dabble in game fixing, it would not be hard to find those who could make it profitable.

47

After the interlude with Burns's turkeys, the Cubs continued their crawl back to the Midwest. Opening Day in St. Louis, on April 16, was the ultimate destination. Each stop was punctuated by games played at war camps before crowds of soldiers in drab uniforms—the "Khaki League" tour. They faced Burns's Santa Rita team at Camp Cody in Deming, and, before the game, the Cubs watched a group of about 20,000 soldiers perform in a review parade. Then it was off to Houston on April 9, to play the Texas League's Buffaloes for the benefit of the Camp Logan soldiers, and to Waco, to play the Navigators at Camp MacArthur. The Cubs were in Dallas on the 11th and began their journey north from there.

As spring training wound down, there was added poignancy to the presence of soldiers. In March, German forces began a major offensive on the Western Front, and, rather quickly, the war turned in the Germans' favor. Leaders in Britain and France wanted more American troops, and the United States would pluck those troops out of the crowds of boys at the Khaki League games. They could be cheering stars like Alexander now and be headed for the front a week later. And it could work both ways. Stars like Alexander could be in a baseball uniform now and be in a khaki uniform a week later.

THE ORIGINAL CURSE: BILL KILLEFER, OTTO KNABE, AND JOHN O. SEYS

Given their geographic proximity to the White Sox, maybe it should not be astonishing that so many Cubs were sucked into the orbit of the 1919 World Series scandal. According to Harry Grabiner's diary, "Knabe who intended betting on the White Sox was told by catcher Killefer (of Cubs) to lay off as the White Sox had been gotten to. Rumors are that games were thrown during 1919 season by . . . Hendrix, Killefer, Cubs."[23] That means, at least according to rumors of the day, that Killefer and Knabe were aware of the fix. And that Killefer may have been up to no good himself.

Cubs secretary John O. Seys—who had such a rough go of things getting the team to California and back in the spring of 1918—certainly was aware of the fix. In July 1921, he was called to testify about his involvement with bets placed on the 1919 World Series. Seys said he met up with Attell in Cincinnati, and, "He told me he was betting on Cincinnati. That was on the first day of the series. [Gambler] Louis Levi was with Attell. He was betting on [Cincinnati]. As we went down an elevator in one building, Attell bet $600 to $500 Cincinnati would win the first game, the second game and the series. I held the stakes."[24]

Seys's involvement with Attell and Levi did not affect his career, though. He remained one of the most respected executives in the Cubs organization until his death in 1938.

FIVE

Sacrifice: Grover Cleveland Alexander

CHICAGO, APRIL 26, 1918

Well, that was it, Aleck thought. Maybe he'd be on a mound again at some point, but who knew when? He'd gotten off a train from Elba, Nebraska, just that morning, shown up at the North Side park intent on throwing a no-hit game for the first time in his life, but dammit, that knocker Hornsby got him. Aleck's right arm was hurling unlike ever before, his speedball jumping, his fadeaway showing great break. But that little sonovabitch Hornsby was a puzzle, standing half a mile from the plate the way he did, and sure enough, Hornsby lammed one of Aleck's best pitches to the left field wall in the first. So long and farewell, no-hitter.[1]

Still, he'd beaten the Cardinals, 3–2, on a two-hitter on Grover Cleveland Alexander and Liberty Day, which should have been a fine send-off for the Cub bugs. They'd leapt the fence—hundreds of them—onto the North Side park field after the game, practically tailing Aleck all the way to the shower. They were still there when he emerged from the clubhouse, forcing him to take refuge in Charley Weeghman's office. His first and only start of 1918 in front of the home fans, and the old right arm had given them quite a memory. But Aleck knew how his mind worked. He would spend the entire train ride back home to Elba considering where he could have better located that pitch to Hornsby, he would spend every idle moment at Camp Funston replaying the sound of Hornsby's bat smashing his fastball, and if he ever did make it to the front, he'd see Hornsby's mug on every Hun he took down.

Aleck turned up his collar as he waited to cross LaSalle Street. It was cold and damp. After the game, he'd had time only for a bit of supper before his train left. He didn't even bother to take his gear out of his locker. It was all still there—shoes, glove, all of it. He wasn't much of speech giver, but he'd given his teammates a few parting words that he'd come up with on the way to the park. He told them he didn't know if he'd be back to play ball, but if he didn't make it back (and he didn't have to spell out what that would mean), then he'd make those Huns dig a lot of holes before they got him.[2] The boys got a chuckle out of that. It was an odd thing to say because Aleck really could not imagine himself across the ocean shooting at Germans. He supposed it was not much different from shooting birds along the banks of the Loup River back home, except that the duck blind was a trench and you wore combat boots instead of hip waders. That, plus gas attacks. Aleck had done a lot of hunting, but he hadn't hunted any species of duck that threw chlorine bombs.

Aleck looked down at his watch, his new watch, a gift from the Cubs. Only a month or so earlier he was planning on buying watches for all his fellow Cubs after he and Wrigley had finally worked out his bonus in the room at the Hotel Green in Pasadena. Mitchell had talked him out of the watches, which was a good thing, because now that he was heading into the army and a $30-per-month paycheck,[3] he needed to give his mother all the money he could. And Aimee—Aleck was going to marry Aimee Arrants before he left for France, and $30 wasn't going to do it. Back in March he had been ready to buy watches for teammates he barely knew, and now he was scrambling to provide for his fiancée. Wrigley and Weeghman, though, said they'd help out. Aleck appreciated that.

What a spring. First Aleck was sky-high in Pasadena, eating fresh oranges on Bill Wrigley's grove, smacking golf balls around the plushest fairways he'd ever seen, counting his bonus money in his head. Then Wrigley was driving Aleck around southern California, to the country club, over to Douglas Fairbanks's place to take photos. There he was, old Dode (as Ma and Pa used to call him) from Nebraska, giving a movie star like Doug Fairbanks a nudge and a wink over his

Grover Cleveland Alexander wound up spending more time in a khaki uniform than a Cubs uniform in 1918. This photo shows Alexander on his way back to America, in 1919. (National Baseball Hall of Fame Library, Cooperstown, N.Y.)

Mary Pickford fling.[4] Aleck knew married ballplayers who had girls on the sly, but leave it to Doug to have Mary Pickford as his side gal!

And then. George died. March 22. His brother George died, and with Pop dead more than a year now, poor Ma couldn't be consoled. Aleck thought the Howard County draft board would be swayed by his brother's death and grant him a draft exemption. But the board was firm—no exemption—and it was off to Camp Funston. Two weeks earlier he was playing in front of Khaki League soldiers. Now he'd be in khaki himself. From shouldering the willow to shouldering the musket. What a spring.

Things had been so busy, going back to the house in Nebraska, seeing Aimee, then to St. Louis and Cincinnati and Chicago with the Cubs, arranging for Ma's well-being, taking care of the billiard parlor back home. Aleck hadn't allowed himself to indulge in comforting thoughts. But now, his baseball season over, his mind wandered. He allowed himself to think that—who knows?—maybe the war would end before he got to the front. Maybe Kaiser Bill would finally give up. Aleck didn't think himself a coward. But he didn't think himself a fool either. He really did not want to go to this fight. That was the funny thing about the war. All these men puffing their chests about how much they wanted to get to war and kill Germans, but most of them crossing their fingers for an exemption. Maybe the young ones, with nothing to lose, were excited. But Aleck had plenty to lose. Men were dying over there. Men were being injured and broken. Aleck wanted to stay and comfort Ma, to marry Aimee, to hunt and fish on the banks of the Loup River, forever. And pitch. He wanted to pitch more than anything.

As Aleck entered the train station, his eye was caught by a billet plastered on a post. There were patriotic posters like this all over town, all over the country, imploring citizens to enlist or buy Liberty Bonds or just hate Germans in general—"Halt the Hun" and "Help Crush the Menace of the Seas" and "Blot Out the Hun." But this one struck Aleck. It was a soldier, seated in a chair. He was smiling, holding a cane, smartly decked in khaki, stretched out and comfortable looking. But something about the uniform was not quite right. It took Aleck a moment to recognize it.

Oh. He saw it now.

The sleeve of the soldier's uniform was pinned to his shoulder. He had no right arm. Some sacrifice. Under the drawing of the soldier: "The Red Cross is spending Ten Million Dollars a Year to help the disabled ex-service man and his family."[5]

Aleck bit his lip, rubbed his arm, and ducked into the LaSalle Street station.

On April 12, just four days before the Cubs were scheduled to open their season in St. Louis, the draft board of Howard County, Nebraska, called Grover Cleveland Alexander as the 10th of a 12-man quota it was required to send to Camp Funston in Kansas. This wasn't entirely unexpected. In the government's ranking system for potential draftees, Alexander had been placed in the first group eligible to be drafted—Class 1A, unmarried and with no dependents. Aleck thought his draft number was low enough to keep him out of the army until much later in the year, if he was drafted at all. He had sought an exemption on the grounds that his elderly mother was dependent on him, especially after the death of his brother, George, in March. But Alexander's appeal was denied. He was told he'd been drafted as the Cubs made the last leg of their spring training journey, from Guthrie, Oklahoma, to Wichita to Opening Day in St. Louis.

Opening Day wasn't as celebratory as usual. Heavy rain seemed to doom the Cubs–Cardinals game at Robison Field, but by midmorning the weather broke. The war dominated the pregame festivities. The Great Lakes military band provided music and a parade, the first ball was thrown out by Colonel Hunter of Jefferson Barracks, and a Liberty Loan skit was put on, in which Uncle Sam struck out Kaiser Bill on three pitches, each representing a loan. A crowd of 20,000 was expected, but only 8,000 showed.

Aleck was to be the day's starter, and he arrived in St. Louis on the morning of the game, agitated and exhausted. He hopped off a train from Chicago, where he'd been trying to nail down the details of his coming trip to Camp Funston. "Alex tried to snatch a nap at the hotel," the *Tribune* reported, "but went to the ball park pretty well worn out."[6] It showed. An error, a triple by Hornsby, and a double put the Cubs in a 2–0 hole in the first inning, and they couldn't recover, suffering a 4–2 loss.

The drafting of Alexander was a sobering reality. He was not the first player to leave baseball because of the war, but he was the biggest star taken by the draft. And he was not easing into the soft duty of naval yards—he was picked for the army, which meant he was destined for the front. In previewing baseball's Opening Day, the *New York Times* wrote, "Peanuts, hot frankfurters and popcorn will no longer have a monopoly, for as side attractions at the ball games, Liberty bonds and Thrift Stamps will also be on sale. . . . Just what sort of a baseball season this is going to be, under war conditions, is problematical. The war had little effect on the game last season, but as the seriousness of the grim struggle becomes more impressed upon the

53

public during the coming season there may be a lack of interest in baseball."[7]

Indeed, the struggle in Europe was getting more and more grim.

When Congress declared war on Germany on April 6, 1917, many assumed that the United States, with its vast wealth and manpower, would quickly turn the tide in favor of the Allies. Broadway writer George M. Cohan popped out a catchy and popular new song, "Over There," that summed up American bravado. When General John Pershing, the head of the American Expeditionary Force, as it was called, arrived in France, he supposedly stated, "Lafayette, we are here," as if the Americans would bail out the French as the French had done for the Americans in the Revolutionary War. (It was actually Pershing's underling who said it.) An editorial in the *Lincoln [Nebraska] Daily Star* read: "What it may mean in loss of life is not now conjecturable. It may mean none. Some are quite sanguine that the war will be over in three months."[8] That sort of optimism was widespread. In Paris, an editorial in *Echo de Paris* stated, "The Americans can give us immediately 500,000 workmen, and let the number include 25,000 specialists capable of building new roads, telegraphic and telephonic systems, saps, mines and all the immense apparatus—what a wonderful contribution to victory this would be!"[9]

But that optimism badly underestimated how unready the United States was for war, especially the kind of war that was being fought in Europe—a war of trenches, barbed wire, tanks, howitzers, machine guns, poison gas attacks, and air warfare. This was a long way from Teddy Roosevelt charging up San Juan Hill in the Spanish-American War, a long way from the Civil War. The U.S. Army stood at 202,510,[10] a pitifully small force whose only recent action had been chasing Pancho Villa's raiders near the Mexican border. In the Battle of the Somme, the British suffered 57,000 casualties *in the battle's first day.*[11] By the time the Battle of the Somme ended in November 1916, nearly 1.3 million soldiers on both sides were casualties. An army of 200,000 could not be expected to have any immediate impact.

After Congress passed the Selective Service Act on May 18, 1917, the nation had its first draft registration, which saw nearly 10 million men get their draft cards in June. It was not until July 20 that Secretary of War Newton Baker drew the draft numbers that would determine which civilians would make up the new army. In the first draft,

687,000 men were called into the service, and the nation prided itself on its speed. In Europe, however, the Allies were less than impressed. In the month that it took Congress to pass the Selective Service Act alone, France lost 187,000 men in the failed Nivelle offensive. By the time of the first registration, a mutiny cost the French another 30,000 soldiers. Meanwhile, the United States was still picking draft numbers. It was clear that the half million workmen the *Echo de Paris* sought immediately were not forthcoming.

Once men were drafted, the nation was faced with the problem of training, housing, clothing, feeding, arming, and transporting those men. Here the government had mixed results. It spent $136 million on 16 cantonments where new soldiers could be trained. Another 16 cantonments were built for the national guard (mostly in tent camps in the South, which, because of an uncharacteristically cold winter nationwide, wound up being a bad idea), plus more for the marines and the navy and for officer training. Construction of the cantonments began in June and was mostly complete by early October, as crews rushed through 30,000 tons of construction materials per day, creating training and living space for 1.5 million soldiers. This was counted as a big success for the War Department.

But clothing and supplies were challenges too. In the first year of the war, the U.S. Army Quartermaster Corps bought 75 million yards of drab olive cloth, 31 million yards of uniform cloth, 20 million blankets, and 49 million pairs of underwear. And, because of the cold winter, it was not enough. One food purchase included 116 million cans of baked beans and 20 million pounds of prunes (which surely made for interesting olfactory conditions in the bunkhouses at night).[12] Even when the men were trained, fed, and clothed, there weren't nearly enough guns. Heavy ordnance was lacking and would remain so. There was a long delay in the nation's air program, hindered by a graft scandal that saw the government essentially throw away $640 million.[13]

Beyond all these shortages was the obvious problem of getting the army over the ocean to Europe, especially with German submarines patrolling the Atlantic. And another problem: General Pershing wanted to amass the army in Europe and have it fight as a unit, rather than simply installing battalions with the French and British armies as they became ready. This further delayed the American effort and further angered the Allies.

Senator George Earle Chamberlain of Oregon, chairman of the Military Affairs Commission, was so disappointed in the progress that he launched a probe into the way the country had been conducting the war effort. For three weeks officials shuffled in to explain themselves. Finally Chamberlain stated flatly in a January 1918 talk with the National Security League, "We are still unprepared, without a definite war program and still without trained men. . . .The military establishment of the United States has broken down. It has almost stopped functioning."[14]

By April 1918, a full year after the declaration of war and under increasing pressure from the disgruntled Allies, the American army began to lurch into action. There wasn't much choice. The situation was worsening. In late 1917, the eastern front shut down when Russia—which had seen Czar Nicholas II overthrown and was now controlled by the Bolsheviks in the wake of the October revolution—agreed to peace with Germany. In March that peace was formalized in the Treaty of Brest-Litovsk and the Germans seized a large swath of Russian land, greatly increasing their store of resources. Germany turned those resources to the stalemated western front, and in late March the reinvigorated German army began a long series of offensives designed to smash Allied lines and win the war before the United States could become a factor.

"Speed up," French high commissioner André Tardieu warned, "but be sure that anyhow you come not too late."[15] The United States began hurrying men across the Atlantic, and as soldiers left the cantonments, the army drafted more civilians. This had a wide-ranging effect. Had Russia not given up the eastern front, had the German offensive not been launched, had German resources continued to erode beneath the strain of a two-front war, the U.S. Army might have continued its snail's crawl into action, and fewer American boys would have been pushed into war. It can be conjectured, then, that the activities of Vladimir Lenin, Leon Trotsky, and the Bolsheviks not only forever changed world political history but changed baseball history too. Grover Cleveland Alexander might have become the greatest pitcher baseball had ever known if war had not intervened. Aleck might have also done the remainder of his hurling in a Cubs uniform. That could have changed history for generations of North Side fans.

Told he'd been drafted before Opening Day, Alexander said, "I am not worried. I am ready to go at once if I am called. No one will have a chance to call me a slacker. However, I hope they will give me a chance to pitch the opening game in St. Louis on Tuesday, as I would like to win one game before going away to join the colors."[16]

He had plenty of motivation for wanting a win. Cubs fans who pinned their 1918 hopes on Alexander's pitching had watched their new star conduct an embarrassing holdout that spring. He wanted a bonus of $10,000, what he considered to be a piece of the money the Phillies received for him. When Baker would not pay, Alexander put the demand to the Cubs. He refused to practice until the bonus was paid. For a week, he watched spring training from the bleachers, hung out at the team's headquarters at the Hotel Green, sat in Killefer's car (Killefer had a house in southern California), and played golf. He was labeled a prima donna, and there was something unsavory about a player conducting a holdout while thousands of young men were being sent to war.

Through it all, Wrigley did most of the talking with Alexander—significantly, with Weeghman in Chicago, Wrigley had the air of Cubs decision maker. Wrigley took Alexander golfing at the Midwick Club, sat with him in the bleachers, and took him to the house of one of the most popular actors in the country, Doug Fairbanks. Finally, it was Wrigley, with Mitchell and Craighead, who worked out the bonus. The day after the agreement, the *Los Angeles Times* wrote, "Mr. Wrigley and the star hurler disappeared at once in the former's touring car, and it was thought possible they went to the bank for a bag of gold."[17]

Alexander, naturally, wanted to show Cubs fans he was worth all that gold. He didn't want baseball fans' last memory of him to be a holdout. After the April 16 loss to start the season in St. Louis, there was good news: Alexander would not have to report for military duty until April 30, which left time for two more starts. In his next outing, Alexander cruised to a 9–1 win in Cincinnati and, two days later, Weeghman's trained seals finally headed home to Chicago after a long, bizarre spring.

There was more excitement for the Cubs' home opener than there had been in St. Louis. Craighead advertised the game in the papers, pointing out that Weeghman Park "is the most comfortable ball garden in America. The ladies can wear their daintiest summer frocks without fear of soiling them."[18] Dainty frocks wouldn't have been a good idea for Opening Day, though, as cold winds limited the crowd to about the 10,000. Before the game, 450 jackies (sailors were called *jackies* and soldiers were called *sammies*) from the Great Lakes training center "went through with some of the fancy stunts taught on the North Shore and wound up in a 'charge bayonets' attitude while the flag was raised to the pennant pole and the band played the national hymn."[19] Illinois governor Frank Lowden threw out the first pitch, joined by powerful federal judge Kenesaw Mountain Landis, who had managed to sneak off the bench for the game. When Lowden uncorked a wild heave, Landis shouted, "Ball one!" There weren't many other bad pitches for the home team—Hippo Vaughn threw a one-hitter and won, 2–0.

Two days later the Cubs hosted Grover Cleveland Alexander and Liberty Day at Weeghman Park. Alexander was bent on throwing his first no-hitter, but Hornsby got in the way with a hit in the first inning. Still, Aleck was brilliant, allowing two hits and two runs in a 3–2 win, the only home game he'd pitch that year. Chilly, wet weather kept attendance down to 6,000, but those who did show were raucous, storming the field after the final out. "[Alexander] went to the firing line amid a thunder of cheers," *The Sporting News* reported, "was fairly smothered with flowers and . . . in a few hours was speeding on his way to join the Army with the plaudits of a cheering multitude ringing in his ears. . . . No man has made greater sacrifice than Grover Alexander."[20]

Alexander's draft tribulations registered with the rest of his teammates, especially those who were also Class 1A. The draft hung like a fog, obscuring the future for nearly every player on every team. Killefer, for one, had been Class 4, because he was married and his wife did not work, but he was reclassified when it was found that he owned land and had earned enough as a ballplayer that his wife was not dependent on his present salary. Killefer was now Class 1A, expecting to be drafted. Backup catcher Rowdy Elliott, second baseman Pete Kilduff, and pitcher Harry Weaver could be drafted at any time. Youngsters Turner Barber, Bill McCabe, and Paul Carter also seemed likely to go. The day after Alexander's debut in St. Louis, the lugubrious Cubs, "spent the day speculating what the team would look like after Uncle Sam gets through drafting men for his big-league affair on the other side of the ocean. With the prospects of losing Alexander and Killefer, the star battery, along with Rowdy Elliott and Pete Kilduff, and the possibility of losing another man or two, it didn't look bright for baseball on the north side in Chicago, but it does look bad for the Kaiser."[21]

The Original Curse: Aleck, Kilduff, and Elliott

Alexander pitched 26 innings in 1918, and when the Cubs suited up for that year's World Series he was an ocean away. But in a way he is an emblem for the misfortune—call it a curse—that defined that year's North Siders. Alexander's 1918 finale was an indication of how dominant a pitcher he was. But by June, Aleck had been whizzed through basic training (and gotten married), he had earned rank as a sergeant, and his unit, the 342nd Field Artillery of the 89th Division, had crossed the Atlantic.[22] By the last week of July, he was at the front. He spent seven weeks in the teeth of German attacks, working heavy artillery and facing relentless bombardment.

When he came back to Chicago in 1919, Alexander wasn't the same pitcher, relying more on finesse than on velocity. He wasn't the same person either. The war had changed him. He described the incongruousness of being at the front and then on the mound: "For many weeks, we had been under fire in France, where there was nobody to see, no matter what we did. There were no cheers, although we might kill or be killed. And now all the people cheering for me when I stepped out and pitched the ball."[23] Exploding artillery rendered him deaf in his left ear. He likely suffered shell shock. In peak condition when he left, he returned subject to epileptic fits and with a serious drinking problem.

Alexander put together one great postwar year, earning the pitching Triple Crown with 27 wins, a 1.91 ERA, and 173 strikeouts for a subpar Cubs team in 1920, but in Chicago he wasn't the pitcher Weeghman hoped he was buying when he laid out that chunk of his $250,000. Alexander managed to pitch until 1930, when he was 43 years old. His wife, Aimee, with whom he had a stormy but loving relationship, would divorce him twice. He could not hold a job because of his drinking, which became an embarrassing problem for baseball. "Certainly, having the man running loose around the country, drinking, carousing, pawning his belongings at every opportunity, is not beneficial to the good name of baseball," NL president Ford Frick wrote to Commissioner Landis in 1935.[24]

In 1939, unable to hold down a regular job during his time out of baseball, Alexander was inducted into the Hall of Fame. "They gave me a tablet up at the Cooperstown Hall of Fame," Alexander said, "but I can't eat any tablet."[25] The same year, he would get a job as a sideshow, telling baseball stories at a cheap flea circus in Times Square. "It is a sad picture for those inclined to be sentimental over the ex-heroes with which the field of sports is strewn, and all such had better stay away from Hubert's Museum, Inc., where Old Pete is working these days," one baseball writer noted.[26] Alexander died in 1947, broke.

Cursed fortune found two other Cubs who joined the colors in '18. Elliott enlisted in the navy in May and would play only one more big-league season. He bounced through minor-league gigs until, on February 12, 1934, at age 43, he (possibly drunk) fell from an apartment window and later died from the injuries. A collection was taken up by friends to keep Elliott, who was penniless, from being buried in a potter's field.[27]

Kilduff joined the navy shortly after Elliott and played three big-league seasons after the war. He was traded to Brooklyn for Lee Magee in 1919, a deal that was cursed for the Cubs in its own way (as we will see). Brooklyn won a pennant with Kilduff at second, but the Dodgers sent him to the Reds. They tried, but failed, to find a taker for Kilduff and shipped him to the Pacific Coast League. Kilduff had agreed to be the manager for Alexandria (Louisiana) in the Cotton States League when, on February 14, 1930, he died on the operating table while having his appendix removed. He was only 36 years old.

SIX

Morality: Max Flack

Chicago, May 11, 1918

Harry Weaver was on the mound, tall and skinny, all elbows and knees. Max settled into his crouch in right field, glove on his knee, absentmindedly scanning the crowd at Weeghman Park. Another weekend date and another bout of bad weather, which had kept the crowd down to about 6,000. Poor Charley Weeghman. The ticket sellers just could not get a break.

But, hey, Max thought, none of us are getting breaks these days. Once spring training was over and the season got under way, Max fell ill, terribly ill. Some kind of flu, but worse than any flu he'd had before. His temperature shot up over 100, for days on end, and his cough was violent.[1] The bug finally passed, and once Max got his strength together, he was able to get back out on the field, and just in time. Max knew the Cubs had paid a handsome sum—$15,000—to get Turner Barber from the Baltimore club, and Max was afraid that if he stayed out too long, Barber would push him right out of a job.

And then what? Max had some training, as a stove maker, but God help him, he did not want to go back to making stoves. His father had worked at the courthouse back home in Belleville, Illinois, and his brother, Jack, had followed him there. Jack was the janitor, and everyone in the place loved him. He was a tenor, and one thing that could be counted on in the Belleville courthouse was the sound of Jack's crooning voice belting out the latest popular numbers.[2] Max could hear Jack singing that sweet, sad song he liked so much:

Joan of Arc, they're calling you,
From each trench, they're calling you.
Far through the haze comes the sweet Marseillaise.
Can't you hear it calling, too?

The lyrics were tinged with sad coincidence—the song, about the war in France, was a favorite of Jack's. And now Jack was preparing to head to war himself. In a few days, he'd leave for Jefferson Barracks. Max could picture it, the employees of the courthouse gathering around, holding a party for his brother, presenting him with a commemorative watch.[3] Aleck had gotten a watch. So had Rowdy Elliott. Now Jack. One group that was surely not complaining about the war, Max thought, was the watchmakers. If Pershing gets a million men, that's a million farewell watches.

Max. Mex. Flack. Flach. They called him Max Flack. Back home, his name was Mex Flach. When Max finally got the chance to play pro baseball, he was so excited for the chance that he didn't bother to make certain that they got his name right. They could have called him Otto von Bismarck for all he cared. Max remembered his mother sending him a newspaper clipping, from the *Belleville News-Democrat*, saying, "On scorecards and in the newspaper, Mex's last name will be distorted to read something like, 'Flack,' but Mex . . . has never taken pains to correct it in his two years of professional baseball."[4]

And why would he correct them? Max was never quite sure he belonged in baseball, never really felt he was all that good a player. He was not going to complain about a minor mangling of his name. He had snuck in through baseball's back door and probably never would have been in the big leagues if not for the chance he got with Chicago's Federal League team in 1914. He hit .314 (fourth in the league) for the Whales in 1915 and was the hero of the season when he knocked a winning double in front of a massive crowd—there were 34,000 on hand, including Mayor Thompson—in the final game of the season, which won the ChiFeds the pennant by one percentage point. But that was the Feds, and honestly, that was not major-league-quality baseball. With the Cubs over the past two years, Max had been somewhat over his head, with averages of .258 and .248.

Max was determined not to go back to Belleville and make stoves, though. His wife, Stella, had just given birth to his first child, Raymond, and Max wanted to provide for his young family. His baseball salary allowed that. He would do anything to provide a good living for them. *Anything.* He had gone to Fred Mitchell and asked him how he could improve, how he could secure his position with the team. Mitchell was blunt, told him he was not much of a hitter, but that if he crouched down more, he could squeeze the pitcher's strike zone, draw more walks, and get on base more, where he could use his speed to steal bases. Max was just five-foot-seven, which was an advantage. He took Mitchell's advice to heart, and Mitchell rewarded him by putting him in the leadoff spot.

Now Max pulled his hat hard over his forehead—his wife always joked that the cap made him look like a little boy selling pink sheets. He smiled and then reminded himself to focus. He was in the middle of a game after all. He was surrounded by Cubs rooters. But he was alone, his head crowded. Mex. Max. Flach. Flack. He absentmindedly watched Weaver on the mound. Wait, how many outs? There's two on. Two out? Top of the third. Who's up? Al Wickland. Wickland can't hit. Weaver pitching. Move in. Too late. Wickland popped a fly ball toward Mex. *Focus.* He started late but ran in and had time to position himself under it. And. Off his glove. Mex muffed it. Two runs scored. The Cubs went on to lose the game, 6–4.

Max was usually so sure on fly balls.[5]

Even without Grover Cleveland Alexander, even in the face of terrible early weather, and even with Flack's unfortunate muff that lost a game to the Braves, the Cubs had a very good start to 1918. Rather than sulking over the loss of Aleck, the team seemed energized. Starting with the home opener, and including Aleck's farewell game, the Cubs won nine in a row. Losing Alexander, it turned out, did not crush their pitching staff. Left-hander Jim Vaughn—called, "Hippo" because of his massive figure and awkward gait—had come into his own since joining the Cubs in 1913 and entered 1918 with an 86–54 record over the five previous seasons. Catcher Bill Killefer would go so far as to call Vaughn an equal of Alexander. "I think Vaughn is as great a left hander as Alexander is a right hander, and I do not say that with any intention of boosting Vaughn undeservingly," Killefer said. "Of course, their styles are different. Alex was a sidearm thrower

63

and Jim delivers his assortment overhanded. As to the speed and the curves of the two, there is no difference. Vaughn is remarkably fast and has as sharp a breaking curve as Alex. The only shade Alexander has is in control."[6]

Lefty Tyler, meanwhile, was not far behind Vaughn. He was a "crossfire" pitcher—he threw from one extreme end of the mound and brought his arm across his body. He had control problems early in his career (he walked 109 batters in 165 innings as a rookie with the Boston Braves) but blossomed when Mitchell became Boston's pitching coach. He was 17–9 with a 2.02 ERA in 1916, but when Mitchell left to take the Cubs job in 1917, Tyler fell to 14–12. Now that he was again with Mitchell, though, Tyler was back in form. Spitballer Claude Hendrix, too, was thriving. Hendrix had one good season with Pittsburgh, going 24–9 in 1912, and had been a star with Chicago's Federal League team, posting a record of 29–10 in 1914. But he slipped to 16–15, and it seemed Hendrix just didn't have big-league stuff—he was 18–28 in '16 and '17 combined. Still, Hendrix had good control. With the Cubs' solid defense and the addition of a smart catcher in Killefer, Hendrix figured to benefit. (Indeed, '18 proved to be one of Hendrix's best seasons.)

The Cubs were not winning with just pitching—they were jelling into a very good offensive team, able to win a slugfest as well as a pitchers' duel. On May 2, they beat the Reds, 12–8, and won again the next day, 9–8, with a thrilling four-run rally in the bottom of the ninth. The offense produced 4.8 runs per game in the first 20 games, impressive for a team that had averaged just 3.5 runs in 1917. When the Cubs won in Pittsburgh, 6–2, on May 9, the *Tribune* noted, "It was one of the strongest offensive games yet played by the new Cubs and rather opened the eyes of local fans who haven't been accustomed to such rough treatment from Chicago."[7]

64

Flack was solid in the leadoff spot, but it was the hitter behind him—new kid Charley Hollocher—who deserved, and got, credit for the team's early offensive output. But like Flack, many Cubs simply started better than expected at the plate. Left fielder Les Mann hit .316 in his first 117 at bats. In center, 36-year-old Dode Paskert hit .299. In the spring, some wondered whether first baseman Fred Merkle, though only 29, was washed up. Merkle ended such talk when he came out slugging, and *Tribune* writer James Crusinberry jokingly began calling him "Mr. Muscle Merkle." By late May, Mr. Muscle

Though 36 years old, center fielder Dode Paskert was one of the hot-hitting Cubs who carried the team throughout the early part of the season. (Chicago History Museum)

was one of the league's top hitters, batting .351 and ably filling the role of cleanup man. The *Chicago American* said of him, "His fielding improved and his hitting went over the .300 mark and he again looked upon the affairs of life with a cheerful countenance."[8]

There was plenty of cheer to go around for the Cubs. Asked early in the season for the secret of the Cubs' success, Mitchell responded, "The hitting of Merkle, Mann, Hollocher, Flack and Paskert has been most excellent, especially in the pinches. Killefer's catching has been wonderful, the fielding steady and the pitching great."[9] Quipped columnist Ring Lardner, poking fun at Mitchell's reputation as a master strategist: "So the mystery no longer exists. But it does seem rather foolish for Mitch to reveal his strategy at this stage of the race, for if the other managers read the interview, there is nothing to prevent their taking advantage of the tip and applying it to their own teams. . . . All that's required to land on top is five hitters hitting most excellent, one catcher catching most wonderful, one team fielding steady and one team's pitchers pitching great. But the other managers evidently didn't think of it."[10]

The pitching staff got a boost on May 12, when Shufflin' Phil Douglas wired Mitchell from Tennessee, telling his manager he had recuperated from his February appendectomy and was ready to report. Four days later, Douglas showed up in Chicago, though he would need a few weeks to get himself ready. Douglas was no star, but he was durable and would give the Cubs a solid fourth pitcher to go with Vaughn, Tyler, and Hendrix. Things were, indeed, cheerful on the North Side.

The perseverance of the Cubs was a comforting story in the spring of 1918, in a city that was in need of comfort. These were stressful, confusing days for Chicagoans, a time of gray areas. America was fighting a war for freedom and democracy but was trampling the First Amendment in support of that war. Citizens were being told of German atrocities, yet Chicago's mayor (pandering to the German vote) had come out as pro-German and antidraft. The federal government was clamping down on vice districts, but the city's police department was loosening the reins on those districts. Inflation had prices skyrocketing, but citizens were pressured to buy Liberty Bonds. Working men were demanding increased rights but in doing so were hindering the war effort. There wasn't much that could be said to be surely right and surely wrong.

One of the great symbols of this moral confusion was the Reverend Billy Sunday, a ballplayer-turned-preacher whose unorthodox style and use of off-color language and violent imagery rankled the religious establishment, even as he drew massive crowds across the country. Sunday had no formal training but packed his speeches with energy—he was accompanied by two thunderous pianos and, as a former athlete, would hurl his lithe body all over the stage, turning somersaults and smashing chairs. He was at his most skillful when he wove the issues of the day into his sermons. That spring, Sunday's travels took him back home to Chicago, and onstage in his massive temporary tabernacle on Lake Michigan there was no question what the issue of the day was: the war in Europe.

War fit Sunday perfectly. First, it gave him a suitable backdrop for his primary aim: outlawing alcohol in the United States. Already, 19 states had backed prohibition, and the war was fueling the dry argument. Not only could alcohol ruin American soldiers, but its manufacture took away resources from the war effort. Besides, most American brewery owners were of German descent. The argument that being antibooze was patriotic gained acceptance, and at one point an amendment that would mandate prohibition during the war was slipped into an agricultural appropriations bill.[11] These were not the moral arguments that people like Billy and other temperance backers favored, but they were effective.

The war also paired well with Sunday's fire-and-brimstone style. The violence of war hit Americans psychologically, and Sunday's inflammatory sermons appealed to that violence. Preaching about pacifists, he said, "Do you know what a pacifist is? He is one too damned cowardly to fight and too damn cowardly to run. He ought to be stood up against a wall with a firing squad in front of him."[12] He said of Germany, "She has used her power to burn cities, sack cathedrals and slay men, murder children, rape women, starve people and inoculate with typhoid and tuberculosis germs. The religion of Germany is the roar of the cannon, the spit of the machine gun, the shrieks of the dying, battlefields drenched with blood. She is happy when she sees these horrors."[13] The previous December, in Atlanta, when a German pacifist harangued Sunday during a sermon, Sunday

67

invited him onto the stage and punched him. A fistfight ensued. Some in Sunday's audience piously shouted, "Sock him! Kill him! Lynch him!"[14]

Sunday's sermons were tracked daily in Chicago's newspapers, and given the contradictions between praising God and executing pacifists, it's little wonder that citizens were having a hard time setting their moral compasses. Sunday was just one symptom of that problem, which was not exactly a new conflict in Chicago. The city's early-20th-century experience, like that of many major American cities, was marked by a back-and-forth between lax moral standards and sporadic campaigns against immorality. The war only intensified that back-and-forth.

When it came to moral laxity, prostitution was a Chicago specialty, but thanks to the efforts of Mont Tennes, Chicago also was a national gambling headquarters. Tennes was the head of the General News Bureau, but the only news the bureau generally disseminated was horse racing information. After a bloody war fought in spurts in 1907–08, Tennes emerged with control over the racing wires in Chicago and eventually across the country. That meant that in the back rooms of hotels, poolhouses, saloons, and "cigar stores" that never sold cigars, men could bet on races across the country—with 50 percent of the take going to Tennes, who also sold police protection. This made Tennes wealthy.

Attempts to expose Tennes were fruitless. He even managed to best Judge Kenesaw Mountain Landis. In October 1916, Landis was investigating a blackmail scam when he stumbled onto witnesses involved at a low level in Tennes's gambling business. Over the course of two days, Landis pressed several hapless witnesses into revealing the inner workings of the General News Bureau. Finally, Tennes himself showed up in court with his lawyer, Clarence Darrow, who had held a conference with those Tennes underlings who had been so loose-lipped in front of Landis. "As a result of this conference," the *Tribune* reported, "the fear of self-incrimination took a strong hold on all the gamblers."[15] Thus ended Landis's confrontation, with no consequences for Tennes. The investigation only fortified the view of the city once expressed by muckraking journalist George Kibbe Turner, who wrote, "Chicago, in the mind of the country, stands notorious for violent crime."[16]

In the early 1910s, Mayor Carter Harrison Jr. tried to stamp out Chicago's crime and graft, but only until William Hale Thompson was elected mayor in 1915. Thompson reverted Chicago to a "wide-open" form of government, with little oversight of vice districts. A little more than a year after Thompson took office, his chief of police, Charles Healey, fired seven of the city's eight morals inspectors. Healey himself was brought up on charges of corruption, facing allegations that he peddled protection to lawbreaking businesses. (One captain complained that because of Healey's influence "he had not been allowed to interfere with all-night cafes in which whites and blacks danced and drank together."[17]) Healey's replacement, John Alcock, picked up the slack, firing tough-minded morals inspector Major M. L. C. Funkhouser—well liked by foes of vice—in May 1918 on flimsy charges.

But while Thompson was loosening the city's oversight of vice, the war gave the federal government, concerned about the moral standards of soldiers, a stake in the vice struggle around the country. Under pressure from the Anti-Saloon League, the sale of liquor to soldiers was banned. The army confronted the widespread problem of venereal disease in the ranks and went to great lengths to ensure its men stayed clean—either by keeping the soldiers clean themselves with extensive prophylaxis inspections or by hitting them with propaganda, such as camp posters that read "A German Bullet Is Cleaner than a Whore" and pamphlets that wondered "How could you look the flag in the face if you were dirty with gonorrhea?"[18]

In wide-open cities like Chicago, federal agents bypassed police and attempted to shut down vice districts, even threatening to take over police forces themselves. Cities across America were undergoing such moral struggles, but Chicago was an especially raucous cauldron, and polarizing figures such as Billy Sunday ensured that it stayed that way. For citizens exposed to this moral back-and-forth, it was increasingly difficult to figure out just what was right and what was wrong.

Boston, though certainly not without its vices, was an older, wealthier city than Chicago and, thus, more morally stable. Or at least the city's advanced age had given it time to find places in which to keep its immorality hidden. Back in 1828, writer and teacher Bronson Alcott (Louisa May Alcott's father) declared Boston "The city that is set on high." Its morality, he said, "is more pure than that of any other city in

America."[19] That self-image stuck. As morality increasingly became a war issue, Boston prided itself on its cleanliness. At a party on April 20, Boston's ex-mayor John "Honey Fitz" Fitzgerald proudly approached Josephus Daniels, secretary of the navy, with a newspaper clipping citing a study that "showed less vice in Boston than ever before and the best moral conditions in the history of the city."[20] (Fitzgerald would go on to serve in Congress and had a grandson who bore his name: John Fitzgerald Kennedy.)

Massachusetts passed the prohibition amendment in early April, cracked down on bootleggers who sold alcohol to soldiers, and passed a law to regulate hotels and lodging houses, keeping them free from prostitution. When the weather warmed, officials at popular Revere Beach (a Babe Ruth favorite) did their best to keep girls pure by "strictly enforcing" the ban preventing men at the beach from lying on their backs, which was apparently too suggestive.[21] The city was much more attuned to the repressed, Puritan attitude of the nation than Chicago. All the wrangling over prostitution and venereal disease in the army, for example, was a strictly American problem. French prime minister Georges Clemenceau offered what he thought was a logical solution: He wrote a letter offering American soldiers use of clean, licensed French brothels. Raymond Fosdick, with the Commission of Training Camp Activities, showed the letter to Secretary of War Newton Baker, upon which Baker said of the prudish Wilson, "For God's sake, Raymond, don't show this to the President or he'll stop the war."[22]

Boston's reconstituted American League team, meanwhile, got off to an even better start than the Cubs. The Red Sox arrived home from spring training to find snow covering the field at Fenway Park but were offered a day of training at the Harvard batting cage, where Boston baseball legend Hugh Duffy coached. Duffy had spent 17 years in pro ball, posting a record .440 batting average for Boston's Beaneaters in 1894, and would later take over the Red Sox as the manager. Fittingly, the Red Sox were to open the season against Connie Mack's Athletics and featured two ex-A's in the starting lineup—Stuffy McInnis at third and Amos Strunk in center. One of the big unknowns for Boston was its cleanup hitter, and Barrow, after much consideration, finally settled on Hoblitzell. "But when he said that [Hoblitzell] had just the nerve that a cleanup hitter required, he was not scaling any asparagus at any of the other boys," Ed Martin of the *Globe* explained.[23] The other boys were, presumably, relieved not to have any asparagus scaled at them.

John Evers was in the stands at Fenway on Opening Day, but he was no longer with the team as a coach or an infielder—in his place, the Red Sox had acquired capable veteran second baseman Dave Shean, a native of Belmont, Massachusetts, from the Reds and brought back well-liked coach Heinie Wagner, who had been fired to make room for Evers. Wagner knew the American League and could help Barrow with strategy. On the mound, Babe Ruth got the nod in the opener and, in front of 10,000 fans, threw a four-hit complete game, driving in two runs for a 7–1 win.

Carl Mays threw a one-hitter in the second game, barely missing a no-hitter when Shean was too slow to get to a grounder (which surely drew the ire of Mays). In the third game, with Mary Pickford on hand to push for the sale of Liberty Bonds, ex-A's catcher Wally Schang knocked in two in the ninth to pull out a 5–4 win. With that, the Red Sox—who had rebuilt their roster by sending $60,000 and some good young players to the A's—started 1918 with a sweep of Mack's bunch.

The Red Sox followed that sweep by taking four out of five from the Yankees, including a game on April 23 in which Boston had been held hitless by rookie Hank Thormahlen in a scoreless game until there was one out in the ninth. Strunk finally broke through with a single, when Barrow pulled a telling maneuver. He removed Hoblitzell for Ruth. This was an odd move. Thormahlen was a left-hander and, theoretically, a more difficult matchup for Ruth, also a left-hander. And Hoblitzell was a right-handed cleanup man, not generally a candidate to be replaced by a pinch-hitter. But Ruth pounded a single, sending Strunk to third. Strunk would score to win the game, 1–0, and sure enough, the notion of subbing in a pitcher for a cleanup hitter now seemed to make some sense—assuming the pitcher in question was Babe Ruth.

The Red Sox were 7–1. Their new players seemed to fit right in. Their pitching staff looked outstanding—with one out-of-shape and distracted flinger being the only exception. Their one loss of the season to that point was an 11–4 blowout in which "The Yanks mauled the offerings of Dutch Leonard . . . mercilessly."[24] It was a bad start to a strange year for Leonard.

71

SEVEN

Cheating: Hubert "Dutch" Leonard

BOSTON, MAY 21, 1918

Hubert let out a deep breath and rubbed a hand over his stomach. All right, he was carrying around a bit more lard than he should. He knew that. Barrow, Frazee, all the beat reporters, they'd been calling him chunky and portly and all that bunk. Of course, the fans jumped right in and mimicked them. There was no ape like a Fenway ape. Dutch had been hearing it since Hot Springs. Portly portsider. Stocky southpaw. He didn't give a damn. He had bigger concerns. Like his own hide. He'd spent most of the off-season getting the vineyards in shape, because if anything was going to keep him out of this hell of a war, it was growing grapes, not tossing horsehides for Barrow and Frazee. Dutch's hope was to pitch in the big leagues for a few more years, gain fame, and capitalize on that fame in business. And that business was good, sweet Fresno raisins.

But he needed to be alive to count raisin money, and being alive meant staying out of the war. This was of chief importance to Dutch Leonard. Last winter he'd looked into signing on with the naval yard in Charlestown, and in Mare Island too, figuring he could call himself a yeoman, get a contract to pitch for the team, drive a rivet every now and then, and keep his backside far, far away from the trenches at Arras or Amiens or wherever the fight was today. He would have done

Dutch Leonard was a talented but enigmatic lefty and did not pitch for the Red Sox after 1918. (National Baseball Hall of Fame Library, Cooperstown, N.Y.)

it, too, if Sybil—the new Mrs. Leonard—hadn't gotten sick almost immediately after their wedding the previous fall.[1]

They're not supposed to call farmers, he figured, which was why Dutch had written it right on his draft registration card. "Do you claim any exemption from draft (specify grounds)?" the card wanted to know. Very carefully, and in large letters, he wrote in script, "Farmer."[2] They'd had him in Class 4 of the draft. But he knew he could, and probably would, be shifted to 1A. Seemed everyone was losing exemptions, getting shifted to 1A—all the married fellows, like Joe Jackson, and some of the farmers, where it was shown that the farm owner was not actually doing the farming, as in Dutch's case. All right, then, he still was not fool enough to march to the gates of Hades to fight Huns. No, no. This war is not for me, thought Dutch Leonard.

He glanced over to third base. Fred Thomas. He was 25, a year younger than Dutch. Class 1A. Behind him, shortstop Everett Scott. He's deferred, married, kids, Class 4, but Scott has money socked away, Dutch thought, enough money so that his dependents aren't really dependent on him. That made Scott a good candidate to move up from Class 4 to 1A. Over his left shoulder, at second base, Dave Shean was 34, too old for the draft. At first, Hobby. Doc Hoblitzell wanted to go to the war, but he was doing it with the Dental Corps. He had been distant all spring, like he was already gone. Good riddance as far as Dutch cared—Hobby was batting one-fifty-something. Dental Corps. Dutch had asked Hobby if they needed dentists at the front. Are cavities a big problem for soldiers? Dutch pictured a fellow in a trench in France, with his leg blown off, gushing blood, screaming for a doctor, and here comes Hobby, saying, "You know, son, we should really take that molar out."

Dutch hadn't expected to be with the Red Sox this year, not until Frazee talked him into it back in February. He was comfortably in Class 4 then. That's why he wasn't in shape. On the slab, Leonard had been getting knocked around by a lot of duck-soup teams, but umpires had been giving him a bum deal. He gave out 10 passes against Philadelphia and walked 7 Tigers last time out. Umps' fault, not his. Besides, Dutch was worn out, and that was Barrow's fault. Big Ed was riding the boxmen too hard. Dutch's speedball had not been hopping, and there wasn't a lot of break in his slants. He needed a rest. But the Big Baboon Babe Ruth was sick, in the Eye and Ear

Infirmary, and Barrow was still too scared to use the young pitchers. There would be no rest.

Ed Miller was in the leadoff hole for the Indians, and Dutch knew that the game was in bad shape when a busher like Miller could make it back into the American League. One of the bugs yelled, "Come on, Lard Pants, even you can get this one out!" Dutch scowled and scanned the crowd. The sky was dark with thunderclouds. Old Jupiter Pluvius had not shown up just yet, but it looked like he was rapping at the door. Place was near empty, not even 2,000 in the cushions, and Dutch knew on a day like this the only arses who showed up were the so-called sporting men of the gambling fraternity. He scanned the first-base bleachers where they sat. From the mound, everyone looked the same to Dutch, pasty-faced and hook-nosed, passing sheets of paper around, wearing $2 straw hats, popping peanuts, downing frankfurters and bottles of soda.

Today, Hubert decided, he was going to take a little extra help. He needed it. His arm was tired. Barrow was on him. The fans were on him. Dutch didn't particularly like the taste of licorice and didn't like the way it blackened his teeth, but it was better than slippery elm bark. He chewed the licorice and worked up a nice ball of sticky saliva in his cheek. He readjusted his hat and, as he did, let the blackened spit fly onto his left palm. Working quickly in the pocket of his glove, he kneaded the licorice spit and a bit of dirt into the ball. Dutch stepped to the mound, looked long at Miller, and then nodded to catcher Wally Schang. He wrapped his fingers around the loaded ball, placing the licorice-and-dirt stain comfortably into his palm. He was ready to pitch.

Spitballs, licorice balls, slippery elm balls, emery balls, shine balls, mud balls, paraffin balls. In 1918, there was no shortage of ways for pitchers to cheat. Only it wasn't really cheating, not until baseball, after years of discussion and foot dragging on the topic, finally outlawed, "freak deliveries" after 1920. There was a fine for "discoloring the ball," but it was minimal. Still, ball doctoring was unseemly, and no pitcher wanted to be blatant about it. It was not done openly. Reds infielder Heinie Groh later described teammate Hod Eller's approach: "Old Hod had what we liked to call a shine ball. What it was, he had a file in his belt and every once in a while he'd rub the ball against that file."[3] Altering the surface of the ball would give it strange movement on its way to the plate.

Use of "freak" pitches was so widespread in 1918 that fed-up Washington manager Clark Griffith, who had long wanted the pitches outlawed, went on a campaign of "shine-balling the American League to death," as The Sporting News put it.[4] He ordered his pitchers to use every available doctoring method—paraffin oil, tar, talcum, licorice—and withheld their pay until they mastered freak pitches. He figured nonstop freakery from Washington pitchers would force the league to do something. He was wrong. The league did nothing. On the bright side, the Senators' team ERA dropped from 2.75 in '17 to 2.14, first in the AL, in '18. That did not much discourage the use of freak pitches.

Dutch Leonard wasn't necessarily a licorice-ball pitcher in 1918 (he would later become one of the "grandfathered" pitchers who were allowed to throw a spitball after the pitch was banned). In fact, it wasn't certain just what kind of pitcher Leonard was. He had burst into the big leagues at 22 with a stunning second season for the 1914 Red Sox, going 19–5 with a 0.96 ERA, lowest in modern baseball history. But after '14, Leonard didn't much apply himself, routinely reporting overweight, earning a reputation as a late-night carouser and chronic complainer. He went just 16–17 in 1917. His slow start in 1918 was no surprise, and it's easy to understand why he, according to Cleveland batters, resorted to smearing balls with licorice on May 21.[5] He had a record of 4–3 at the time, including a couple of lucky wins. He had allowed 57 hits, 32 runs, and way too many walks (31) in his seven starts. Throughout the start against Cleveland, batters protested to umpire Dick Nallin that the ball was marked with licorice. All Nallin could do was look at the balls, toss them aside, and issue limp warnings to the Boston dugout.

As a whole, the Red Sox had gotten off to an impressive start, having swept the A's and going on to win 11 of their first 13 games. But they quickly tired and fell into a 6-game losing streak. By mid-May, pitching depth behind the big four of Babe Ruth, Carl Mays, Leonard, and Joe Bush was a problem. Nick Flatley wrote in the Boston American, "Lack of substitute material, more than the beatings, is greying the hairs of Manager Barrow just now. . . . [For Leonard] a rest would be the best thing in the world, but when there are no other pitchers handy there can be no rests."[6] Barrow used only two other pitchers—Sam Jones made two relief appearances, and Weldon Wyckoff made one. Barrow had so little faith in his second-stringers that while letting up 14 hits and seven runs in Washington on May 7, Leonard was left in to absorb the pummeling.

The Red Sox had one pitching advantage: their ace was Babe Ruth, and no player dominated early 1918 quite like Ruth. Short rosters and Hooper's badgering induced Barrow to use Ruth at first base and in the outfield throughout spring training, and Ruth responded by consistently clubbing home runs. Those displays were not forgotten. Barrow used Ruth as a pinch hitter in April, but Hooper pressed Barrow to have Ruth hit more. Barrow resisted, telling Hooper, "I would be the laughingstock of the league if I took the best lefthanded pitcher in the league and put him in the outfield."[7] While pitching and batting ninth on May 5, Ruth knocked his first home run. The next day, Hoblitzell sat out with what would become a swollen thumb of historic significance, because the injury forced Barrow to turn to Ruth. On May 6, for the first time in his career, Ruth started a game at a position other than pitcher. Batting sixth, Ruth hit another home run. The next day, with Hoblitzell still injured, Barrow moved Ruth to cleanup. He hit another home run. In one game on May 10, Ruth tallied five hits, including a triple and three doubles. He was hitting a league-best .407 by May 20, while still serving as the Red Sox ace pitcher.

Ruth was obviously a wonder at swinging the willow, but in the minds of many he was a pitcher and that should not change. The *Boston American* commented, "[Ruth] was forced to dally around first base while Hobby was on the shelf. He carved a dent in the season's history while doing it, but star pitchers never will flourish under that sort of treatment."[8] Still, Ruth's hitting excited fans. Barrow was the manager, but he was a front-office man at heart, and he knew the importance of putting people in the cushions. Hooper made that appeal to Barrow—fans wanted to see Babe hit, not pitch. "[Ruth] is applauded every time he steps to the plate," reported Burt Whitman in *The Sporting News*, "and the simple snare of a spent fly out there in left also draws the plaudits of the enthusiasts. They are all wild about the big fellow; they all want him in every game and Barrow has felt the pulse of the fans and is giving them just what they desire."[9]

Barrow began playing Ruth in the outfield, making Hooper responsible for teaching Ruth to play the field. Ruth's scorching performance in May was soon derailed by a bout with tonsillitis, commonly—and carefully—treated with silver nitrate at the time. Open a copy of the *American Journal of Clinical Medicine* from 1914, though, and find the following note on using silver nitrate with tonsil patients: "Caution: Great care must be exercised that no excess silver-nitrate solution oozing from the swab drops into the throat, lest serious results might follow; for, as we know, cases are on record in which edema of the glottis, severe spasms of the larynx and other spastic affections of the throat, even suffocation, resulted from such accidents."[10] With such dire consequences, the Red Sox trainer had no business administering silver nitrate to Ruth's throat. That should have been left to a doctor. Still, the trainer tried, and, sure enough, some excess oozed off the swab. Ruth's throat closed up, he collapsed, and he would spend the next week at the Massachusetts Eye and Ear Infirmary. Ruth struggled to speak but kept his sense of humor. When Barrow and Frazee visited his hospital room, where a stream of delivery men had piled up floral arrangements, Ruth pointed out, "The time to get flowers is when you are alive."[11] Barrow, though, did not keep his humor. He fired the trainer.[12]

Even with their depth problems, the Red Sox shaped up to be the class of the league. Entering the year, the White Sox were expected to defend the AL championship, but Chicago's roster took an irreparable hit in mid-May when outfielder Joe Jackson was bumped up from Class 4 to Class 1A (after the first draft wave, the government narrowed and simplified its classification system, removing many of the marriage exemptions, and local draft boards pushed previously deferred men into Class 1A). Rather than wait to be called into the army, Jackson accepted an offer to paint ships for the Harlan & Hollingsworth Shipbuilding Company in Delaware, part of the nationalized Emergency Fleet Corporation, which was building a modern American navy. Losing Jackson, who was hitting .354 at the time, was the start of an exodus that pretty much sank the champs' season, leaving inexperienced upstarts such as Cleveland and the Yankees—neither team had ever won a pennant at that point—as the Red Sox's main challengers.

Jackson's move brought attention to a brewing problem. Once he punched in for his shipyard job, Jackson was supposed to paint ships, which qualified him for a draft exemption on the grounds that he was employed in a field useful to the war effort. It's unlikely, though, that Jackson so much as fingered a brush. See, it so happened that Harlan & Hollingsworth had a competitive baseball team. In fact, all six of the government's shipbuilding yards had competitive baseball teams. The shipyards pursued Class 1A big-league players such as Jackson, offering hefty wages to top players, plus exemption from army service. The *Boston American* reported, "As much as $900 a month has been offered to more than one star player, while propositions of $500 are numerous."[13]

There was bluster and outrage about the draft-dodging scheme. When Jackson left, Ban Johnson claimed that more than 20 players had been taken by shipyards. Columnist Hugh Fullerton wrote, "The recent movement of the players to the shipyards of private companies, where the majority are to play on ball teams rather than drive rivets, is a sad commentary on the patriotism of the players."[14] When two more White Sox players, Claude Williams and Byrd Lynn, jumped to the shipyards the following month, an angry Charles Comiskey said, "I don't consider them fit to play on my ball club."[15] Brooklyn owner Charles Ebbets, who lost pitcher Al Mamaux to a shipyard, wrote, in a letter to *Baseball Magazine*, "I would not care to re-employ any of our men who enter such plants."[16] These were empty threats. In 1919, Jackson, Williams, and Lynn were back with the White Sox, and Mamaux was pitching for Ebbets.

The shipyard lure was strong. The money was good, the competition tough, and the war distant. That winter, Leonard nearly signed up with a naval yard team, and for all the struggles he was having by the time the Indians were accusing him of giving his fastball a little licorice, he probably wished he had done so. Leonard did pull himself together, throwing a no-hitter on June 3 and pitching better as the weather warmed. But Leonard had to be thinking about getting out all along. Eventually, on June 22, Leonard signed with the Fore River shipyard in Quincy, Massachusetts. Two days later he was moved up to Class 1A. He did not play again in 1918, but neither did he go to war.

Which, perhaps, was selfish and unpatriotic, though consistent with Leonard's me-first reputation. But Leonard's choices were difficult. Remember, when Alexander returned from the front, he was a shell-shocked epileptic with an alcohol problem, who died broke.

When Leonard died in 1952, he was a raisin magnate, living on 2,500 acres of lush California land. He left his heirs an estate worth $2.1 million.[17]

Draft dodging and ball doctoring were known problems in 1918, but baseball rarely handled problems head-on. Broad proclamations were quickly ignored (as with the quick re-signing of players who jumped to shipyards), and complicated issues were shrugged off (as with pitchers' use of freak deliveries). Baseball had risen to American sporting supremacy. It had little competition. Fans were satisfied with the game as it was. Solving problems meant delving into negatives, and why delve into negatives?

Gambling was one of baseball's great negatives, and the city of Boston was its epicenter. Rumors of crookedness had been cropping up in the city for years, and there was active and open gambling in Boston's ball parks, but the problem was presented merely as one of too much betting in the stands, not as a problem of gamblers influencing players. Baseball was loath to admit that there was interaction between gamblers and the game itself. Rewind to the summer of 1917, though, and find that baseball's gambling problem literally spilled onto the field at Fenway Park.

The scene on June 16, 1917, was surreal—a cool, wet day at Fenway, the Red Sox playing an important afternoon game against the White Sox. Boston was in second place, trailing Chicago by 2.5 games. Ninety-four hundred fans were on hand, including several officers from the French army, in town to help train American soldiers. The pitching matchup was a beauty—32-year-old Chicago shine-baller Eddie Cicotte against fire-throwing 22-year-old Babe Ruth. The White Sox took a 2–0 lead in the top of the fourth when rain began to fall, muddying the field. Fans in the right-field bleachers chanted, "Call the game!"

For a game to be official, five innings must be completed. With two out in the fifth and the White Sox winning—just one more out would make the game count in the books—the frustrated chants of "Call the game!" grew louder. Then 300 fans overran the fence and stormed the field. The *Globe* reported, "Sgt. Louis C. Lutz and five patrolmen from the Boylston St. station were powerless against the mob, which drew many recruits from the left-field bleachers."[18] In the mayhem, a fight broke out between Red Sox fans and White Sox players. One fan let out three cheers for the Red Sox and claimed he was attacked by Chicago's Buck Weaver and Fred McMullin for it. White Sox catcher Ray Schalk got into a scuffle with one of the cops. There was a 45-minute delay to clear the fans. The field was soaked, but play continued. The White Sox won, 7–2. The French officers must have thought baseball a very strange game.

If a game ends before it is official, any wager placed on that game becomes null and void—which is why the "Call the game!" chanters were so persistent. They wanted to rescue their losing bets on the Red Sox. Right field in Fenway was notorious as a gambling hub (gamblers were equally active at the home of the NL's Boston Braves). With the Red Sox down, 2–0, all bets on Boston officially would be losers if the umpire waited until the next inning to call the game. The gamblers attempted a human rain delay.

In a stern column on the subject, James Crusinberry wrote in the *Tribune*:

> Later investigation made it practically certain that the trouble was started by the horde of gamblers that assembles each day in the right field pavilion and carries on operations with as much vigor and vim as one would see in the wheat pit of the Chicago board of trade. The same condition prevails at the National league park, and although gambling may take place more or less in all big league parks, there is no other city in which it is allowed to flourish so openly. . . .
>
> Just why this betting ring is allowed in Boston and not tolerated in other cities never has been explained by the baseball magnates, but it is supposed to carry a political angle which has the hands of the magnates tied. The attention of major league presidents has been called to it in the past and even has brought forth statements from the baseball heads that there was no open gambling. Any one present, however, can see the transactions and hear them plainly.[19]

81

Boston gambling had been brought to the attention of Ban Johnson years earlier. In August 1915, when stories appeared about betting at the park, Johnson set out to address the problem. "We stopped gambling there a few years ago," Johnson said at the time. "There is nothing more harmful to baseball than gambling and I think we have it pretty well rooted out. When we started after the gamblers in Boston . . . we had all kinds of obstacles thrown in our way. Influential politicians and others tried their best to protect these leeches, but we stopped at nothing and soon had the regulars suppressed."[20]

Evidently not, because two years later gamblers made a farce of the game at Fenway. Outraged and embarrassed, Johnson began an antigambling crusade in August 1917. He hired Pinkerton detectives, and by August 24 nine men had been convicted of gambling at Boston's two parks, and others were awaiting hearings. Four days later, at Braves Field, police manned the bleacher gates and denied admission to 25 men suspected of being gamblers. The crackdown was swift but utterly lacked teeth. The convicted gamblers had to pay only a small fine, and off they went.

The hubbub around Johnson's fight against gamblers subsided, and when 1918 opened, not much had changed. Fenway was still infested with gamblers. When the White Sox—with Weaver and McMullin in tow—returned to Boston for a late-May series, Weaver was hounded by Fenway gamblers. "Those money changers who ply their trade brazenly in the face of authority at major-league ball games remembered the incidents of last season—one in particular—when they tried to stop a ball game by force, when they stood to lose some shekels on the series with the White Sox," one story in the *Daily News* read. "[Weaver] had been booed before in the Hub, but since that incident gamblers who infest the park have paid particular attention to Buck at practically every appearance. . . . This was the case in the series that ended [May 28]."[21]

Nothing changed at Braves Field either. During one game in 1918, according to the *Tribune,* "It was so hot the spectators in the open-faced seats were invited into the shade of the grand stand. Most of them belonged to the gambling squad which still maintains headquarters high up in the first base pavilion. The jitney bettors accepted the invitation and established a temporary clearinghouse near the quickest grand stand exit."[22] Johnson's brief crusade, readily abandoned, was typical of baseball's approach to hard-to-solve problems: talk big, take minimal action, move on. There was talk but no action on shipyard draft dodgers and on freak pitches. This was just how baseball dealt with the tricky issues of the day. It didn't.

Gambling was the trickiest issue, and the problem was bigger than Boston. Later in 1918, *The Sporting News* charged, "In the St. Louis National League club's grand stand, with a club operated by a highly moral set of citizens and officials, for instance, the passages were often blocked by known professional gamblers in such numbers, openly taking bets, that the ordinary patron could scarcely make his way."[23] In Pittsburgh, "there is a clique at Forbes Field which operates openly to the amazement of spectators and the management, which provides and pays policemen to prevent this practice. . . . Why they can't be stopped is a mystery."[24]

Probably because no one really *wanted* them to stop. The attitude of the game's magnates was not universally supportive of Johnson's gambling fight. There was little impetus to root out gamblers. They were, after all, reliable ticket buyers. Besides, loudly conducting an antigambling campaign only made fans aware that there was a gambling problem. Comiskey "sharply suggests that it does the game no good to parade the fact that there is an evil difficult to eliminate."[25] Maybe Comiskey and the other magnates should have had the foresight to tackle baseball's gambling issue, but why? Keeping quiet about gambling and keeping baseball profitable were more immediate concerns. (Comiskey stuck to his hush-hush approach even after he found out that his own team threw the 1919 World Series.) Rumors of players fixing games were persistent, but there were no solid cases in which players and gamblers could be linked directly. As long as those connections stayed in the shadows, there seemed to be no danger.

In *Eight Men Out*, Eliot Asinof summed up the thinking of Comiskey and other magnates: "Most likely, the cloak of secrecy was maintained by the power of the owners themselves. They knew, as all baseball men came to know. They knew, but pretended they didn't. Terrified of exposing dishonest practices in major-league ball games, their solution was no solution at all. It was simply an evasion. Whenever there was talk of some fresh incident, they would combine to hush it up. The probing sportswriter would be instructed—or paid off—to stop his digging. Ballplayers would be thanked for their information—and disregarded. Always, the owners claimed, for the good of baseball. Their greatest fear was that the American fan might suspect there was something crooked about the National Pastime. Who, then, would pay good money to see a game?"[26]

In Boston, gamblers and ballplayers had an easy time crossing paths, and the events of June 1917 brandished the city's claim as the capital of baseball betting. In July 1918, we will see, two players would cross paths with a well-known Boston gambler at the Oxford Hotel. Bets would be placed, double crosses would be attempted, and one player's career would end. But not before baseball tried to cover it up, of course.

The Original Curse: Dutch Leonard

Leonard's life did not end in tragedy or destitution, but his baseball career ended in ignominy and embarrassment. Leonard finished his playing days in Detroit, under manager Ty Cobb. Despite an 11–4 record, Cobb released Leonard in July 1925, and Leonard was frustrated to find that no other team would pick him up—not even the Indians, managed by his old Red Sox teammate Tris Speaker. The following spring Leonard went to Ban Johnson, alleging that late in September 1919 he and Cobb had conspired with Speaker and Indians outfielder Joe Wood (another ex-teammate) to have Cleveland lose a game to help Detroit finish in third place. Leonard produced letters that—vaguely—backed his claim.

Johnson investigated, called an AL meeting, and decided that Speaker and Cobb should be forced out by quiet "retirement." But new baseball commissioner Kenesaw Mountain Landis, no friend of Johnson, investigated the matter himself. Both Speaker and Cobb declared their innocence. Landis visited Leonard in California, but when Leonard was asked to come to Chicago to testify, he refused. Because of that refusal, Landis overturned the AL's decision and declared Cobb and Speaker, two of the game's most popular heroes, innocent. That left Leonard forever remembered as the goat. "Only a miserable thirst for vengeance actuated Leonard's attack on Cobb and Speaker," former umpire Billy Evans claimed. "It is a crime that men of the stature of Ty and Tris should be blackened by a man of this caliber with charges that every baseballer knows to be utterly false."[27]

EIGHT

Usefulness: Newton D. Baker

WASHINGTON, D.C., MAY 23, 1918

Newton Baker hadn't really wanted to be secretary of war. He was a pacifist and had taken the job at the request of President Wilson in 1916, promising to stay aboard for just one year before he returned to his old job as mayor of Cleveland. He'd obviously broken that promise. And the job had grown on him.

Baker was back in the United States after having spent seven weeks in Europe. *Seven weeks*, in the heart of the war, traveling from the English Channel to Venice. Never had an American secretary of war had that kind of experience. He saw a German shell land, cleanly, 50 yards from him, one of the 105-millimeter, long-range jobs, leaving a crater in its wake. He'd climbed down into a trench. He'd worn a gas mask and a shrapnel helmet. He saw graves, thousands of them. He'd set his boot in mud tinged red with blood, saw limbs dangling from the barbed wire of no-man's-land. He heard the low thud of heavy artillery, the metal groan of advancing tanks, the crackling putt-putt-putt of Browning guns. Even now, back in the States, the sounds of the front were easy to conjure. It was emotional. In France he was told about a woman who went to the intelligence office to inquire about her husband. He was dead. She staggered to the sidewalk, where one of the officers caught up to her and offered his condolences. Baker would never forget what the woman said: "Sir, under these circumstances there is only one proper sentiment to express. *Vive la France!*"[1]

This was what Baker had seen. He'd been back in America for little more than a month, but his fellow American citizens didn't seem to grasp the way the war had descended into a stalemated slaughter that no one would have bargained for when the thing began. It had to end. America had to end it, and had to end it with a wave of soldiers and equipment so massive that victory would be inevitable. Baker had just gone before Congress and asked that Wilson be allowed to draft an unlimited army rather than the million-man force that had originally been authorized. Congress agreed.

The nation needed men. Throughout the country, there were still healthy young layabouts of draft age, plodding on as if there were no war, making no apologies for their slackerism. It seemed wrong that these men should continue in their cushioned jobs while others were fighting. If they weren't at the front, they should be helping those at the front—farming their food, making their guns, building their supply ships. While Baker was making his request for an unlimited army, General Enoch Crowder made a corresponding change to the Selective Service Act, dictating that any man of draft age who was not in the military would have to give up his job and either enlist or get a useful occupation. If you are not shouldering a Browning gun in France, you should be making a Browning gun in America. Fight. Or work.

It was a profound moment for the United States, the army receiving permission to grow to an unlimited size, all men of draft age called to duty, at home or abroad, without exception. It would put America in a new light, show her strength to the rest of the world. Yet it seemed all anyone wanted to ask Baker was whether the rule would apply to the nation's sports—especially baseball. The German offensive was pushing west, the Allies were struggling, the scene in Europe was gruesome, and this was the most crucial moment in America's history, perhaps in the history of the world.

86

But over and over again, Baker was asked, *What's going to happen to baseball?*

IN THE LOBBY OF THE SHERIDAN HOTEL, CHICAGO, MAY 24

Jess Barnes, right-handed pitcher of the Giants, leaned forward in a high-backed chair. He was scheduled to pitch that afternoon against the Cubs, but heavy rain was pounding the streets outside. Jess fingered the text on the front page of the newspaper, surrounded by several of his teammates, cleared his throat, and read aloud. "'Baseball players all over the United States last night were wondering whether on July 1, the government would make them go to work on farms, in shipyards or munitions factories, or take up other pursuits with a more direct bearing on the war,'"[2] Barnes said in his dusty Oklahoma twang. When he pronounced *United*, it came out, "You-nighted."

Benny Kauff bent down to flick a bit of dirt off his freshly polished (and quite expensive, he told anyone who asked) shoes. "Looks like you'll be taking some of us with you, Barnes," Kauff said. Kauff was Class 1A.

Barnes was not only 1A but had already been drafted. In less than a week he would head to Camp Funston for training. That left time to pitch one more game with the Giants. Figures. Barnes had knocked around with the Braves for three years, went 22–36, and now that he was having a great year—6–1—he was off to war. The Giants' other top pitcher, Rube Benton, was already gone. Jess didn't think the Giants could hold the pennant without two of their top pitchers. "What do the big gizzazzers say?" asked Heinie Zimmerman.

"Who?" Barnes asked.

"You know, Baker and Crowder."

"Well, here's what this one says," Jess said, picking up another paper. "'That baseball, as a business institution, will enter into the government's decision on the question was indicated by Secretary of War Baker yesterday. He explained that the status of baseball players had been discussed before the regulation was approved and it was agreed that the question could not be disposed of until all the facts relating to the effect upon the baseball business had been brought out through a test case. The Secretary did not know that a large majority of the major league players were of draft age, but on the contrary, was under the impression that most of them were outside the draft limits.'"[3]

Laughter broke out. "Outside draft limits?" Art Fletcher asked. "What's the matter with this Baker? He thinks we are all 16!"

"Maybe he thinks we're tottering old men like you, Fletcher," Kauff said, drawing a grim stare from Fletcher, who, at 33, was beyond draft age but never opposed to a fight. "He doesn't seem to think we're in our 20s, that's for sure."

"What's all that mean, a 'test case'?"

"It means we'll play till July 1," Fletcher said. "After that, it might be illegal to play ball for a living if you are Class 1A. Not for me. But one of the draft boards will call one of you fellows, or just any player, I guess, and it'll be up to that player to prove that baseball is useful in the war. If the draft boards say we're doing something that helps the war, they'll let us play. It'll probably go all the way up to Baker, or even Wilson."

Jess grabbed another newspaper. "There is a statement from Garry Herrmann in here. Let me read it," he said. "'If the new order should be strictly enforced, it would certainly cause the closing of all ball parks. It would be impossible to fill the places of the men in the draft age'"—here Jess slowed and spoke loudly—"'so that the game would have to be abandoned.'"[4]

Some commotion rose. "Unbelievable."

"So they'll shut us down starting on July 1? Until when?"

"Until after the war," Kauff answered.

"When's that?"

"When's the war going to be over? Do I look like Pershing to you, Ivory Dome? It might be over tomorrow. It might be over in 1925."

Outside, more rain. It was useless. The Giants and Cubs would not play today.

IN THE HOME DUGOUT, WEEGHMAN PARK, MAY 26

There were so many fans, they couldn't all fit into the stands. This is what Fred Merkle had been expecting since he was traded to the Cubs the previous year. A lot had happened over the years, but now it was Cubs vs. Giants for first place in the National League, and it was the closest thing to '08 anyone could remember. Fans swarmed the park, coming by car up Addison Street from Lake Shore Drive, pouring out of the 'L' at the Addison stop, and sardined into the Clark Street streetcar. There were no more seats, so the cops and ushers lined up fans on the outfield grass. Looked like 15 deep.[5] Merkle had been having a good year. Hitting .350. Mr. Muscle Merkle. But the Giants were in town, and the old '08 Cubs–Giants rivalry was stoked up, and Merkle knew what that meant. Bonehead. Boner. It was 10 years since the end of '08 and he had played *nine seasons* since that one bone play. Sometimes, Merkle thought, it seemed that no matter what he did in this game, all anyone would remember about him in 10 years, 20 years, 100 years was not touching the base in the key game of a pennant race back when he was 19 years old.

"Hey, Merkle," one of the haw-hawing fans shouted. "How about you don't forget to touch second base if you have the chance to reach it?"

Merkle, usually such a gentleman, leaning on the top stair of the dugout, shot back: "How about you don't forget to shut your yap so I don't have the chance to lodge my spikes in it?"

Shufflin' Phil Douglas, in the corner of the dugout near the water cooler, heard Merkle above the dugout chatter and began to laugh. Just then, Les Mann came bounding and whistling down the dugout stairs. He went to the cooler, pouring himself some water. Mann had finished his setting-up exercises. He patted the laughing Douglas on the knee.

"You're in good spirits, Phil. How are you feeling? Near ready to pitch?"

"Almost, almost," Phil said. "Crowd like this makes me want to get on the slab."

"Can't hurry a removed appendix," Mann said. "Are you taking that nuxated iron I gave you? Good for the blood. You need that iron, coming back from surgery."

Phil smiled. He was almost as big sitting down as Mann was standing up. "Is there nuximated iron in sour mash?" he said.

Les sighed. "No, Phil," he said, shaking his head.

"Then I haven't been taking nuximated iron," Phil said, his laugh picking up again.[6] Douglas gave an elbow to Dode Paskert, who was sitting next to him, spitting tobacco onto his bat, rubbing the brown saliva into the handle, and talking with Rollie Zeider. Paskert half-heard Douglas's joke before turning his attention back to Zeider.

"Suppose Baker orders ballplayers to go to work," Paskert said. "And suppose they don't shut it down. Suppose they try to go with players outside draft age. You see what I mean? All these young ones would be out. They'd be drafted. It'd just be me and you, Rollie! What do you think, Rollie? Can we win a pennant, me and you?"

Zeider shook his head. "They'll probably sign up half a team of teenaged Yannigans and half a team of grandpas like us," he said. "Keep it balanced."

"Makes it nice to be 36 years old; I will tell you that much," Paskert said.

With a pregnant wife and an awkward gait, Hippo Vaughn did not figure to be a prime target for the army. But he was a key in the Cubs' crucial May sweep of the Giants. (NATIONAL BASEBALL HALL OF FAME LIBRARY, COOPERSTOWN, N.Y.)

"I think we'd have Vaughn too," Zeider said, nodding toward the edge of the grass, where Hippo Vaughn and Lefty Tyler were standing side by side, warming up their arms. "The army would never take him, not with a pregnant wife and that hippo gait of his." Zeider raised his voice to Vaughn. "Isn't that right, Hippo?"

Vaughn paused and looked in at Zeider. "I did not hear you, Rollie, but I am sure it was an insult," he said, shaking his head. "So, my response is, no, it is *not* right."

Tyler watched Vaughn throw and then asked, "What are you going to do, Jim, when they shut us down in July?"

"Head on back to Texas, back to the farm," Vaughn answered. "I think I can be useful enough there. How about you? Are you joining up with the sammies?"

"No," Tyler said. "Back to the farm too. Uncle Sam would not take me anyway."

"Why not?"

Tyler paused, putting the ball into his glove. He opened his mouth and reached in with his thumb and forefinger. With only a slight tug, he pulled out a yellowed tooth and held it up for Vaughn. "Bad teeth," he said. Vaughn blanched. Tyler popped his tooth back into place and smiled.[7]

As the players bantered, fans kept piling in. The war was raging, the order that all men should work or fight was official, and baseball might soon be ruled a nonuseful occupation. But it was Cubs–Giants weekend, and Weeghman Park was packed.

With a solid early-season record and signs of a good club, the Cubs had been looking ahead to the series against the Giants (slated to start May 24 but delayed by rain) for two reasons. First, Cubs fans considered John McGraw's bunch the arch nemesis, going back to the thrilling 1908 pennant race. The Cubs won in part because of a controversial play in which Giants rookie Fred Merkle—now a veteran Cub—failed to run to second base on an otherwise game-winning hit. The other reason the Cubs bugs were worked up was that the series was a measuring stick. The Giants were champions. At 19–11, the Cubs were good, but they trailed New York by four games, and if they wanted to prove they were championship class, this weekend offered the opportunity.

Just before the series started, though, everything changed. Now that America had plunged into the war, more soldiers were needed, and more men were needed to work jobs that supported the soldiers. On May 23, General Crowder made it a legal obligation, as of July 1, for men of draft age either to work in a useful industry or to be drafted immediately. Crowder noted the impetus behind the order: "One of the unanswerable criticisms of the draft has been that it takes men from the farms and from all useful employments and marches them past crowds of idlers and loafers away to the army," he said. "The remedy is . . . to require that any man pleading exemption on any ground shall also show that he is contributing effectively to the industrial welfare of the nation."[8]

Idlers and loafers were, in most cases, easy to define. If a young man was hanging around a poolroom, he was obviously loafing and would have to answer for why he was not employed in a useful trade. Those who held jobs as bartenders or hotel doormen, too, would be collared and required to get essential work. But what about baseball players? Was theirs a useful industry? Baseball did not contribute directly to the war effort, and when Johnson made his plea for the exemption of 288 players, Crowder had laughed him down. Baseball had, however, helped raise money for the Red Cross and contributed to the purchase of Liberty Bonds. Fans attending games paid a war tax, which was useful. Besides, actors were granted exemption so that the population could continue to get much-needed diversion at theaters and in the movies. Shouldn't baseball players, too, be exempted because of the entertainment they provided?

Baker and Crowder had considered baseball before writing the order. Neither felt sure enough about the game to take a definitive stance on baseball's status—Baker was under the mistaken belief that most players were older than draft age—so they decided to wait until an appeal of an actual case could be made. Which put baseball and its players in a precarious position. From May 23 until Crowder's order would take effect on July 1, baseball would continue with no inkling as to whether the government approved or disapproved, no inkling of whether players were considered slackers, that most dread label in 1918 America. Whenever Crowder did rule on the subject, it was understood that there were three possible outcomes. Crowder could call the game nonessential, and owners could end the season abruptly. Or Crowder could call the game nonessential, baseball could lose all of its players of draft age, and owners could sign up teams of players outside draft age, younger than 21 and older than 31. Or Crowder could smile upon the sport, recognize its usefulness to a country at war, and exempt its players. There were signs that the government would rule in favor of baseball. Wilson had, in the summer of '17, expressed his support, and two days after the work-or-fight order was handed down, Wilson threw out the first pitch at a Senators game in Washington.

Still, the future was questionable. If all players of draft age were forced to find useful work, according to one estimate, 70–80 percent of rosters would be gone. Frank J. Navin, president of the Tigers, said, "Such an order would cause us to close our park. The order would leave me [41-year-old Bill] Donovan as a pitcher, [35-year-old Oscar] Stanage behind the bat, [34-year-old Tubby] Spencer at first and [49-year-old manager Hughie] Jennings at short. How does that sound for a pennant winner?"[9]

But, for Giants–Cubs weekend, work-or-fight was easily pushed aside. There were 14,000 on hand for the opening of the series on Saturday, and it was a tense crowd as things got off to an iffy start for Lefty Tyler. Leadoff man Ross Youngs rapped a single, and Benny Kauff (who would be drafted in late June) drove a Tyler pitch deep to left for a double, scoring Youngs. George Burns followed with a single, and just like that, Tyler let up three hits and two runs to the first three men he faced. But he braced himself, getting two infield outs before striking out Walter Holke. In the bottom of the first inning, with Barnes taking the mound for the last time before he joined the army, Flack scored on a double by Mann. When Merkle crushed a Barnes fastball foul past third base, McGraw pulled out Barnes, sparing him the embarrassment of getting knocked around in his final start. Al Demaree took the slab, and the Cubs built a 5–4 lead before Demaree was replaced by Floridian reliever Red Causey. Here's how the *Tribune's* James Crusinberry described Causey: "Mr. Cecil Algernon 'Red' Causey is six feet in height, ten and a half inches wide, has ambitions, is too young for the war, and too old to stay on the Everglades. . . . The Cubs didn't do much in the way of prowess after he entered the arena in search of fame."[10] The Cubs had enough prowess to wind up with a 7–4 win, though.

Vaughn took the mound for the second game, on Sunday. Chicago was bustling in anticipation. Tickets were sold out by 3:15, for a game that was to start at 4:00. The Cubs kept selling tickets, though—fans stood in the aisles, they packed under the stands and peeked out when they could, and ushers lined up fans along the outfield wall and behind the plate in foul ground, technically in the field of play, forcing the managers and umpires to agree on ground rules for balls that struck fans. The rooftops and windows of the apartment buildings across Clark Street were packed.[11] A throng of about 25,000 showed up, the biggest crowd the Cubs had ever drawn to Weeghman Park. They saw a mint performance from Vaughn, who allowed two hits and a run in the first, but shut the Giants down after that, giving up only two more hits and grabbing a 5–1 win.

The Sunday fans also heard the band play "The Star-Spangled Banner" in the seventh inning. The *Chicago Herald Examiner* reported, "All hands, with the exception of one rash youth, stood up and saluted. He probably will stand up for a week with or without music. Indignant patriots grabbed the slacker, rushed him down the center of the aisle of the stand and into the street. Other patriots stepped into the aisle behind the procession and landed a series of swift kicks where they would do the most good."[12]

By the third game the Giants were deflated and frustrated—particularly ex-Cub Heinie Zimmerman, now New York's third baseman, who was alternately cheered and booed throughout the series. The Giants grabbed a quick lead, but the Cubs scraped back. As the Cubs were pulling even, Mann went hard into third base and Zimmerman gave him a forceful tag to the stomach. Mann grabbed Zimmerman's knees, pulling him to the ground. The two exchanged blows before being separated without ejections. But the Cubs kept up their assault, giving Claude Hendrix a 7–3 win. After the game, a ticked-off Zimmerman waited for Mann in street clothes on Addison Street. A group of fans watched eagerly. Alas, Zimmerman's pugilistic intentions were short-circuited by the fairer sex. "Later Mann came out," Crusinberry reported, "but Mrs. Mann had been waiting for him and walked alongside of him, past Heinie and the expectant crowd. Strong arms weren't needed this time. Mrs. Mann marched her husband home, and Heinie grabbed a taxi and beat it."[13]

The Cubs had humiliated the NL champs. In three games they outscored the McGraws, 19–8, outhit them, 40–24, outplayed them in the field, and showed far more class on the mound. Mann's bout with Zimmerman might have been exactly what the Cubs needed.

The Giants had a bullying reputation that reflected the disposition of McGraw, their hard-boiled manager. The Cubs would not be cowed. Later in the week, Bill Killefer got into a dustup after Cincinnati's Greasy Neale—future Hall of Fame football coach—delivered a sucker punch to Killefer's jaw, laying out the sturdy catcher in the middle of a game. An onrush of Cubs players came to their catcher's defense, and Neale was thrown out for the punch. Incensed Cubs fans threw glass soda bottles at Reds outfielder Rube Bressler, thinking he was Neale, and showing that these Cubs and their fans were not afraid of rough play.

Indeed, baseball was not a game for the meek in 1918, on the field or in the stands. Not until the 1923 season did baseball, tired of seeing umpires attacked with projectiles, ban glass bottles in parks. During the '18 season, after two women were injured by fans who threw seat cushions during Cubs games, Charley Weeghman pushed Chicago's aldermen to make it a crime to throw bottles and other objects from the stands. He failed. The aldermen decided that "the enraged fan was within his rights in heaving a bottle at Catfish the umpire." One alderman, incredibly, argued, "Our ancestors fought and died for certain unalienable rights. Just now our boys are fighting in France for freedom and democracy. Why should not the baseball fan have freedom to innocently express his sentiment?"[14]

The Cubs were 23–12 when they left the friendly, flying-bottle confines of Weeghman Park to set out on the road for a 23-day junket to the East on May 31. The train ride was miserable—it was hot, and war restrictions meant all 30 members of the Cubs traveling party were crammed into one car, which made even grabbing a seat a challenge. Teddy Roosevelt was on the train, with a car to himself. Several players stopped to visit the ex-president, who had been a loud critic of the administration's war effort. Roosevelt's disdain for Wilson and Baker was widely known (rooted in the fact that they hadn't allowed Roosevelt, 59 years old and not exactly in peak shape, to put together his own fighting division to take to France). When players asked what Roosevelt thought about the work-or-fight order and how it would affect ballplayers after July 1, they were probably expecting T.R. to deliver a scathing rebuke. They were disappointed. Roosevelt told them he had been too busy to think about baseball's situation.[15]

The Cubs swept the Braves and Phillies to start the trip, which boosted them to the top of the standings. They were greeted in Phila-

95

delphia by Bill Wrigley, who gave each player a first-place reward—$5 to spend on new clothes, which they gladly did the following day. "Haberdashers on Chestnut Street did some business," the *Daily News* reported. "The boys came back with new ties, hats, socks and shirts, which they sported on the Sabbath."[16] To close the trip, the Cubs split the rematch with the Giants, won two of three from Brooklyn, and split with Pittsburgh. They went 13–5, returning to Chicago with a 36–17 record and a tight grip on first place.

NINE

Loyalty: The *Texel*

OFF THE NEW YORK COAST, SUNDAY, JUNE 2, 1918

It was just after 4:00 P.M. by the watch of K. B. Lowry, the Brooklynite captain of the *Texel*, a Dutch steamship that had been loaded up with 42,000 tons of sugar from the Caribbean. The sea was calm, the afternoon was warm, and Lowry had the boat about 60 miles from its destination, New York harbor. That's when he saw ripples radiate in the water, just yards from the *Texel*'s bow. The smooth surface of the ocean convulsed and split, and suddenly Lowry was looking at the massive gray deck of a submarine. Without warning, the sub aimed its gun and fired a shell packed with shrapnel at the clumsy body of the *Texel*. Panic set in among the crew. *What was a submarine doing firing shells on an unarmed sugar boat 60 miles off the New York coast?* The men took cover. One of the crew, Frank Ryan, scrambled back on deck to rescue the ship's mascot, a Maltese cat. Just in time. The sub's guns fired again, a rain of debris spraying the *Texel*'s deck. And then a third blast. Lowry pulled the *Texel* to a stop. The U-boat's captain boarded, demanding to see the ship's papers. Looking them over, he said to Lowry, "We will give you time to get off. Then we shall sink your vessel."[1]

The 36-man crew crammed into two lifeboats. The cat too. They began to row to shore, a two-day ordeal. Behind them, the U-boat blasted the *Texel*, which tipped to its side and slowly eased into the water.

June 2 was a bad day for ships in American waters. The *Texel* was one of six ships sunk off the East Coast that day. In the past, German submarines had occasionally slipped into U.S. waters to cause mischief and create a scare, but this was different. Between May 25 and May 28, four nonmilitary ships had been mysteriously sunk, and the June 2 tally brought the total to 10 in a span of just eight days. This wave of U-boat marauding would end in mid-June, with ships attacked from the waters of Massachusetts down to Virginia, but in the wake of the sinking of the *Texel* and others, there was no way to tell what, exactly, was going on or when it would stop. It very much appeared that the United States was under German assault. Word spread that there were as many as five U-boats off the coast, and a mother ship, maybe even disguised under an American flag, supplying them.[2]

It was easy to tie these rumors to another rumor, which held that a shipment of one million Mauser rifles and a billion cartridges had reached American shores and was hidden in storage in the United States, waiting for a German-American uprising. Both rumors had credibility. New York's deputy attorney general held hearings on the Mauser rifle shipment,[3] and the U.S. Congress thought enough of the U-boat threat that it passed a $16 million appropriation for balloon and seaplane stations to track enemy subs. In New York, fear spread that the submarine attacks could be a precursor to German air attacks. For the first time, the city established an air raid siren and required businesses on major thoroughfares—such as Broadway and Fifth Avenue—to dim their lights at night to make the streets harder to see from above.[4]

The ship sinkings were not part of a German invasion. There was no air assault, and there were no Mauser rifles. The attacks of late May and early June were the work of just one very efficient sub, the U-151, which was sent to America to lay mines off the coast and, when it was finished, went on a three-week rampage that hit 20 ships. But the heightened reaction to U-151 was revealing—rational Americans were afraid that the war "over there" would open a front over here. There was much to drive that fear. Americans had been spooked the previous year by the Zimmerman telegram, in which Germany recruited Mexico as an ally in war on America. German saboteurs and propagandists had been found to be working in the country (though not to the degree many claimed). After leaving his ambassadorship in Germany in 1917, American statesman James Gerard became a great force for fear in the nation. His story was adapted into a movie, *My Four Years in Germany,* and in a speech he gave all around the country Gerard said, "The foreign minister of Germany once said to me, 'Your country does not dare do anything against Germany, because we have in your country 500,000 German reservists who will rise in arms against your government if you dare make a move against Germany.'"

There were not 500,000 German reservists in the United States, but Gerard didn't let facts muddle a rousing speech. Gerard continued: "I told him that that might be so, but that we had 500,001 lamp posts in this country, and that that was where the reservists would be hanging the day after they tried to rise. If there are any German-Americans here who are so ungrateful for all the benefits they have received that they are still for the Kaiser, there is only one thing to do with them. And that is to hog-tie them, give them back the wooden shoes and rags they landed in and ship them back to the Fatherland."[5]

Gerard's speech was titled "Loyalty," and it was emblematic of the mood of the nation. Legitimate fear of German invasion became distorted into rabid hatred of all things German. This was driven in part by domestic propaganda efforts, which were so successful that overzealous Americans were inspired to acts ranging from silly to bone-chilling, under the guise of loyalty. Schools dropped German from the curriculum, the Bismarck School in Chicago was renamed "Funston School," sauerkraut was renamed "liberty cabbage," and even German measles were called "liberty measles." The statue of the writer Friedrich von Schiller in Chicago was painted yellow by vandals, and a statue of Goethe was put into storage for its own protection. One congressman from Michigan introduced a bill eliminating all American town names containing the word *Berlin* or *Germany* and replacing them with the word *victory* or *liberty.*[6] Books by German writers were burned publicly, and recordings of Beethoven and Bach were smashed.

Some expressions of loyalty went further. In May, Wilson had pushed the Sedition Act through Congress, making it illegal to "willfully utter, print, write or publish any disloyal, profane, scurrilous, or abusive language" about the government. Criticism became a crime. Everywhere Americans squealed on fellow citizens for making disloyal comments. John Anderson, of Quincy, Massachusetts, was riding on a train near Boston when he was overheard saying that the war in Europe was a family affair in which the United States should not be involved. Enraged fellow passengers "were at the point of throwing [him] from the train."[7] Instead, they turned him over to police at the next stop. When children trying to sell thrift stamps to Dr. Ruth Lighthall of Chicago were turned away, they told authorities that she said the war was one for capitalists. Lighthall confirmed that sentiment, added that she thought President Wilson a traitor—and she was sentenced to jail for 10 years for it.[8] Millionaire Rose Pastor Stokes was sent to jail for 10 years after making an antiwar speech in Kansas City. Respected film producer Robert Goldstein had his movie *The Spirit of '76* seized because it showed British soldiers committing war atrocities—which should be expected in a patriotic movie set in the American Revolution. But the British were American allies now. Goldstein was sentenced to 10 years in prison.[9]

Before the war, German-Americans were one of the proudest, most assimilated ethnic groups in the nation, especially in Chicago. History professor Melvin Holli notes that, before the war, "No ethnic group was so numerous in Chicago or the nation or had made such rapid and solid economic progress, dominating and monopolizing in many cases the middle rungs of the occupational ladder."[10] But the spasm of patriotism that accompanied the war erased that. German-Americans became targets. Early in the morning of April 5, Robert Prager, a 29-year-old unemployed baker, was lynched by a mob of 350 in Collinsville, Illinois. Prager allegedly made a "disloyal" comment while seeking work at a local mine. A growing mob menaced him throughout the day and evening, finally tracking down Prager after midnight. Originally, the plan was to tar and feather him, but with no tar or feathers handy at that hour, the mob hanged Prager instead. Five men brought to trial for the lynching were found not guilty after the jury deliberated for just 45 minutes.[11] The incident was a national disgrace. But, then, hadn't Gerard promised the German foreign secretary that his countrymen would hang from American lampposts?

In the midst of the U-151 raids, Red Sox first baseman Dick Hoblitzell—himself partly of German descent—finally left the team to join the army's Dental Corps as a lieutenant, to be trained at Fort Oglethorpe in Georgia. Attached to Fort Oglethorpe, Hoblitzell would have found an internment camp, one of three across the country that held Germans who had been living peacefully but were now held as enemy aliens. In that camp was another famous Bostonian, 58-year-old Dr. Karl Muck, the conductor of the Boston Symphony. Or ex-conductor. Muck had been arrested in late March on the charge of being German (though Muck had Swiss citizenship). Muck allegedly refused to lead "The Star-Spangled Banner" at a concert in Providence and had been criticized across the country for it—though witnesses confirmed that Muck did play it. But Muck was German, he was suspect, and he was sent to Fort Oglethorpe.

If Hoblitzell had listened carefully when he arrived in Georgia, he might have heard the sounds of Beethoven's Fifth coming from the jail. That's because Muck wasn't alone. Many of the nation's orchestras were stocked with Germans, and Muck found so many musicians among his fellow prisoners that he started a Fort Oglethorpe orchestra.[12]

The Red Sox started June in first place and headed on a long western trip, with stops in Detroit, Cleveland, Chicago, and St. Louis. The team Hoblitzell left was not in bad shape. Ruth was out of the infirmary, healthy again. Hobby was the captain, but he had been injured and slumped under the mental strain of his impending army service. Stuffy McInnis had been playing out of position at third base, and when Hoblitzell left he slid over to his natural first-base spot. Fred Thomas, Class 1A and waiting for the call to war, took over at third. Hoblitzell's captaincy went to Harry Hooper, who was batting .330, was popular with teammates and fans, had a good relationship with Barrow, and was suited for the job. Hoblitzell had already yielded his spot in the lineup—cleanup hitter—to Ruth, and his departure cemented Ruth's place as the team's top run producer.

Ruth's stay in the infirmary did have a benefit. It forced Barrow to use one of the young pitchers he trusted so little—Sam Jones, who had gone just 0–2 in two big-league seasons. But without Ruth, Barrow was so desperate as to insert Jones on May 23, and Jones responded by allowing just one run in a complete-game loss to Cleveland. It was a good enough showing to warrant another start, and Jones beat Washington great Walter Johnson, 3–0, on May 29. This was quite a turn in Jones's young career. He had been so deep on the Boston bench that, when the team reported for spring training that March, few noticed Jones hadn't shown up. The Red Sox assumed Jones had been drafted by the army. He hadn't, and, according to *The Sporting News*, "The team was at Hot Springs when owner Harry Frazee received a message from Sam which expressed itself thusly: 'Forgotten

101

me altogether? Not worth a contract of any sort? If I am through, let me in on it.'"[13]

Barrow's confidence in Jones grew, and for a short time the Red Sox had pitching depth, a rare commodity in 1918. On June 6, Jones took the mound at Cleveland. Seated in the press box was 51-year-old Cy Young, baseball's lifetime leader in pitching wins. As Young watched Jones, he lamented the lack of pitching around the league. When told the Senators resorted to giving some starts to Nick Altrock, their noodle-armed 41-year-old coach, Young "declared that if his arm were a little stronger, he would come back and try to pitch again himself."[14] He probably could have. An inordinate number of pitchers were in the service of Uncle Sam. In his syndicated column, Reds manager Christy Mathewson wrote, "If the other big-league managers are having the same trouble I am, and I guess most of them are in the same boat, they must go to bed at night praying for some young hurler to rise up over night as a Moses to lead them out of their difficulty."[15] For Barrow and the Red Sox, that Moses was Sam Jones. In that game against Cleveland, Cy Young himself watched Jones hurl a five-hit shutout.

The rise of Jones provided an opening for Ruth, who had become fond enough of hitting that he did not want to pitch anymore. After returning from the tonsil problem, he kept himself off the mound by complaining about arm injuries of dubious legitimacy. Even with Jones pitching well, the Red Sox slumped to a 3–5 start on their June trip—one of those wins was Dutch Leonard's no-hitter in Detroit—and the surprising Yankees moved into a tie for the top spot in the AL. That's when Boston rolled into Chicago's South Side for a four-game series against the defending champions, a series that should have been of the same magnitude as Cubs–Giants. But the White Sox were engulfed in turmoil. Jackson was gone to the shipyard, Byrd Lynn and Lefty Williams were preparing to follow, and Red Faber enlisted in the navy. It was an opportunity for the Red Sox. Joe Bush opened the series with his best performance of the year, yielding two hits in a 1–0 win. In the second game, Faber—making one last start—shut down Boston, 4–1. But Carl Mays and Leonard dominated the last two games with shutout wins, and over the four games Boston outscored Chicago, 15–4. The South Siders were booed by their home fans. It was so windy on the final day of the series that the 1917 AL pennant the White Sox had hung in the outfield ripped and had to be taken down for repairs. "The Red Sox are putting bigger holes in it than the wind did," the *Globe* noted.[16]

Boston split four games in St. Louis to wrap the trip 9–8, good enough to keep them slightly ahead of the Yankees. Leonard was a tough-luck loser, 2–1, on June 16, in what would be his last appearance for the Red Sox—he bolted from the trip early and suited up for the Fore River shipyard team. So much for pitching depth. And, perhaps, so much for Babe Ruth's brief career as a hitter. Ruth had pitched just one game since his silver nitrate incident. Leonard's departure, though, meant Ruth would head back to the mound. "No longer will [Ruth] be called upon to fill utility roles," the *Boston American* stated, "playing first base one day and the outfield the next."[17] Well, maybe.

For players, the work-or-fight order could be seen as a loyalty issue. The patriotic mania that surged through the nation made conditions such that adequately supporting the war was almost impossible, especially for public figures. Being behind the U.S. cause wasn't enough; buying Liberty Bonds wasn't enough; donating to the Red Cross wasn't enough. You had to be doing something to show not only that you supported the war but that you truly *hated* Germany. You had to burn something—effigies, books, anything. You had to deface statues. You had to kick a dachshund and contract liberty measles. You had to spy on your neighbors and scream in terror or throw someone off a train should you overhear a disloyal utterance.

Ballplayers weren't doing these kinds of things. They were just playing the game, which didn't seem very patriotic. Baseball's leaders floated the argument that players and magnates had made great investments in Liberty Bonds and that the war tax collected from fans at the gates helped fatten the nation's coffers. But that was a difficult sell. Though no ruling had been made on baseball's usefulness in the war effort, the sight of healthy young players frolicking on ball fields while American soldiers were being pressed to war and workers in other occupations were forced into war industries didn't sit well. Nor did the publicity that cropped up as more and more players took shipyard jobs.

Attendance began to flag—in part because the draft and work-or-fight order had sapped the fan base, but also because the charge of baseball slackerism had begun to stick. Good teams and holidays (such as July 4) still were big draws, but in many cities enthusiasm for the game vanished. Over the course of the Red Sox's trip through the AL's

Of all the pleasant surprises for the Cubs in early 1918, first baseman Fred Merkle—considered washed up by some before the season—was perhaps the most surprising. (NATIONAL BASEBALL HALL OF FAME LIBRARY, COOPERSTOWN, N.Y.)

western locales, some crowds were pitiful. One game in Detroit drew 2,500. A game in Cleveland drew 1,800. When Comiskey ordered Lynn and Williams out of his park after learning of their plans to join a shipyard team, the South Side fan base was so disgusted that only 1,000 turned up the next day to watch the champs.

The Cubs experienced much the same thing in the National League. They were in first place and played great baseball throughout

June, bolstering the pitching staff with the return of Phil Douglas—who tossed a three-hit shutout in his first outing—and getting exceptional performances from unexpected sources. Hendrix, who might have been bumped from the rotation had Alexander not been drafted, went on a seven-game win streak, and the offense, from the sprightly Hollocher to the sagely Paskert, was unstoppable. The *New York Times* wrote, "How Manager Fred Mitchell has enticed this collection of ancient and youthful players to play winning ball is something of a mystery. Such familiar relics as Rollie Zeider, Dode Paskert and Fred Merkle perform as if they had discovered some kind of tonic which laughs at the advancing years. This young Charley Hollocher . . . is a whirlwind with his hands and feet. Charley Deal, who is no Spring chicken, manages to insert hits at the proper time and Claude Hendrix blooms forth into a better pitching commodity than he has been for half a dozen years."[18]

Still, fans weren't flocking to see the Cubs on the road. Even in New York, with first place on the line, crowds were modest. Over four games at the Polo Grounds, the Cubs and Giants attracted about 6,700 fans per game, which was not great but was big business relative to other teams. An article in the *Boston American* stated, "If the Giants and Cubs had not played to big crowds last week, it might have been time to admit that baseball had lost something of the glamour that once surrounded it. . . . Naturally, there are many things more interesting than the performance of talented teams, and war news is one of those things."[19] When the June 18 game in Brooklyn drew about 1,900, Crusinberry joked, "this means that business is picking up tremendously in Brooklyn."[20]

Business was about to decline all over, though. That's because, 10 days before work-or-fight was to become the law of the land, General Crowder decided to say a few more things about his fateful directive. Throughout June, hints from Washington suggested Crowder would recommend that the War Department allow baseball to finish its season and then impose the work-or-fight ruling on players. But on June 21, Crowder issued more detailed definitions on the productiveness of several occupations. Crowder's statement put the slacker label on "all persons engaged and occupied in games, sports and amusements, except actual performers in legitimate concerts, operas or theatrical performances." But he didn't specifically address professional baseball. Crowder left the game plowing uncertainly toward the all-important

July 1 date, when his order would become law. The appeal process still would have to play itself out.

But Crowder's noncommittal statement cemented the opinion that baseball was shirking its duty, that players were not showing the requisite patriotic zeal of truly loyal Americans.

Across the country the public soured on the game. Many evening papers stopped printing sports extras that featured the day's final baseball scores. When the Cubs were in Cincinnati on June 27, the *Tribune* reported, "Only a few hundred fans were out and they were as silent as deafmutes."[21]

The sport pressed on through the final week of June, resigned to the reality that the deck would be reshuffled in the coming month and that, until the reshuffling was settled (and perhaps beyond then), many would look on ballplayers as slackers. For the Red Sox on the field, the rise of Jones was offset by the loss of Leonard, which added pressure on Barrow to return Ruth to pitching. Ruth didn't want to pitch, though. Besides, the loss of Hoblitzell meant Boston had no cleanup hitter, and with the way Ruth was slugging, there was no better cleanup hitter. Barrow needed two Ruths.

On June 28, Ruth knocked his 10th home run of the season, but, because he wouldn't pitch, Barrow was forced to use an overmatched journeyman as his starting pitcher—30-year-old Lore Bader, who had made just two previous big-league starts in his career. The Red Sox lost. Still, the following day, columnist Hugh Fullerton wrote that Ruth hit the ball harder than any player he'd ever seen. Fullerton, obviously badly misinformed, went on to praise Ruth's willingness to do whatever the team asked of him: "Ruth is one of the most likable fellows in the world, and he possesses one quality that makes him a great friend and a great ball player—loyalty. He is the most loyal man to his manager, to his team and to his fellow players in the world."[22]

But loyalty was a tricky thing in 1918, for citizens and for ballplayers. In the coming days, Ruth would prove that.

THE ORIGINAL CURSE: THE 1920 BUNCH

For the Cubs, Hendrix and Merkle were among the pleasant surprises who pushed the team to a fast start. But two-and-a-half years later, both would get their Cubs release amid suspicion that they were part of a group of players who participated in a game-fixing plot that drew such attention that a grand jury was called in Cook County court. When that grand jury began digging into baseball gambling in Chicago, it brought the Black Sox scandal to light—and never fully probed the Cubs scandal.

On August 31, 1920, the Cubs were to play the Phillies. Just before that game, team president William Veeck Sr. received six telegrams and two phone calls from mysterious sources in Detroit, warning him of abnormal betting on the Phillies. The messages advised pulling that day's pitcher, Claude Hendrix. On orders from Veeck, manager Fred Mitchell benched Hendrix, inserting Grover Cleveland Alexander in his place. Veeck offered Aleck a $500 bonus to win. Merkle, too, was mysteriously benched.

The Cubs still lost, thanks in large part to a late error by second baseman Buck Herzog. As details of the suspected plot became public in the following days, Hendrix, Merkle, Herzog, and relief pitcher Paul Carter were sent home and were expected to testify about the scandal— until the Black Sox discoveries got in the way. Thus the truth of the alleged August 31 fix is lost to history. But the grand jury's investigation did bring to light earlier accusations that Herzog and Hal Chase had offered $800 to pitcher Rube Benton to lose a game in 1919, an accusation that had been brought to NL president John Heydler in June and covered up. The Cubs released Herzog in the off-season.

Additionally, a letter from Kansas City sportswriter Otto Floto accused Hendrix (who, according to Harry Grabiner's diary, had been suspected of fixing games in 1919) of sending a telegram to Kansas City gambler Frog Thompson. The text of the telegram, according to Floto: "Bet $5,000 on opposition." The telegram itself was never produced, though, and both Hendrix and Thompson denied it. When Hendrix was released by the Cubs in February 1921, three weeks after Merkle, the *Tribune* wrote, "While no convincing evidence against Hendrix ever was presented in the investigation of crookedness in the game, his name was mentioned in an incident that started the big fireworks which culminated in the confessions of three White Sox players that the World's Series of 1919 was thrown. . . . President Veeck stated yesterday that Hendrix wasn't released because of any evidence against him, but was let out with the general idea of disposing of veteran material."[23] Hendrix died young, at age 52, of tuberculosis.

No charges were made against Merkle or Carter. Merkle later returned as a coach for the Yankees and even played eight games in his late 30s. He, of course, still bears the burden of his own curse— to be remembered solely for the one "bonehead" play that cost the Giants the 1908 pennant race, despite a solid record in 1,638 career games over 16 seasons. Hendrix, Herzog, and Carter never appeared in the majors again. Why the four were sent home from the Cubs was never explained.

Asked during the Black Sox investigation whether he believed the Cubs–Phillies game was fixed, NL president John Heydler said, "I am not in a humor to say any game is fixed or isn't fixed. . . . I've heard so much about crookedness in baseball in the last year that I wouldn't say anything any more, but I am in favor of running down to the end every rumor of crookedness from now on, and doing it openly and above board."[24]

Note that Heydler used the phrase "from now on." Inherent in those three words is the admission that it had not been baseball's custom to run down crookedness, openly and above board, before that.

TEN

Strategy: Harry Hooper

PHILADELPHIA, JULY 3, 1918

The Strategy Board was what Arthur Duffey from the *Boston Post* called them,[1] and they—that group of Red Sox players who would meet a few times each week to track the progress of the war in Europe—rather liked the moniker. They were seated in the dining room of the Aldine Hotel, a converted mansion on Chestnut Street. A stack of newspapers and evening extras sat on the table. Harry Hooper, in the center chair as usual, opened up maps from old newspapers on the table while two other Strategy Board members, George Whiteman and Wally Mayer, huddled around him. (Amos Strunk also was an avid Strategy Board member, but he lived in Philadelphia and was likely off with his wife.) Dinner was over. Their sleeves were rolled up, collars loosened. Cigars were passed. Other Red Sox were locked in poker games and Quaker-town nightlife, but for the Strategy Board this was an opportunity to catch up on the activity of the armies overseas.

"All right, men, what do we have?" Hooper said, opening the map of the front before him and testing the tip of his pen. "What's happening with our boys in France?" That's what these meetings were all about—tracking the movements of the American Expeditionary Force and the Allies all over the globe. Maybe it was because the members of the Strategy Board were older than the other Red Sox players, but they seemed to understand better just what was at stake in the war in Europe, and they understood that a pursuit like baseball was largely meaningless. So they'd meet, read the papers, mark maps, and give each other their recommendations on war strategy. Not that General Pershing was listening. But playing baseball every day with a war on felt so futile. This was a way, however small, for the players on the Strategy Board to feel they were part of things, as if by simply studying and understanding the war they could somehow give themselves a stake in it.

"Here now," Whiteman said. "The Americans made an attack on German positions just outside of, er, Chat-tow Thee-rey. Vowks Village and Boys day la Roach were taken by Americans. Zow-wee. That's good news."

Whiteman pointed to the map in front of Hooper, locating Chateau Thierry. "It's Vaux Village," Hooper said, "and Bois de la Roche." Whiteman nodded. He was accustomed to being corrected during these meetings. French wasn't his strong suit.

"Right," Whiteman said. "Now move the line up a mile. The American line now should run from, uh, Boo-res-chess to Chat-tow Thee-rey." Hooper carefully put his pen to the villages. He drew with a steady hand, precisely.

Hooper shaded the territory the Americans had gained in the attack. "And this was? When?" Hooper asked.

"July 2," Whiteman said. Hooper noted the date.

"What does the paper say about it?" Hooper asked.

"Says it's the most important operation American troops have taken on so far. Planned for 10 days. Says Vowks is vital to the Germans holding Chat-tow Thee-rey. The sammies used big guns, high explosives, and gas. We wiped that village out!"[2]

"A big one, and we ought to remember it," Hooper said, putting a star next to the just-marked American advance. This was Harry in his element.

110

"They've got to drive the Huns away from Paris," Mayer said. "That's got to be the top priority, don't you think? It looks to be only 70 miles to Paris from there."

Hooper eyed the map. "More like 50 miles," he said. "And, you're right; it's got the Paris road running through." He tapped his pen along the Paris road. Hoop was eager to keep drawing. It came naturally to him. When he entered school in California, Hoop's teachers had recognized his knack for mathematics and talked his parents into putting Harry into a baccalaureate program.[3] He'd been trained as

Red Sox right fielder Harry Hooper proved himself adept at strategy off the field, but the 1918 season might have been the best on-field performance of his Hall of Fame career. (NATIONAL BASEBALL HALL OF FAME LIBRARY, COOPERSTOWN, N.Y.)

an engineer at St. Mary's College, even got a job as a land surveyor,[4] and though he gave it up for baseball, working with angles and movement and maps thrilled him. Engineering was strategy, defining what needed to be done and using math to determine the best way to do it. That was how Harry saw the world—angles to be measured, distances to be covered, problems to be solved.

Every day in right field, Hoop was challenged with decisions: what path to take to a fly ball, what was the best angle to throw to third base, where he should be positioned when an outside fastball was coming to a right-handed hitter. Every pitch was a miniature engineering problem. And he had become darned good at solving those problems. He was a fine leadoff hitter, but he was known to Sox bugs for two things: getting key hits and making big catches. Hoop was not one to boast. But he knew Boston had beat the Giants in the 1912 World Series because of his astonishing catch of a Larry Doyle smash in the deciding game. What had Hughie Jennings said? "Hooper's judgment of the course of the ball was perfect, and he had to get away on the instant and exactly under the path that the ball was taking through the air,"[5] as Harry remembered. He liked that. Jennings recognized that it wasn't athleticism that made a great catch. It was strategy.

Hoop saw strategy everywhere. The flight of a baseball, the contours of land to be surveyed, the waltz of armies along maps of the front, even the way you approached a hand of bridge (few could beat Hooper at bridge). Plenty of players could play baseball. Hoop knew how to *think* the game. This had been an important aspect of Hooper's place on another Strategy Board—the one that ran the Red Sox. Barrow was no field manager, so it was shortstop Everett Scott, coach Heinie Wagner, and Hooper who made the baseball decisions for the team.[6] Hooper had been loudest in insisting that Babe Ruth play the field. Barrow gave in but had said, "Mark my word. The first time he gets in a slump, he will be down on his knees begging to pitch."[7]

Actually, Ruth had been slumping, and his reaction was much worse than begging to pitch again. The previous afternoon had been a real bust for the Red Sox. They were in Washington. Ruth committed an error and struck out, twice, against Harry Harper. Ruth had been swinging wildly, eschewing the time-honored Red Sox approach, which called for taking the first strike and making the pitcher work. After the second strikeout, Barrow went after Ruth. Called him a bum and worse. Ruth threatened to punch Barrow on the nose, and history

112

suggested this was not an idle threat. Barrow was a puncher too. He fined Ruth $500 on the spot.[8] Barrow was right, Hooper knew. Ruth was swinging like a gate up there. But Barrow was all iron fist—the players called him "Simon Legree" after the vicious plantation owner in *Uncle Tom's Cabin*.[9] It had been obvious to Hooper that Ruth was getting fed up with being fought with all the time.

So Ruth left. Took off his uniform. Did not get on the train to Philadelphia. Some of the reporters showed up with word that Ruth was in Baltimore and had signed up with the Chester shipyard team. Harry Frazee went nuts, said he would sue the shipyard. Barrow seethed.

Hooper saw the team was in trouble. Without Ruth, the Red Sox ran out a team of pikers against Connie Mack that afternoon, July 3, and showed no pep. The lineup was barely recognizable. Heinie Wagner at second. One of the new fellows, Jack Stansbury, in center. Two other bushers named Bluhm and Barbare, with the rag-armed Bader on the slab. It wasn't a big-league team. They made errors, they got just four hits, they lost, 6–0, and it was obvious that Barrow needed Babe more than Babe needed Barrow.

The Strategy Board was working on the movements of General Pershing, but they really wanted word on the movements of Private Ruth. Especially Harry. He, however, was trying not to think about that just now. The war was more important, he told himself. "What else?" Hooper asked.

"Baker sent out word that there are a million American soldiers in Europe now," Mayer said, whistling. "That's some reserves. They're talking about a counterattack."

Harry sat back and looked at the map, envisioned the slow progress of Allied gains, imagined the angles and lines he'd draw as the front was pushed back toward the Hindenburg Line. Back and forth. Germany and the Allies. Ruth and Barrow. Offensives, fronts, angles, lines, maps, fly balls. It was all the same. Harry nodded. "Yes," he said. "A counteroffensive—that would be a good strategy."

When the Red Sox went north from Washington to Philadelphia on the evening of July 2, Babe Ruth went south, to his father's house in Baltimore. He hadn't really wanted to quit, and though he did wire the shipyard team at Chester, he wanted to be with the Red Sox. But he'd lost patience with Barrow. Ruth contacted Wagner—who had served as Ruth's quasi-chaperone early in his career—and told him so.

Wagner took a late train to Baltimore, talking the wayward star into rejoining the team in Philadelphia. Wagner and Ruth arrived at the Aldine after 2:00 A.M. on July 4.[10] The Red Sox had a doubleheader that day, and Ruth, happy to be back, showed up at Shibe Park in the morning. But Barrow continued the iron-fist act and refused to speak to him. He kept Ruth on the bench for the entire first game, letting the slugger stew through a long, 11–9 Red Sox victory.

Déjà vu. Ruth "didn't seem highly pleased at not being received with open arms" and again took off his uniform between games, again saying he was leaving.[11] Hooper and some teammates talked Ruth back into the park before the second game and went to Barrow, persuading him to come to some kind of détente. Barrow put Ruth back in the lineup, in center field. From the *Globe*: "So far as is known, Ruth is resigned to his hard fate with the Boston Red Sox and Manager Barrow. It is not believed that he had any serious intention of jumping the team. His fellow players strongly resent his actions. They think he should remain loyal to the Sox."[12]

July 4 was the bottom for the Red Sox. Not only was the Ruth-Barrow situation tugging at the team, but Cleveland moved into first place. Boston lost third baseman Fred Thomas, who had been called to war two days earlier, and now the Red Sox were getting very thin very fast. Barrow had begun purchasing minor-leaguers to bolster his roster—utility man Jack Stansbury, outfielder Walter Barbare, pitcher Vince Molyneaux, pinch hitter Red Bluhm, Cuban infielder Eusebio Gonzalez (several teams signed Cubans, because they were not enemy aliens and not subject to the draft), infielder Frank Truesdale, and later infielder George Cochran and veteran pitcher Jean Dubuc. None helped. Thomas was no star at third base, but he was adequate, far better than any in Barrow's new crop. (Thomas was rejected by the army because of diabetes, but, afraid of being labeled a draft dodger,[13] he enlisted in the navy, which did not require a physical exam.)

Nothing was going right. Pitcher Carl Mays was moved into Class 1A and was harangued daily by agents of the shipyard league. Shortstop Everett Scott, it appeared, would not win his exemption appeal and would remain in Class 1A too. Stuffy McInnis struggled and missed time after an "attack of boils."[14] Barrow bought the rights of outfielder Hughey High—who had left the Yankees to join the shipyards—hoping to play High in left field and move Ruth back to the mound. High consented to join the Sox but failed to show up in Philadelphia. When contacted by Barrow, High said, "My wife won't let me." Even spousal duty was conspiring against the Red Sox.[15]

But the outlook brightened after July 4. Ruth, Barrow, and Frazee had a meeting, and Frazee agreed to give Ruth a bonus of $1,000 for pulling double duty on the mound and in the field. Ruth agreed to pitch when Barrow needed him—and Barrow wasted no time, calling on Ruth to pitch July 5. For the first time in over a month, Ruth was in the box, finishing the forgettable trip by pitching the Red Sox to a 4–3 win. Back in Boston and facing second-place Cleveland, Ruth had the day off, but Barrow could not resist pinch-hitting him with two men on base and the Red Sox down, 4–2, in the sixth. Ruth smacked a triple and scored on an errant throw. That gave Boston a 5–4 win and put the Red Sox back in first place. Ruth solidified that lead on July 8, when he hit what would have been, under modern scoring rules, his 12th home run, into Fenway's right-field bleachers in the 10th inning of a scoreless game. Under old rules, the batter stopped when the winning run scored, even if the ball left the park. Because there was a man on first, Ruth's hit counted only as a triple. But the Red Sox won, 1–0, part of a July string in which they won 15 out of 18. Ruth would stay stuck at 11 home runs.

Hooper, in his 10th season with the Red Sox, finished the year in a bit of a slump (he was batting over .320 on July 1 but hit .249 the rest of the way). Still, the 1918 season was his best all-around year. Hooper tutored Ruth, helped defuse the Barrow-Ruth situation, advised Barrow, and got comfortable as a team leader. For the first time in his career he was the best, most polished everyday player on his team. Hooper thrived. He hit .289, finishing second in the AL in doubles and triples and third in walks and runs. And, he noted, "Barrow was technically the manager, but I ran the team on the field."[16]

A fact that surely made the Strategy Board proud.

Crowder's work-or-fight order went into effect as soon as July 1 arrived, but men of draft age had a 10-day grace period to secure essential work. On July 11 the grace period was up. That day the Cubs took the first half of a home doubleheader from the Braves, 4–3, and between games, as some fans made for the exits, an announcement went up by megaphone: no one would be allowed to leave the park without giving an account of their draft status. The gates were locked and manned by federal agents. If draft-eligible men were found not carrying their cards, they were taken to the nearby Town Hall police station and jammed into the squad room until they could adequately explain their circumstances. This was part of a "slacker sweep" around Chicago that day. Movie houses, theaters, railway stations, cabarets, and poolrooms were swept, and more than 5,000 suspected slackers were detained. Of those, 500 had been at the Cubs game.[17]

While there was rancor in the stands, there was anxiety on the field. The Cubs and Braves played the second game of their double-header (the Cubs won, 3–2, behind Phil Douglas), but players had to wonder what was to stop officials from asking *them* to show they were not slackers. Ten days after work-or-fight became law, the question of baseball's usefulness remained unanswered. The notion that the fans who drove the game's popularity were subject to arrest simply by being in the stands could not have been comforting. Baseball was still waiting for a test case that could be appealed to the War Department and decide the sport's fate.

A few candidates emerged. The Brighton, Massachusetts, draft board, which oversaw the district in which Braves Field was located, summoned the entire team (eventually modified so that only catcher John Henry had to appear). The board found that baseball was not essential, and an appeal to Washington was prepared. In St. Louis, Rogers Hornsby received word from his home draft board in Fort Worth, Texas, that he needed an essential occupation. He, too, readied an appeal. But the first appeal to reach Baker and Crowder was that of a player in their backyard—Washington catcher Eddie Ainsmith. Manager Clark Griffith filed the appeal for Ainsmith the next day. (In a strange and sad twist, Ainsmith's wife had died just one week earlier after a long illness, leaving him with a young daughter.)

Griffith was generally a good representative of baseball. The Old Fox was smart and moved easily in Washington's political circles. His appeal was based on three precepts. First, that baseball was a big business, and enforcing the work-or-fight edict would cripple the business—part of Crowder's order exempted workers from the mandate if removal of those workers would ruin an entire industry. Baseball would be ruined without players. Second, Griffith noted that players are specialized. Few had skills outside of baseball that could be useful to the government. Because of those limited skills, they could get only menial new jobs in useful fields, which would cause severe financial hardship (another cause for work-or-fight exemption). Third, baseball

116

was the national sport, and to stop it would end the country's most popular form of outdoor recreation. Additionally, Griffith pointed out, baseball was not seeking special exemptions for players. It just wanted baseball to be considered an acceptable way to fill the "work" part of the work-or-fight order. Players who were already Class 1A would continue to join the army as called.

Griffith may have made a miscalculation or two in his brief, though. He did not make clear to the War Department just how many of baseball's players were of draft age—remember, in May, Baker had said he thought most players were outside draft age. Surely, too, Griffith slipped by bringing up the willingness of baseball men to answer the draft call. It was true that many players had joined the colors. But the War Department was also well aware of the many players who had skipped the draft to play for shipyard teams, which had been an embarrassment for the military as well as for baseball.

As Baker considered Griffith's brief, players kept playing, with their eyes on Washington, their minds on shipyards, and their tired bodies going through the motions on the diamond. "So long as Washington officials keep the players in suspense, there is certain to be bad baseball," Hugh Fullerton wrote. "The uncertainty and worry already have affected not only individual players, but entire clubs."[18] The Cubs, without ace Grover Cleveland Alexander and wondering when they might lose catcher Bill Killefer, got more worrisome news when Charley Hollocher was ordered to appear before his draft board on July 15 for a physical that, if he passed, would make him eligible to be immediately called. Little-used pitcher Vic Aldridge, who had made three relief appearances, got a jump on his draft board and left the Cubs to join the navy.

The Braves were so short of material that, when they played the Cubs on July 12, manager George Stallings sent Ed Konetchy to the mound and Hugh Canavan to the outfield. Konetchy was a first baseman, and Canavan was a pitcher (who happened to go 0–4 with a 6.36 ERA in 1918, his only major-league season). The Cubs won, 8–0. When the Cubs played Philadelphia two days later, tempers were so testy that Phillies manager Pat Moran nearly came to blows with Otto Knabe, Moran's teammate for four years in Philadelphia. The Cubs were exhausted but had to play a doubleheader against the Phillies the next day. They were swept. The fatigue got worse. On July 17 the Cubs and Phillies played a 21-inning game, second-longest in NL history at the time, with Lefty Tyler throwing a complete game (now, there's an understatement) in a 2–1 win. It got even worse. The next day the Cubs and Dodgers played a 16-inning game, with Hippo Vaughn throwing all 16. In three days, the Cubs played 55 innings, part of their worst stretch of the season with six losses in seven games.

But some rest was on its way, whether the players liked it or not.

Baker wasn't buying Griffith's plea. On July 19, well past the halfway point of the 1918 season, the government finally gave baseball the advice that Ban Johnson had been seeking for a year. And that advice was a bombshell. In the War Department's eyes, the game was not essential. Baker shot down Griffith's three major points. He started by noting that baseball had enough players outside of draft age to make the game viable (which was, of course, not true). He mocked Griffith's notion that ballplayers could do nothing else but play ball—"It is quite inconceivable," Baker said, "that occupations cannot be found by these men."[19] He did take the recreation angle seriously, but he decided that in war citizens should and would sacrifice recreation for the good of the country. Baker had made it official: every ballplayer of draft age was a slacker and should get useful work or be forced to join the army.

Chaos followed. Baker's ruling came out late on a Friday, and little could be resolved over the weekend. Baseball was unprepared for Baker's decision. The National League scrambled to call a meeting in New York the following Wednesday but moved it to Tuesday in Pittsburgh. Johnson, with no authority to do so, said the American League would shut down immediately. Griffith countered that Johnson was "talking through his hat,"[20] and Harry Frazee, of course, criticized Johnson sharply. Johnson saved face by sending out a telegram directing AL teams to keep playing their schedule, which they were already doing. Barrow seemed as unimpressed with the big-league magnates as he had been with those of the International League. "Barrow was all het up," the *Globe* reported. "His impression was that the baseball men had bungled the job."[21]

When business opened on Monday, things looked grim. The Cubs and Reds canceled their doubleheader. At Fenway, 10,000 fans were sure they were giving their Red Sox a wartime send-off. Down in Washington, though, NL president John Tener, Giants owner Harry Hempstead, and Indiana senator Harry New visited Crowder, essentially asking him to overturn the decision the War Department had just handed out.[22] Crowder got another group of baseball visitors: Griffith and Senators owner Ben Minor, along with Ohio representative Nicholas Longworth.[23] They employed a different strategy, asking that Crowder give baseball enough time to finish the season before enforcing the ruling. (Interesting that baseball's leaders took along two very partisan Republican congressmen who were critics of Baker and Wilson—Longworth, in fact, was the son-in-law of the administration's bane, Teddy Roosevelt.) Crowder, hoping to settle the thing once and for all, told the baseball men to get organized and present a brief that Wednesday.

In a rare show of unity, 15 of baseball's leaders, including Frazee and Weeghman, gathered at Ben Minor's office to work out their request to Crowder. Even Johnson and Tener made nice. Their disdain for each other had grown over the course of the year, in part because of an interleague contract squabble involving the rights to pitcher Scott Perry. Two weeks later Tener would resign, but for now Johnson and Tener were all handshakes and guffaws. The 15 arrived at Crowder's office and presented their brief. One of the key points was that only 63 big-league players were *not* within the draft ages, finally disabusing Baker of his notion that baseball would not be disorganized by the work-or-fight order. They requested that baseball be given an extension through October 15, enough time to finish the year, play the World Series, and settle their business.

In the midst of the chaos, the Red Sox players looked to Captain Hooper, who called a team meeting in the clubhouse at Fenway Park. Hooper, like most players, would have taken a serious financial hit if the season had stopped. He had a wife and two children at home in California, where he had also built up some farmland holdings. The previous winter his farm's foreman urged Hooper to buy more land. Hooper took out loans and did so.[24] With that debt hanging over him, the thought of losing his Red Sox income, including probable postseason pay, was surely worrisome. But, at the same time, players were worried about whether they should be playing at all after Baker's ruling.

Harry and his teammates decided to play until the final word came from Washington. On July 22 they played a doubleheader at home against Detroit and swept both games with shutouts. Two days later the Red Sox headed west to play Chicago, unsure of whether the AL would still be running when they got there. They lost the series opener, 4–2, in what the *Globe* described as "about as quiet a victory as ever was won on the South Side grounds. The 2,000 persons present seemed afraid to cheer, for they didn't know just how Sec. of War Baker would take such actions."[25]

On July 26, Crowder and Baker denied baseball's request for an extension to October 15. They did, however, grant an extension to September 1, enough time to allow the game to wrap up its business affairs. After that, both leagues would shut down for the rest of 1918 and, it seemed, for all of 1919.

THE ORIGINAL CURSE: JEAN DUBUC

As the Red Sox ranks were thinned by the draft, Barrow began signing players from minor leagues that shut down because of the work-or-fight order. One of those players was Jean Dubuc, a so-so, 29-year-old right-handed pitcher who had slipped out of the big leagues after seven seasons. Dubuc didn't pitch much for the Red Sox—only two games, though he was used as a pinch hitter. He was signed by the Giants the next year and had some success as a reliever.

In 1912 Dubuc had befriended a teammate with the Tigers, little-used pitcher Bill Burns. Yes, the same Bill Burns who fed the Cubs wild turkey in spring training and gained further fame as briber of the Black Sox. During the trial, Giants pitcher Rube Benton testified that Dubuc had received telegrams—presumably from Burns—telling him how to bet on the 1919 World Series. His friendship with Burns convinced manager John McGraw to drop Dubuc from the Giants after his solid 1919 season. In 1920, after news of the Black Sox scandal broke, McGraw would explain: "Bill Burns, also indicted in Chicago, hung around the Giants the latter part of the 1919 campaign. He was trying to interest me in a Texas oil proposition, he said, but when the season ended and the Reds had clinched the pennant, he disappeared. He constantly associated with one of our pitchers, Jean Dubuc, for which reason I finally decided to release Dubuc unconditionally."[26]

120

Dubuc, though not formally banned, never played in the big leagues again. He did go on to become a very popular figure in New England sports. He was Brown University's baseball and hockey coach and had success establishing a pro hockey team in Providence, Rhode Island. He also did well for his former team, the Tigers, as a scout—among the players he signed was Hank Greenberg.

ELEVEN

Money: Recollection of Boston Gambler James Costello

POOLROOM OF THE OXFORD HOTEL, JULY 24, 1918

Q: I wish you would describe what was said between you and Lee Magee, if anything was said, on or about July 24, 1918.

A: On the evening of July 24, about eight o'clock, Magee came into my place looking for me, and he called me aside and told me he had a proposition for me. I says, "What is it?" He says, "On tomorrow's ball game," he says. "We can't talk details just now," he says, "but I will have another man tomorrow with me and we will talk it over." I says, "What time?" He says, "Ten o'clock." The next morning, about ten o'clock Magee and the other party comes in the room and we go down in the far part of my room.

Q: Before you come to the next morning, what was said, if anything, by Magee, as to what was to be done?

A: He said it was in regard to a ball game the next day; they were going to "fix" a ball game. By "tossing" a game it means your own side loses the game—bet against his own side.

Q: Did he come back the next day?

A: The next morning at ten o'clock Magee and the other party came in my room and we go down in the corner and talk things over.

Q: Who was the other party?

A: The other party was Hal Chase. He says, "The proposition is this," he says. "How much money can you place on a ball game in Boston?" I says, "I can bet an unlimited amount." "Well," he says, "I think we can do business with you, Jim." I says, "I don't do business on ball games myself, so I will get somebody else." He says, "What will we do?" I says, "I want you to understand this in the first place: if you are going to throw a ball game, you have to bet some of your own money, because the gamblers won't bet unless you do." I says, "I have a gambler that can handle the thing for you." I asked them how much they wanted to bet themselves. "Well," they says, "we haven't got the money with us, will you take our check?" "Yes," I says, "I will take your check," I says, "for any amount, with this agreement—if you lose that ball game according to the agreement, I will give you your checks back and the amount equivalent to your check and one-third of what the gamblers win." That satisfied them. So then I walked down to my safe, took out my own checkbook on the Old Colony Trust Company of Boston, and gave them each a check. They crossed out the "Old Colony Trust Company" and filled their own banks in for five hundred dollars apiece. I took them checks and put them in my safe and took out one thousand dollars.

Q: Well, then you found out the Reds didn't lose the first game.

A: Well, I had a ticker across the street and I sent the boys over to see the ticker, and they came back and reported that the Reds had won the game. So that night, nobody comes and sees me. The next morning, Chase comes in and sees me. He says, "It was a tough break we had, Jim; we tried awful hard." I says, "Yes, the gamblers are satisfied you tried, both of you." He says, "Put them checks through." I put them checks through my bank, the Old Colony Trust Company. In a few days, them checks came back, one of the checks came back— Magee's check came back and the other check went through. So I says to my brother, "What are you doing Saturday?" He says, "Nothing." I says, "Drive me to New York." So I take the machine and drive to New York. At that time, Cincinnati was playing Brooklyn. . . .

[Two days later] I go up to the hotel and we all three met. Magee says, "There is Matty going across the room. Look out he don't see us." So we walked down Seventy-First Street to West End Avenue, and down West End Avenue to Sixty-Fifth Street, and there we talked the thing over. I says, "What are you going to do?" He says, "Well, the best I can do is send you reports of different games we are going to fix. You can do business on them." I says, "That don't satisfy me." I says, "I don't gamble on baseball myself." He says, "That is the best I can do." I says, "If you don't take this check up immediately, I will take it up with the club." Chase and Magee got a little ways away and talked the thing over among themselves. They says, "Why not stay here in New York today? We are going to play New York and that game is fixed." I says, "I don't gamble on baseball." They talked the thing over. He says, "I will tell you what I will do, Jim. You go back to Boston and we will send you half of that check, and the other half when we get home to Cincinnati." I says to Chase, "Will you stand good for that check and make Magee pay it?" He says, "Yes." I says, "I will take your word, Hal."

Q: When Magee was talking to you about this gambling, for how long, if it all, did he say it had been continuing on his part?
A: I asked the boys down at Sixty-Fifth Street how long this thing was going on. They said, "Oh, it has been going on in the Cincinnati Club for two years."[1]

This was the actual, word-for-word testimony of Jim Costello, a well-known Boston gambler who had been subpoenaed as a witness in a lawsuit filed by Lee Magee in 1920. The circumstances were unusual. Magee had been the second baseman for the Reds in 1918, and in July of that year Magee and his Cincinnati teammate—first baseman Hal Chase—visited Costello's poolroom with the proposal to throw a game against the Braves the following afternoon. The fix failed, though, and Magee did not settle his debt to Costello. Magee was traded to Brooklyn after the 1918 season and to the Cubs in the summer of 1919. Costello, finally ticked off over not having been paid, hit Magee with a court order and took his story about the bet to baseball officials. He even took along the crossed-out Old Colony Trust check as proof. Not only did Costello have evidence against Magee and Chase, but he had an added nugget: the pair told him that, among the Reds, game fixing had been going on for two years.

When Cubs president Bill Veeck (the father of the Bill Veeck who discovered Harry Grabiner's diary) was shown the evidence against Magee, baseball tradition dictated his next move. He confronted

123

Magee, who confessed, and in February 1920 the Cubs abruptly released Magee without public explanation. This was just the baseball way. Problem players—whether drinkers, gamblers, or fighters—did not have their problems brought before the public. They were simply shuffled along with closed lips. To protect the greatest-game-in-the-world image, baseball never acknowledged that its players were even capable of transgressions.

The problem for the Cubs—and baseball—was that Magee refused to follow the script. If he had, he would have accepted his release and gone off to find work with some minor-league team, never again speaking of the incident. But Magee insisted that, when he and Chase visited Costello, he had intended to bet on the Reds, not against them, and that Chase had double-crossed him. As Magee saw it, the Cubs had terminated his contract without just cause. He wasn't going to go quietly. Magee sued the Cubs.

This created a difficult tangle. Baseball had to do whatever it could to win the case—the right of owners to release players at any time, for any reason, was a crucial power for the magnates. But, in doing so, baseball had to acknowledge that gambling was the reason for Magee's release, that gamblers and players easily crossed paths, and that players had attempted to throw games. Worse, baseball had to call Costello to the stand. The game worked so hard to keep gambling in the shadows, but Magee's suit brought to light a voice from those shadows.

Costello's testimony doomed Magee's case, and the jury needed just 45 minutes to find in favor of the Cubs. But to get that win, baseball allowed the first crack to show in the barrier that had shielded the public from the problem of players mingling with gamblers. That barrier already had been trembling beneath the weight of suspicions about the honesty of the 1919 World Series, but it would not be utterly demolished until months later, in 1920, when Veeck would receive word that a Cubs–Phillies game had been fixed—which led to the uncovering of the previous year's Black Sox conspiracy. (Funny how the Cubs always seemed to be on the periphery of the juiciest gambling scandals of the era, isn't it?)

But at the time, Costello's testimony went largely overlooked. The magnates celebrated the verdict and took the opportunity to pat themselves on the back. The National League issued a commendation to the Cubs for "forcing into the full light of publicity its reasons for the discharge of player Lee Magee."[2] The commendation failed to mention that the Cubs had intended to keep the reasons for Magee's discharge secret and that the Magee issue would have been swept neatly under the rug, as usual, if not for the fact that Magee had filed a lawsuit. Magee was subject to the full light of publicity, but the Cubs hardly forced it.

What the magnates also did not want to mention was the fact that, in the summer of 1918, a couple of players could walk into a poolroom and attempt to fix a game. They surely did not want to mention that neither the players nor the gambler seemed to find this circumstance all that unusual. And, of course, they completely shrugged off Costello's suggestion that the Reds may have been throwing games as far back as 1916.

The game that Chase and Magee attempted to fix in Boston took place on July 25, just as the 1918 season was crumbling and the game's leaders were looking for one last boost from Washington. It was the day before Baker granted baseball the September 1 extension, and both leagues were mired in War Department purgatory. No one knew how much longer the season would continue, if at all—if you were gamblers like Chase and Magee, why not try to make one last big score?

All around baseball, players were taking the game lightly. In Chicago, the first-place Cubs tentatively left for a trip east, unsure whether they'd actually play any of the scheduled games. Some players didn't even show up for the trip. Lefty Tyler left the Cubs to return to his farm in New England. Bill Killefer went home to Michigan for a fishing trip. Charley Deal quit to go into government service. After Baker's extension was announced on July 26, Tyler, Killefer, and Deal returned to the team, but the games were a farce. A 7–1 win over the Braves was, according to the *Boston American*, "a fitful, absentminded game [featuring] many boob plays."[3] Players were understandably distracted. But, make no mistake, it wasn't the integrity of baseball itself that concerned the players. Nor was it worry over the progress of the war or anxiety about the dwindling recreational choices faced by Americans in wartime. It was money.

In the wake of Baker's ruling, a number of questions were left unanswered, and they all seemed to concern money. Would players be paid for the whole season or only through September 1? What would happen to multiyear contracts? Would there be a 1919 season? And the

125

big question: was there time to play a World Series? That was most important, for players and magnates alike. As Colonel T. L. Huston had called it, the World Series was a "financial orgy." Owners made bushels, as their teams played in front of packed houses with jacked-up ticket prices, and the National Commission got a cut of the receipts too. But the World Series mattered most to the players. The winners' share for the 1917 World Series had been almost $3,700, which was as much as some players made in a whole season. This year, with the members of the top four teams in each league sharing in the receipts, more players than usual were especially concerned about the playing of the World Series.

The money question dominated when the Cubs arrived in Boston to play the Braves on July 27, just two days after Costello's encounter with Chase and Magee. A heat-and-humidity wave had hit the East Coast, and the dead-tired Cubs had lost 8 of their previous 11 games, allowing the Giants to pull within 2 games of first place. Manager Fred Mitchell called a meeting. His players admitted that, in addition to being fatigued, they were worried about salaries. The following day, *Tribune* writer I. E. Sanborn scolded some of the Cubs for their pecuniary focus. He wrote: "While all the rest of the world is wrapped up in the monster game between democracy and autocracy, 'over there,' some of the ball players cannot see beyond the wings of the American dollar bill. With the nation's pastime about to be interred for the duration of the war their minds are centered on wringing the last possible nickel out of it before the blow-off."[4] Sanborn later expanded on that notion, saying that the Cubs' only motivation was to have the World Series played so that they could collect the extra pay. "Some of them," he wrote, "go so far as to declare that if there is to be no World's [Series] they will quit right away."[5]

If the Cubs were looking for a bright side, Mitchell was the wrong guy to ask. He didn't see a rosy outlook. "Big league baseball will be run much less expensively after the war," Mitchell said. "New contracts will be drawn and ball players will be forced to play for smaller salaries than they now get. . . . Contracts which have two and three years to run probably will be void after Sept. 1. When these contracts are drawn after the war men who have been receiving fabulous salaries probably will have to accept big cuts."[6]

For all the questions around baseball's future, it seemed certain that when the game did return after the war it would be on a much different basis, without the fabulous salaries. And, yes, the salaries in 1918 were fairly fabulous. That might not square with the assessment of Eddie Ainsmith—who, remember, had noted that most players bet in that era to make up for "the little we were paid." But Ainsmith was comparing salaries across eras, putting his paycheck up against those that came decades later, after free agency drove up contract values in baseball. At the time, ballplayers did pretty well for themselves. Ty Cobb was the game's highest-paid player and had made $20,000 in 1917. Grover Cleveland Alexander was the highest-paid Cub in 1918, at $12,000 per year. Ruth had signed for $7,000. When writer Eliot Asinof wrote to ex–Reds pitcher Dutch Ruether, inquiring as to his salary in 1919, Ruether wrote back sarcastically, "My salary was a huge $8,400 per season."[7] According to the Department of Labor's consumer price index, Cobb's '17 salary of $20,000 would work out to $330,000 in 2008 dollars. Ruth's $7,000 in 1918 was the equivalent of about $98,000 nine decades later. Aleck would have been making $168,000 (before the $10,000 spring bonus, that is).[8]

These were not astronomical incomes by today's standards. But against other 1918 professions, baseball players' salaries put them firmly in the upper middle class. A typical bartender made $3,000. A union bricklayer in Chicago made $1,700. A coal driver in Boston made $1,560. And teachers were woefully underpaid, earning an average of just $630, or what would be $8,800 in 2008 money.[9] (Some things never change.)

But, from the start of the war in Europe back in August 1914, there was a problem with money, and players were finding that their fabulous salaries were not going as far as they had before. They were not alone. Across America, the dollar was losing value. The war had created such an immense demand for basic necessities at home and for the Allies in Europe that the domestic supply chain could not keep up. The United States was providing Britain, France, and Italy with everything from wheat and lard to coal and clothing. Herbert Hoover's Meatless Mondays and Wheatless Wednesdays were not enough to stem the overwhelming demand. Meanwhile, credit policies were relaxed to help fund the purchase of Liberty Bonds, leading to an increase in the amount of cash printed. Prices soared. Inflation hammered the economy. Overall, 1918 registered the second-highest single-year inflation rate in U.S. history, at 17.26 percent. The only worse year was 1917, when inflation was 17.80 percent. (The inflation rate in 2007, by way of comparison, was typical—2.85 percent—and even the severe inflation of 1980 was only 13.58 percent). In fact, it was this problem that spurred the government to begin measuring inflation rates and cost-of-living indexes. A report released in August 1918 showed that from August 1914 until June 1918, the cost of living in America rose 50 to 55 percent. Food prices rose 62 percent. Clothing was up 77 percent. The price for a pair of men's overalls, the report stated, rose 161 percent.[10]

Money was a problem, for everyone in America. But ballplayers had reason to be particularly concerned. After all, someone who was a chauffeur or bartender before the war could be a chauffeur or bartender after the war. No one could say whether ballplayers could be ballplayers again once the war was over.

The details of the game that Lee Magee and Hal Chase attempted to throw are dosed with irony. Costello claimed Magee and Chase had the Reds' scheduled pitcher, Pete Schneider, in on the fix, but Schneider went to Mathewson before the game and asked to sit out. Matty inserted shine-baller Hod Eller, who threw a great game and would have won a 2–1 decision except that, with two out in the ninth, Magee made a wild throw that allowed the tying run to score. The score was still 2–2 in the 13th inning when Magee (who had been 0-for-5) hit a routine grounder that took "a crazy bound and hit [shortstop Johnny Rawlings] on the nose for a knockout blow."[11] Rawlings, his face bloody, was taken to the clubhouse to have his broken nose set and later came out wrapped up in adhesive tape. One of the Reds wisecracked, "What battle were you in?"

It wasn't humorous for Magee, because the bad bounce put him on first base. With Rawlings out and their roster already depleted, the Braves moved outfielder Roy Massey to shortstop, putting pitcher Art Nehf in center field and another pitcher, Hugh Canavan (who had also manned the outfield against the Cubs on the day of the slacker sweep in Chicago), in left. The next batter, Edd Roush, took advantage of the makeshift outfield, knocking a deep hit between Nehf and Canavan. Magee did his best to foul up the works by running slowly, but with two pitchers in the outfield it was impossible for Magee to move slowly enough not to score. Thus, it was Magee himself who scored the winning run that cost him his $500 bet with Costello and, eventually, his career.

128

Though Costello's testimony indicates that Magee led the plot to throw the game in Boston, it's no surprise to find Chase with a hand in the fix. This was the hallmark of his career. Chase was a very talented and popular player, dubbed "Prince Hal" almost from the start of his career in 1905, with the New York Highlanders (later renamed the Yankees). An excellent hitter, Chase was best known for his fielding, where his speed and athleticism made him, arguably, the greatest ever to play first base. For all his talent, though, Chase racked up a suspicious number of errors—402 in 1,815 games at first base, or one error for every 4.5 games. Compare that to Fred Merkle, who was not a great fielder but made only one error every 6.1 games. Or Red Sox first baseman Stuffy McInnis, an excellent fielder, who made an error every 12.5 games. And yet, when McInnis was asked, in 1942, who was the best first baseman he ever saw, he said, "Without question, Hal Chase."[12]

In 1910, Chase was accused by Yankees manager George Stallings of "laying down." Stallings was right—Chase was loafing because he wanted Stallings's job. Chase got it and got what he was really after: more money. "It is understood that his [managerial] duties will bring him a fat increase in pay," the *New York Times* reported.[13] Chase struggled as a manager, though, and the Yankees brought in Frank Chance to run the team. But Chase did not give up his habit of laying down. Early in the 1913 season, Chance visited the press box after a game and asked two reporters, "Did you notice some of the balls that got away from Chase today? They weren't wild throws; they were only made to look that way. He's been doing that right along. He's throwing games on me!"[14] The reporters didn't print Chance's accusation, fearing a libel lawsuit. Still, even bringing up Chase's suspicious play was a dangerous break from baseball protocol for Chance. Gambling players were not to be discussed—they were to be swept under the rug. Sure enough, two days after Chance's outburst, the Yankees traded Chase to Chicago, and the game-throwing accusation was never mentioned again. Problem solved.

In 1918, suspicions around Chase oozed into plain sight. If Costello's testimony is to be believed, the failed July 25 fix was not an isolated incident. Magee and Chase were also planning a game-fixing spree during Cincinnati's August trip to New York and Brooklyn. Everyone seemed to know something was odd about the Reds, but none dared call them crooked. "The Reds . . . can beat anything in

129

the whole league if they wish to go in and do their best," *The Sporting News* wrote. "In every defeat, the Reds looked stronger than their conquerors, and it was infuriating to the fans to see games dubbed away by blunders mixed with pop flies and failure to take advantage of the hits. . . . They blunder so often and so maddeningly!"[15]

It was especially maddening for manager Christy Mathewson, a legendary pitcher and one of baseball's best-liked figures. He knew about the game fixing. "We all knew," Roush would later recall. "But Matty, he wouldn't do anything about it."[16] Matty certainly knew about Chase in 1917. That summer, pitcher Jimmy Ring approached Mathewson and told him that Chase had offered him a bribe to throw a game. Ring turned him down, but when the Reds wound up losing, Chase still paid Ring. After Ring told Mathewson his story, though, the manager did exactly what was expected of him: nothing.

We'll never know the full extent of gambling that took place in baseball before the 1919 Black Sox, because there was such a culture of silence on the subject among players, among owners, and among managers. But something was different for Mathewson in August 1918, something that made him break with tradition. His job seemed to be in danger—an on-field fight between Magee and Greasy Neale on August 5 in Brooklyn seemed to confirm the feeling that Mathewson had lost control of the team. In addition, Matty had been under pressure all year to go to France with the YMCA to teach soldiers baseball, but he had consistently ducked the issue.

Finally, Mathewson decided to join the army as an officer with the chemical warfare division. He would leave at the end of August, and he'd leave the Reds behind. Mathewson was only 37, so it could have been that he wanted to rescue his reputation before he left and show that the Reds' problems were not his fault. Or perhaps the prospect of going to war gave him some sort of psychological liberation. But, on August 6, Mathewson did something unusual for a manager—he suspended Chase for "indifferent playing," a common euphemism for throwing games.

Even without Ring's accusation, it would have been obvious to any manager that Chase was up to no good. According to *The Sporting News*, "Prince Hal's fielding lapses, more frequent this year than formerly, have exasperated the other players. . . .These mishaps have hurt the team's chances and caused more or less friction between Chase and the pitchers." *TSN* also pointed out, "In the East recently things got so bad that opposing players would yell at him, 'Well, Hal, what are the odds today?'"[17] Mathewson collected testimony against Chase from Ring, Heinie Groh, Neale, Mike Regan, and Sherry Magee (no relation to Lee). Giants pitcher Pol Perritt testified that Chase had approached him, asking him to throw a game. *That* was bold—attempting to collude with an opposing pitcher on a fix. Giants manager John McGraw confirmed that Perritt told him about the conversation with Chase. McGraw did, however, add that if Chase were exonerated of the charges, McGraw wanted him on the Giants.

When Chase's case was heard in January 1919, he did beat the charges. NL president John Heydler (who took over after Tener's resignation) found that, with Mathewson in France and unable to testify, there was insufficient evidence to support Chase's banishment. Chase was reinstated and signed by McGraw that spring.

Chase was crooked, and his case shows pretty clearly that baseball had a gambling problem in 1918—and well before. Chase is often cited as an inspiration for the Black Sox scandal, because, as the logic goes, players who watched the NL whitewash Chase's suspension felt safer doing some of their own game fixing. But Chase was not the only gambler in baseball in 1918. He was just the only one who got caught. It's likely that there were other Hal Chases who managed to stay out of the spotlight. Chase was, like most, driven by the dollar. But he was more willing than most to bend his morals in the name of finances. Shortly before his death, Chase (who always maintained he never bet against his own team) said in an interview with *The Sporting News*:

> I wasn't satisfied with what the club owners paid me. Like others, I had to have a bet on the side and we used to bet with the other team and the gamblers who sat in the boxes. It was easy to get a bet. Sometimes collections were hard to make. Players would pass out IOUs and often be in debt for their entire salaries. That wasn't a healthy condition. Once the evil started, there was no stopping it and the club owners were not strong enough to cope with the evil.[18]

As Donald Dewey and Nicholas Acocella wrote in their Hal Chase biography, *The Black Prince of Baseball*, "For all the glamour attached to his profession, Chase never lost sight of the fact that ballplayers were hired help whose contracted pay was as much a brief security against the day they were jettisoned as it was an acknowledgment of their present usefulness. . . . For Chase, baseball and money were inseparable."[19]

With inflation putting unprecedented pressure on the money players did have, and with the sport expected to fall dormant the following season, baseball and money had never seemed so inseparable as they were in 1918. Not just for Hal Chase. For all players.

TWELVE

Labor: Charley Hollocher

Polo Grounds, New York, August 5, 1918

It was hot at the Polo Grounds. It had been hot all week, hot all summer, hot in every city across the country. The mercury was tapping 91 in New York, which would have been bad enough, but the humidity was awful, worse, even, than anything Charley had felt back home in St. Louis, where they knew something about humidity. The game hadn't even started, and Charley's uniform was nearly soaked with sweat. He must have lost 10 pounds in perspiration just walking through the city this afternoon, and a skinny fellow like Charley Hollocher didn't really have 10 pounds to lose. It was so hot and humid that in midtown Manhattan he had seen lines of men, five deep in spots and winding around whole city blocks, waiting just to get into the bathhouse. He had heard that almost a half million people were on their way to Coney Island's beaches today.[1] Charley couldn't imagine any island able to jam half a million people on the beach alone. There weren't any islands like that in St. Louis or even in Chicago.

No place was comfortable. The few Cubs who had ventured to sit in the stagnant dugout were crowded around the watercooler. Charley's other teammates were all back in the clubhouse trying to stay cool. It wasn't Charley's place to go and knock the older players out of the watercooler spots, and he didn't feel comfortable staying in the clubhouse. The game would be starting soon, and Charley had to get his arm warmed up. He was supposed to be out on the field, practicing, working. But here he was standing around, practically alone, being broiled by the sun.

Still, heat and all, Charley was just where he wanted to be. Playing ball, in the big leagues. That was the good life for a young man, his father had always told him. Ballplayer, a real living. The kind of work other men looked up to. Charley had always felt there was some envy in his father's tone when he spoke that way, as if he wished he were the ballplayer, as if maybe Charley didn't appreciate the opportunity as much as he should. Charley could understand. His father—Jacob Hollocher—had grown up on a farm near St. Louis, and from the time he could stand, Jacob was helping his stern German father in the field. When Charley's father was still just a kid, he left the farm and went to work for his older brother, Joseph, in a dry-goods store in Bonhomme Township. Then Charley's dad settled into the life insurance game as a young man and, well, he had been at it for more than 20 years now.[2] Life insurance was good, solid work, Jacob would say. But there was no excitement, no pep. When Jacob Hollocher would tell his son he wanted him to be a ballplayer, Charley knew what he was really saying: don't be an insurance broker.

It was easy advice to follow, because baseball came naturally to Charley. His father would push him to practice, but going all the way back to his days at Central High, it was as if Charley did not need practice. His hitting was something he had worked on, cutting down his swing, making consistent contact, from his first pro games at Keokuk in 1915, right through all 200 games he'd played in the previous year with Portland in the PCL. Charley's talent was there. It was just that sometimes his brain seemed to interfere. Charley had a tendency to put too much pressure on himself, and when he did that he would bungle and dub. He had done it at Keokuk, had done it in his first stop as a pinch hitter in Portland. But he hadn't done that here in his first year in the big leagues. He was free and easy in Chicago—so free and easy that the rest of the team, even the older guys like Merkle and Paskert, seemed to take after him.

So his father's message had sunk in. Charley loved his job. Milton had gotten the message, too, but Charley always knew his little brother was impatient. Milt wanted to play ball, in the big leagues, but he wanted it *immediately*. He had followed Charley to the minors that spring and played 28 games out in Spokane. But Milton pretty quickly got an itch for some real adventure and decided to go to war,

From left, Fred Merkle, Rollie Zeider, Charley Hollocher, and Charley Deal stand in front of the Cubs dugout. Though Hollocher was far younger than most of his teammates, he seemed to set a positive tone for the Cubs. (CHICAGO HISTORY MUSEUM)

even though he was only 19 and not even eligible for the draft. But that was Milt. Impatient. He quit baseball, hurried himself into a marriage, and, just like that, got a new line of work: he signed up with the marines. He had been writing to Charley from Parris Island, telling him about the life and work of a soldier.[3] Charley read the letters with great interest. He had been placed in Class 1A, so, soon enough, he'd give up his job as a ballplayer and become a soldier himself. Probably would not be much different from his job now, anyway. At games throughout the season, it seemed players were always surrounded by soldiers.

135

Charley, leaning on the dugout rail, waved to one of the jackies sitting in a box. "How was the cigar?" Charley asked. The other day, Charley had won a prize from the jackies on hand for Sailors Day. The player who got the first hit, it was announced, won a box of cigars. It was an awkward presentation. Charley had hit an inside-the-park home run, hustling all the way. He was winded. The last thing anyone would want, panting and sweating under a hot sun, was a batch of cigars, and all the gratitude Charley could muster was a breathless "Thank you." Besides, Charley didn't touch tobacco. He didn't meddle in the stuff other men on the team did—smoking, drinking, chewing tobacco, playing poker and craps, staying out until dawn. So Charley had opened the cigars and passed them out to the sailors in the crowd. He'd gotten a warm ovation for his efforts.[4]

Now one of the sailors he'd met was back. "Oh, it was a fine cigar," the jackie said. "You should have at least kept one for yourself. Don't tell me you never smoke."

"No, it's true," Holly said. "Never smoke. No booze, either. Something about it. I don't quite know. Things like that give me these strange stomach pains."

Charley shrugged and patted his stomach, smiling up at the jackie.

July had been a funk for the Cubs. They'd gone 18–14, their worst month of the season. They were tired. They were unsure about the future. They'd lost their momentum. Throughout the month several Cubs who had been performing far above their abilities slumped their way back to more pedestrian numbers. On July 4, Fred Merkle was hitting .347, Dode Paskert was hitting .320, and Leslie Mann was hitting .317. All three were among the National League leaders. Just three weeks later, though, Merkle was down to .310, Paskert was at .296, and Mann fell to .281. Hendrix, after an 11–3 start, went 2–3 in his next five outings. Douglas evened out too—his record dropped from 5–1 to 8–4.

But, through it all, Hollocher never stopped hitting. He hit .376 in April. At the end of May he was at .324. End of June: .310. And while it seemed that every other Cub was free-falling through July, Hollocher actually bumped up his average to .312, among the best in baseball. For the Cubs, this was a pleasant surprise. Hollocher had shown hitting potential in the minor leagues and in spring training, but it was his fine fielding, not his bat, that seemed to secure his future. He had batted just .229 in his first minor-league season, with Keokuk in '15. He improved to .289 for Rock Island the next year and was at .276 for Portland in '17. When he reached Chicago, though, he simply seemed to find hits. He was one of the hardest batters in the league to strike out, and he excelled as the number-two hitter in Chicago's lineup, behind leadoff man Max Flack.

Hollocher's consistency and ebullience rubbed off on his older teammates. He did not miss a game, even after the magnates—who were coping with the shortened season that had been decided on after Baker's ruling—began compacting the schedule, squeezing in as many doubleheaders as they could during a brutally hot August. The Cubs, for example, played 10 doubleheaders in the month, and under those conditions managers had to rest their players frequently. But not Hollocher. In the *Tribune*, Crusinberry wrote, "[Hollocher] has struck such a merry stride he has inspired confidence in all of the others. As a result, they are going at top speed in every inning of every game."[5]

Once August hit and the magnates finally settled the rest of the season, the Cubs and Hollocher reclaimed that merry stride. Just in time, too, because the team was in New York to face the Giants, who had overcome player losses at nearly every position to pull within 3.5 games of the Cubs, heading into a crucial 5-game series. But if there was a hallmark of the Cubs' 1918 season, it was the way they were consistently able to rip through the defending NL champion Giants. This key series in early August would be no different. Hippo Vaughn tossed a one-hitter in the opener, not letting a batter past second base in an easy 5–0 win. The second game of the series—Sailors Day at the Polo Grounds, with a box of cigars for the batter who notched the first hit—showed what a mess the Giants' pitching staff had become in the absence of regulars Jess Barnes, Jeff Tesreau, and Rube Benton. Starter Pol Perritt was knocked around for three runs in the first three innings, and the best reliever McGraw had handy was Ferdie Schupp. The Cubs battered him for 14 hits and 8 runs, giving Lefty Tyler an 11–1 win.

On a warm August 3 afternoon, the Cubs and Giants split a doubleheader in front of 25,000 fans. But warm turned hot. Temperatures topped 90 for four days, and a record was set on August 7, when thermometers in New York registered 102 degrees. It was especially humid on August 5. "Furnace is right," the *Tribune* reported, "for the mercury went up without making even the express stops, and the humidity hugged the century mark all day, making a mammoth stew pot of the Polo Grounds."[6] This would be a key game for the Cubs, because by now the Giants had fallen 5.5 games out of first. A win

137

would almost seal the pennant. Fred Mitchell had an idea—he would use the heat to his advantage. Hippo Vaughn was to start against the Giants' Fred Toney, a matchup that tickled fans, because in a head-to-head matchup the previous summer Toney and Vaughn had both thrown no-hitters through nine innings, with Vaughn and the Cubs finally losing in the 10th. There would be no no-hitter for Vaughn today, though, because Mitchell entered the game planning to pull him after five innings, before the heat could wear him down. Then he'd insert Paul Carter for two innings and Douglas for two more.

When the Cubs were at the plate, Mitchell wanted to exploit a known weakness of Toney's: fielding. Toney had been a notable player in 1918, and not because of his talent. He went 24–16 for the Reds in 1917 but became a pariah after he was arrested for attempting to dodge the draft. Facing nonstop virulence from Cincinnati fans, Toney started 6–10, and the Reds traded him. Typical of McGraw's acquisitions, Toney got back on track, notching a record of 58–30 over the next three and a half years. Mitchell, though, knew that Toney struggled to field bunts. After the Cubs fell behind, 3–0, Chicago's batters began bunting, sending Toney scampering all over the infield. The Cubs did not score, but the bunts had Toney drenched in sweat. With two outs in the eighth, the tactic paid off as the Cubs rallied for five runs off Toney and won, 5–3. The Cubs left the Polo Grounds with a 6.5-game lead. The pennant was all but theirs.

Hollocher's steady fielding, hitting, and enthusiasm helped pull the Cubs out of their July rut, but the roster was boosted by reinforcements. In the wake of the work-or-fight order, the Pacific Coast League had broken up, and Mitchell plucked a pair of useful players in the aftermath: infielder Charley Pick and right-hander Speed Martin. Pick, who had been playing for San Francisco, was a decent hitter, but in his only full big-league season, with the Athletics in 1916, he had committed 42 errors in 108 games at third base. With the more sure-handed Charley Deal at third, Mitchell inserted Pick at second base, where the Cubs had lost Pete Kilduff to the draft and had been trying to get by with Rollie Zeider and Bill McCabe (a pair who combined to hit .216). Pick was lacking in the field but hit .326 in 29 games with the Cubs. Martin, signed from Oakland, also had value. With Hendrix and Douglas sliding, Mitchell needed another right-hander. Martin served well. Tall and thin, his nickname was ironic—he mostly used curveballs delivered from a variety of arm angles, as well as a slowball. "Pick and Martin are delighted to be with the Cubs," Oscar Reichow wrote in the *Daily News*. "It is not often that many players join a ball club in time to 'horn in' on a World's Series as they have."[7]

After the Giants series, it seemed inevitable that Pick and Martin would, indeed, horn in on the World Series. If it was played, that is. As August passed, the question of whether baseball would put on a World Series continued to go unanswered. Players would have until September 1 to find useful work, and Baker had given baseball that much time to settle its business affairs. But just how to finish the business was a puzzle. The pleasant unity the magnates had shown in making their final plea to Baker and Crowder at the end of July didn't even last till August 1. Ban Johnson, sticking to the letter of Baker's revised ruling, proposed a plan to end the season on August 20 and play a World Series that could be over by September 1. But again, the magnates coalesced into factions. Johnson got no support from the National League (even good friend Garry Herrmann panned Ban's plan), plus a thumbs-down from Clark Griffith, Charles Comiskey, and, of course, Harry Frazee. When AL leaders met in Cleveland on August 3, Comiskey delivered a rousing speech that swayed the other magnates to vote against Johnson's August 20 arrangement and support finishing the season on Labor Day (September 2), with a World Series starting on September 4. The NL agreed.

Johnson, not accustomed to being so freely defied, issued a statement: "If the club owners wish to take a chance on acting contrary to the ruling of the War Department, that is their business."[8] That brought a scathing rebuke signed by Frazee, Griffith, and Comiskey, accusing Johnson of bungling the work-or-fight situation and adding something like an AL magnates' declaration of independence: "From now on, the club owners are going to run the American League. We criticise [sic] Mr. Johnson merely as an official. We have nothing against him personally, but from now on we intend to take a hand in the management of the league. His rule or ruin policy is shelved."[9] A week later, though, Comiskey and Griffith said they did not authorize the statement.[10] This is what a mess the game's leadership had become. Even the anti-Johnson faction had factions.

But Johnson was right. Baseball's owners were taking a chance defying Baker. It was a reasonable guess that the War Department would allow two teams an extra 10 days to play out the championship. Play-

139

ers, though, were not willing to abide by guesses. They wanted Baker's written approval. "It may be all right for the magnates to assume the government will not object to a world's series after Sept. 1," one Cub told the *Tribune*. "They won't be taking any chances, because no penalty will be imposed on them. The players are the ones who will get it in the neck if the work or fight order is not obeyed, and I for one am going to obey it."[11]

All haggling and convulsions about the World Series caused a stir among the two league leaders—the Cubs in the NL and the Red Sox in the AL. Through it all, though, Hollocher was a touchstone. He just kept hitting. When the Cubs left the Polo Grounds, having won 4 of 5 from the Giants, Hollocher had hit in seven straight games. Arriving in Pittsburgh to play a one-day series—one of the odd contortions of the newfangled schedule—Holly had hit in 11 straight. Over a 6-game, four-day series at home in Chicago, Holly kept playing and hitting, running his streak to 18 straight. In a doubleheader against Philadelphia on August 17, Hollocher tallied five hits and pushed his hitting streak to 20 games.

This should have been a big story. But there was bigger news in Chicago on August 17, and Hollocher's run was pushed to the inside pages of the newspapers.

While Hollocher was pushing his hitting streak to 20 games on Chicago's North Side, down in the Loop high drama was playing out in the Federal Building courtroom of Judge Kenesaw Mountain Landis. The biggest court case of 1918—the federal government's arrest and trial, on charges of sedition and undermining the draft, of 100 members of the radical Industrial Workers of the World labor union—was coming to a sudden close. Indeed, it may have been the biggest case in the history of the American courts, believed to be the largest group of defendants ever tried before a federal jury. The estimated cost of the trial, which began with jury selection back on April 1, was $1 million. By the time it was over, more than 30,000 pages of records had been typewritten, and stenographers had entered 7.5 million words into the court log.

The trial of the Wobblies—the nickname of the IWW—had loomed over Chicago throughout the spring and summer. It was expected to be a tense affair, especially after Landis was assigned the case. Few judges were as far away from the IWW on the political spectrum as Landis. The Wobblies were strongly antiwar and differed from the mainstream labor movement, headed by Samuel Gompers and the American Federation of Labor, in that they were not looking for moderate, incremental improvements to the condition of workers but for a wholesale overthrow of the wage system as it existed. The AFL had actually been very supportive of the war effort and had leveraged the overall shortage of labor into widespread improvements for its members. The IWW, though, pushed its members to resist the war. This was not a stance appreciated by Landis, who had been making strongly pro-war speeches around Chicago and had a son, Reed Landis, serving at the front as one of America's first fighter pilots.

But Landis had been surprisingly respectful and even indulgent when it came to the Wobblies. At the start of the trial, Landis, a chewer himself, made a tobacco concession to the largely foreign-born and generally rough-hewn defendants. "I think we will have a row of spittoons moved in tomorrow," he said. "We must not deprive these men of their comforts."[12] Landis listened to complaints about the food that the IWW defendants were being served and ordered them to be well fed. He also ordered they be given razors and a place to shave each day. Over the course of the trial, Landis allowed about 70 of the defendants out of jail on their own recognizance.

The case presented by the government, though, was not so kind. Federal prosecutors presented the IWW as an extremely violent organization bent on the overthrow of the U.S. government. Prosecutors freely mixed truth and fiction. The Wobblies were antiwar and sought to fight against the war through the sabotage of industry. An IWW tract read during the trial described the use of sabotage: "It may mean the destroying of raw materials destined for a scab factory or shop. It may mean the spoiling of a finished product. It may mean the destruction of parts of machinery or the disarrangement of a whole machine. . . . In the case of wars, which every intelligent worker knows are wholesale murders of workers to enrich the master class, there is no weapon so forceful to defeat the employers as sabotage by the rebellious workers."[13]

141

The government wove in actual words and pamphlets from the Wobblies with grotesque exaggerations. It was charged that IWW was plotting to replace President Wilson with Kaiser Wilhelm, that they were funded by Germany, that they were planning to invade Arizona with the help of Mexico, that they had plotted with the Irish rebel group Sinn Fein in Butte, Montana, that they were run by the Russian Bolsheviks. No actual evidence of any of these plots or associations was presented, but merely mentioning them in court helped the government accomplish its real aim in the case—to make the Wobblies look so scary that no one could sympathize with them.

It worked. Though many around the country supported the goal of workers' rights, the labor situation was tricky during wartime. Even unions that were members of the AFL were subject to public scorn, because strikes threatened to slow down production to support the Allied armies. And there were plenty of strikes across the country. Around Boston at least 10 groups were on strike in August alone—shoe cutters in Brockton, followed by shoe lasters in Brockton, Bridgewater, and Rockland; city workers in Lawrence; General Electric workers, twice, in Lynn; blacksmiths in Watertown; operators of the Middlesex & Boston Street Railway; bellboys in Swampscott; employees of E. A. Henchley and Co., makers of life rafts, in Cambridge.

But Wobblies were different from East Coast strikers, who had specific and reasonable goals. Wobblies were plain *scary* to many. The union's headquarters were located at 1001 W. Madison Street in Chicago—that's why the trial was now before Landis's court—but the Wobblies were not a strong presence among Chicago workers. The rank-and-file IWW generally worked in mining and logging companies of the West and were almost always unskilled laborers. Some measure of the Wobblies' scary reputation was earned. Violent outbursts between employers and the IWW were common (often initiated by employers), but in big cities those violent outbursts were just distant legends, taking place in far-flung locales such as Colorado, Arizona, and Washington. The IWW trial brought those tales to life in Chicago. There was fear that the city would become the scene of Wobbly vengeance. On April 14, a *Tribune* editorial warned, "Farther West, on the coast, there is a different idea of the I.W.W. There people know what the virtual terrorization of a town by the incursion of violent revolutionaries can be. . . . The indulgent humor of this region is not found where the I.W.W. has been felt as an applied force and where it is not known solely as a ludicrous vagary, pink whiskered and long haired."[14]

This was not unjustified alarmism. Bombs linked to labor—some to the IWW, some to other unions—were being found all over Chicago. In January, a girl was arrested at Union Station, armed with 50 pounds of dynamite and a loaded automatic pistol. Known as "Dynamite Girl," she had IWW connections and, according to the *Tribune*, "With the great I.W.W. trial coming up next month, the police saw a possible motive in the efforts to bring contraband explosive to Chicago."[15] (Dynamite Girl was actually anarchist Ella Antolini, 18, who was sent to a Missouri prison, where her cellmate was famed anarchist Emma Goldman.) In March a bombing campaign that was part of the strike against the Lyon & Healy music company led to murder indictments for union officials. Also in March, a bomb had been found in the Federal Building office of attorneys Frank Nebeker and Claude Porter, who would be prosecuting the IWW trial. It was the second bomb found in the building in the previous two months. In April a man believed to be an anarchist or a Wobbly was arrested for making bombs in his South Side home. In July, as part of an internal dispute in the Cobblers Union, a bomb on the North Side exploded at 1:00 A.M., driving hundreds of locals into the street. There was paranoia when it came to domestic terrorism, but it was rooted in daily headlines. The presence of the IWW made Chicagoans nervous.

The climax of the IWW trial came with the testimony of the union's leader, massive, one-eyed organizer "Big Bill" Haywood. On the stand, Haywood lobbed his own sensational accusations, including the claim that lumber bosses were getting black workers hooked on cocaine and heroin so that they'd become addicted and agree to work for low wages. Haywood stridently denied the government's assertion that the Wobblies supported the kaiser and made a pretty good point in response: if the IWW was antiwar, how could it be pro German? "I regard the German socialists as more responsible for the war than any other body," Haywood said. "They refused to vote for the general strike against the war. If they had refused to fight in August 1914, this war would never have been. . . . I have learned to despise autocracies of all kinds and that includes governmental autocracies. Germany today is the worst autocracy in the world."[16]

Haywood's testimony ended August 13. Four days later, as Hollocher hit in his 20th straight game, the trial jolted to a stop. The prosecution made its final argument, and the defense, in a move that sent a wave of surprise through the courtroom, declined to present a final argument. Just after 4:00 P.M., with the trial having dragged over four and a half months, the jury retired for what was expected

143

to be a proportionately long deliberation. But they returned in just 65 minutes. All 100 defendants were found guilty. "It had been feared by court attaches that, were the 100 convicted, there would be a riot in court," the *Tribune* reported. "Instead, there was a dead, almost breathless silence."[17]

Shock fell over the room. Haywood, in a move to calm his disciples, praised Landis and agreed that the IWW had gotten a fair trial. If there was outrage over the guilty verdict, it would apparently be expressed another time.

THE ORIGINAL CURSE: CHARLEY HOLLOCHER

Charley Hollocher batted .316 as a rookie, fourth in the NL, and by the end of the year he seemed destined to become one of the greatest shortstops the game had known. But Hollocher's story would take a strange, tragic turn.

By 1923, Hollocher was in his prime. He was team captain, coming off a year in which he had hit .340 for the Cubs and, incredibly, struck out just five times in 592 at bats. At spring training in California, though, he suffered an attack of the flu. He went back to St. Louis and was examined by Dr. Robert Hyland, who sent Hollocher to a specialist. Hollocher never explained what was wrong with him but later said, "They advised me that I would ruin my health if I played baseball that season."[18] Still, Bill Killefer, who was by then manager of the Cubs, persuaded Hollocher to rejoin the team. Hollocher hit .342 in 66 games but continued to have stomach pain. Finally he left a note saying, "Feeling pretty rotten, so made up my mind to go home and take a rest and forget baseball for the rest of the year. No hard feelings, just didn't feel like playing anymore. Good luck."[19] And that was it. Holly left.

He returned for 76 games in 1924, but his stomach still hurt, and he quit for good. He worked at a number of odd jobs around St. Louis and spent a year as a scout for the Cubs. But he did not play ball again. Hollocher might have been a hypochondriac, might have had a legitimate but undiagnosed stomach condition, or—as has been more recently speculated—might have been suffering from depression. The latter reasoning makes sense in light of what later became of Hollocher.

On August 14, 1940, at age 43, Hollocher, who had been complaining to his wife about abdominal pains, slid into the front seat of his car and parked in a driveway near Lindbergh Boulevard in St. Louis County. He took off his sunglasses and took out his membership card for the Association of Professional Baseball Players. He pulled out his new shotgun—so new that the tag was still attached—scrawled out a note, and placed it on the dashboard. The note read: "Call Walnut 4123, Mrs. Ruth Hollocher." He then put the barrel of his shotgun to his neck and pulled the trigger.[20]

THIRTEEEN

Death: Carl Mays

Fenway Park, Boston, August 10, 1918

Carl leaned back on the bench in the corner of the home dugout,
watching George Mogridge hurl for the Yankees. Another southpaw,
and everyone in Beantown knew what that meant: the Red Sox would
not score—they could not beat lefties at all—and they would lose.
Carl's arms were folded against his chest. The heat wave had passed,
and now it was a chilly Saturday at Fenway, maybe 60 degrees. Fans
wore overcoats. Carl's teammates were not bothering him, which was
customary. Carl was pitching the second game of that afternoon's
doubleheader against New York, and most players steered clear of the
boxman on the day he was pitching, leaving him time to get his focus.
But the truth was Carl's teammates steered clear of him even when
he was not pitching.

It was OK, though. Carl had other worries on his mind.

Babe Ruth was coming to bat, and Carl heaved a sigh when the
crowd went into the usual convulsion of cheering. After the run-in
with Barrow in the beginning of July, Ruth's temper had cooled, and
he was now pitching his turn in the rotation and playing the outfield
when he was not on the slab. And even Carl had to credit him—Ruth
had been performing quite well. Still, Carl had never liked the man,
though they'd been acquainted for a long time. He hadn't liked Ruth
when they both joined the Providence club in 1914, hadn't liked him
when they came up to the Red Sox together later that year, hadn't

146

liked him when they were battling for a spot in the pitching rotation as rookies in 1915, and did not like him now that they were big-league stars. Carl could not explain why. Ruth was big, loud, and brash; he did not seem to care a whit about anything except satisfying whatever desire happened to grab him at that moment. What baffled Carl was that people seemed to *love* the big ape for it. Ruth would do something childish—steal a car, eat two raw steaks, punch a man on the train, fight with Barrow—and he'd get that dumb grin on his moon face, and everyone would laugh and say, "Oh, Babe."

Maybe this was the reason Carl disliked Ruth. Babe was popular. Carl was not. One thing Carl knew was this: there is such a thing as popularity. We all know people who are popular without being able to explain why they should be. We also know people who are not popular, and yet they may be even more deserving of respect. Popularity does not necessarily rest on merit. Nor is unpopularity necessarily deserved. It was long ago made very apparent to Carl that he was not one of those individuals who were fated to be popular. It used to bother him some, for he supposed there are none of us who wouldn't prefer to be well thought of.[1]

Maybe it was the death of his father that was behind his persistent unpopularity. Carl was just 12 when William Henry Mays, a stern Methodist minister who had moved the family from Kentucky to Missouri, was returning from a day of preaching, got caught in a rainstorm, got sick, and died. After that, it seemed, Carl never learned how to get in good with other men. It's a bad outlook for a boy of 12 to have a dead father. Everywhere he went in the years following his father's death, he was immediately disliked. When he was with Boise, Idaho, he didn't have a pal on the club until the season was half over. When he went to Portland, Oregon, he got the same cold shoulder until the fellows understood him better. But when he came East and joined the Providence club, he got a still bigger dose of the same unpleasant medicine, and that began to get on his nerves.[2]

It was OK, though. Carl had other worries on his mind.

Maybe, it's true, he should not belittle the other men when plays were bungled behind him. But Carl didn't stand for failure. That could be attributed to his uncle Pierce—who actually wasn't Carl's uncle. In 1913, when Carl was 21, he signed with Portland. One afternoon Pierce Mays showed up at a game. He approached Carl, wondering if they were related. Maybe, they concluded, there was a distant

147

relation. But Carl and Pierce took to each other immediately, and (with his wife, "Auntie" Genevieve) it was as if he had a new set of parents. The way he clung to Pierce made Carl suspect that losing his father at a young age had been more difficult than he had originally supposed. Perhaps the bond with Uncle Pierce was forged on death itself—it probably was no coincidence that Pierce's only son had died too. Why else could Carl make no friends among his teammates but immediately make friends with Pierce?

At one point, when Carl had been particularly frustrated with his unpopularity in Providence, he wrote to Uncle Pierce, telling him that baseball was a game where you had to swim continually against the current and that he had perhaps better get out, go back to Oregon, and see what he could do in some other profession where the waters weren't quite so deep.[3] Carl got a letter back saying that he could surely return to Portland, only he would no longer be welcome at the home of Pierce and Genevieve Mays. They did not tolerate quitters. So Carl stayed, but now he got angry at himself when things did not go well. He was not going to let down Uncle Pierce. He got angry when his teammates showed ineptitude in the field. Why shouldn't he? When they failed, weren't they letting Uncle Pierce down too?

Ah, it was OK, though. Carl had other worries on his mind.

Like his right arm, which was not hurling as it usually did. Carl had been lammed in his past four starts. His arm was sore, and he was showing signs of wear and tear.

And he was worried about Freddie Madden, his longtime girlfriend who would become his wife in just a little more than a month. Carl wanted to support her with a nice honeymoon and, eventually, a new house.

And the Red Sox, whose grip on first and the attending slice of World Series coin was slipping.

148

And the World Series itself—that it would take place at all was looking more and more doubtful. When the Red Sox won in 1916, Carl had gotten more than $3,900. He needed that money.

And the men from the shipyard league, who had been pressuring him for two months now to join Dutch Leonard and get himself out of the way of the war.

And Carl was worried about his Class 1A status. He'd gotten word to report to his draft board in Mansfield, Missouri, for a physical. He was trying to arrange for the physical to be moved to Boston so

Carl Mays married Freddie Madden after the 1918 season but left Boston in a controversial trade in 1919. Here, Mays and his young family are shown in New York shortly after the trade. (NATIONAL BASEBALL HALL OF FAME LIBRARY, COOPERSTOWN, N.Y.)

that he could continue pitching.[4] Either way, after the physical, he'd probably be drafted, maybe before the season ended. Even if the Red Sox won the pennant, even if the World Series was put on, there was a good chance Carl would be the property of General Pershing and relocated to the front by the time it started. He could win a pennant, get married, and be dead, all in the same year.

Carl squinted out at the field and furrowed his brow. He looked like a man with a toothache.[5]

149

Manager Miller Huggins once summed up his feelings for Carl Mays, pointing out that if just about any player Huggins had ever coached was in need, he would offer help. But not Carl Mays. "If [Mays] was in the gutter," Huggins said, "I'd kick him."

Mays was not a well-liked man, not by teammates who did not appreciate being berated after a bad play in the field and not by opponents who took offense at Mays's aggressiveness and willingness to throw inside at batters. But he was not a brute or a drunk or an all-hours carouser, like so many players around him. In a particularly insightful interview he did with *Baseball Magazine* in 1920, Mays revealed—even as he claimed it did not bother him—that he wrestled with the reasons he'd always been widely reviled. "I always have wondered why I have encountered this antipathy from so many people wherever I have been," he said. "And I have never been able to explain it even to myself, though I have one or two theories on the subject. . . . I have been told I lack tact, which is probably true. But that is no crime."[6]

Popularity aside, Mays was in his prime in 1918, just 26 years old. He was also unique. Mays was a submarine pitcher. He would rear back, drop his hand to his shoe top, and fire the ball up from the ground, his knuckles scraping the dirt. He did not have an overpowering fastball, but he was able to keep his pitches low and force ground balls. His delivery confounded hitters. "Carl slings the pill from his toes, has a weird looking wind-up and in action, looks like a cross between an octopus and a bowler," *Baseball Magazine* wrote. "He shoots the ball in at the batter at such unexpected angles that his delivery is hard to find, generally, until along about 5 o'clock, when the hitters get accustomed to it—and when the game is about over."[7]

Mays had been off to a great start in 1918—he was 17–7 in late July—when the pressures of the season began wearing on him. After losing his third straight start on August 2, to the Indians, who were unexpectedly gaining ground on the Red Sox, it was clear that Mays was struggling. Reporter Burt Whitman wrote, "Carl unquestionably is more or less up in the air over his future path. He has been one of the most eagerly and persistently sought of big league pitchers by [the shipyard teams]. But he did not throw over his team. He said that he would stick through the season, or as long as he could, and that he would wait for the draft to get him, but would not dodge, neither would he duck. He expects to be inducted into the Army at any moment now."[8]

By the time Mays took the mound in the second game of a doubleheader on August 10, he had finally broken through and won his previous start. But now, against the Yankees, the hard times were back. Mays gave up just one run in the first five innings, but after getting two out in the sixth, he lost focus and control. He walked a batter. Then he hit two others with pitches. This was not unusual—Mays's penchant for throwing inside caused him to finish first in hit bats-men in '17 and second in 1918. With the bases loaded, the Yankees' Jack Fournier knocked a Mays pitch for a two-run double, putting the Yankees up, 3–0. They'd win, 4–1, sweeping the doubleheader and knocking Boston's lead over Cleveland down to two games. Barrow, ticked off, called for a morning practice before the Red Sox's next game. "Any club that can't put up a better brand of ball than the Red Sox did this afternoon needs all the practice they can get," Barrow said. "So I ran the risk of offending our star players by telling them to report for duty Monday morning."[9]

Monday didn't go any better, even though the Red Sox were sched-uled to face 30-year-old journeyman Hank Robinson, who hadn't pitched in the majors since 1915 but was signed by the Yankees as a war fill-in. Robinson did have one thing going for him, though—he was left-handed, and Boston could not beat lefties. Sure enough, he beat the Red Sox, 2–1, with Babe Ruth on the mound. Umpire Billy Evans worked that series and would later comment, "Left handed pitching has made a lot of trouble for the Red Sox this year. With Ruth playing the outfield, it is made up entirely of left handed hit-ters—Ruth, Strunk and Hooper. . . . Considerable of the punch of the club is in the outfield, and as left handed pitching is not pleasing to them as right-handers, the club naturally suffers."[10]

Of course, it was brought to Evans's attention that, should the Red Sox hold on and win the pennant, they would get a heavy dose of southpaw pitching in the World Series—the Cubs were tops in the NL, anchored by two lefties, Hippo Vaughn and Lefty Tyler. But three weeks after the extension granted by Baker, the World Series was *still* a mystery. There were rumors that Clark Griffith had used his political connections to ensure the War Department would accept the Series, but nothing had been decreed formally. Time was running short. Baseball was planning to run games until Labor Day, Septem-ber 2, and start the World Series two days later—the logic, according to Griffith, being that players would have 10 days as a grace period to settle their affairs.

But, on August 13, the Red Sox got jolting news. Ruth, Strunk, and catcher Sam Agnew received notices from their draft boards inform-ing them that they were to get useful work after September 1 or be immediately subject to the draft. Thus, if they showed up on Sep-tember 4 for the opening of the World Series, they could be dragged off the field and inducted into the army. This was shortly after the expected NL-champion Cubs had been talking about boycotting the World Series. Players wanted assurance—they wanted Baker's written approval. Baseball was slow to ask for it.

Each day the Cubs and Red Sox put aside the uncertainty and kept playing. The Cubs went on a mid-August run of seven wins in eight games, removing any doubt about their pennant prospects. The Red Sox rallied, too, after the early August sweep by the Yankees. Boston took two of three over the White Sox and knocked some of the air out of the Indians' pursuit by beating Cleveland twice in three games. Finally, on August 23, word came from Baker's office: Yes, two teams of players could have till September 15 to play a World Series. The decision came 12 days before the scheduled starting date. The next day the Cubs swept a doubleheader from Brooklyn to clinch the National League pennant and secure their place in the Baker-approved championship.

The whole thing had a farcical quality. Nearly every nation in the civilized world was taking part in the most destructive war in history, basic American rights were being trampled, the economy was in flux, a battle between labor and management was simmering, another battle between radical workers and capitalism itself was raging, domestic terrorism was on the rise, a wave of hypermorality was gaining force, women were fighting for suffrage—but, for baseball, what mattered was whether extra time could be allotted for a cash-orgy World Series. "In one way, the present contention . . . is amusing," *The Sporting News* wrote, "and, perhaps, when the war is over and all regain a normal attitude, we can have a good laugh over the commotion that has been caused over such a trivial thing as whether 50 ordinary—very ordinary—day laborers should have been permitted six or eight days of grace in quitting one job and taking up another. . . . The ridiculousness of the thing should have been pointed out before."[11]

Baseball wasn't very perceptive, though, when it came to perspective. The game kept plowing toward the finish line of a fairly miserable season, and those in baseball made what seemed to be important decisions. But few in the game grasped how insignificant those decisions were when compared with other happenings throughout the world. That was the strangest of realizations—no one really *needed* baseball. No matter what went on with the sport, the rest of the world just kept on going. And so, baseball men wrapped up their business, as promised, in the waning weeks of August, while elsewhere life just kept happening, news just kept being made:

- One month after a difficult hernia surgery, the Reverend Billy Sunday received tough news—the War Department's Priorities Committee ruled that his work was not essential and that he should not be given priority when it came to obtaining the materials necessary to build a tabernacle in Providence, Rhode Island, where he was scheduled to hold a revival in September.
- In mid-August, Mayor Big Bill Thompson's wide-open administration allowed the problem of cabarets and brothels catering to soldiers to become so out of control that Judge Harry Fisher warned aldermen, "Chicago's police department is in danger of being taken over by the government."[12]
- Days later, the World Series schedule was approved by the National Commission. It would start with three games in Chicago, and the rest—four, maximum—at the home of the AL champ. The commission also considered changing World Series payouts to match war conditions. But it declined to act.
- On August 25, Babe Ruth's father, George Ruth, took a family dispute outside the saloon he owned in Baltimore. He fought with his brother-in-law, who hit George, knocking him down. As the elder Ruth tried to get up—according to the brother-in-law—he fell back down and hit his head on the street. He fractured his skull and died, at age 45. On August 28, Babe Ruth stood by his father's grave and cried.
- On the same day as George Ruth's funeral, Cubs secretary Walter Craighead announced that the team had received enough requests for World Series reservations that the Chicago games would be moved south to Comiskey Park, which could hold 32,000 spectators, far more than Weeghman Park.
- Also on the 28th, according to the diary of one soldier, the 89th Division of the American army was training in DeMange, France, preparing to hike for a week to St.-Mihiel.[13] There they would prepare for a crucial offensive in the dangerous Argonne Forest. Among the solders of the 89th was Grover Cleveland Alexander, who had earlier sent off a letter to friend and teammate Bill Killefer. "There are a lot of interesting things to write about the war," Alexander wrote, "but we are not permitted to

153

say anything and we can't even tell where we are, but maybe they'll let me say we can hear the big guns booming on a still night."[14]

- On August 29, gamblers in New York announced that the Cubs were the World Series favorite, with the *Globe* reporting, "Percy Guard, a Curb betting commissioner, today was offering $10,000 to $9,000 that Chicago wins the World's Baseball Series. Some small bets were made. Guard states there is plenty of Chicago money, but very little Boston."[15]

- On August 30, manager Ed Barrow inserted Carl Mays for the second game of a doubleheader against Philadelphia, even though Mays had just pitched the first game and took an easy complete-game win, 12–1. Mays won the second game too, 4–0. They were his 20th and 21st wins of the year, earning him a $1,500 contract bonus. The next day, the Red Sox wrapped up the pennant, and Mays entered the World Series with renewed confidence. "Carl Mays no longer has the submarine delivery," Whitman wrote in the *Boston Herald*. "Hereafter, it must be called an all-American, low-range barrage and nothing so suggestive of the Teutonic evil genius as that implied in the word, 'submarine,' must be used hereafter in reference to Blond Carl."[16]

- While Mays was pulling his iron-man feat, a sentencing decision was being handed down in the government's criminal case against 100 members of the Industrial Workers of the World in Chicago. Kenesaw Mountain Landis, who had been so accommodating throughout the trial of the IWW, doled out onerous punishment to union chief Bill Haywood and 14 of his top deputies—20 years in the federal penitentiary at Leavenworth, Kansas, plus a fine of $20,000 each. Landis sentenced 33 others to 10 years in prison, including Ben Fletcher, the trial's only black defendant. Afterward, Fletcher employed some gallows humor. "Judge Landis uses poor English," he said. "His sentences are too long."[17]

- On August 31, Dutch Leonard pitched a three-hit shutout for the Fore River shipyard team in the Bethlehem Steel League play-offs. He beat another left-hander, 43-year-old future Hall of Famer Eddie Plank.

- On September 1, writer I. E. Sanborn looked over the rubble of the 1918 baseball season and chose an apt phrase to wrap it up: "Slow curtain."[18]

At the end of August, players in both leagues received official letters from their teams: They were fired. All contracts were void after September 2, and all players were, technically, unemployed. Multiyear contracts that extended beyond 1918 were simply torn up. The White Sox received their letters on August 23 in Philadelphia, just after the A's had gotten theirs. A few players attempted to take their teams to court over the matter, without success. If baseball was played next year—Brooklyn Dodgers management thought baseball in 1919 was so unlikely that they agreed to let the government use Ebbets Field as a storage facility—it would be on much different terms, with lower salaries and, possibly, fewer players. In retrospect, we might think of baseball in the early 20th century as in its adolescence, but in late 1918 the game looked to be in its grave. "Baseball Collapse Due, War or No War," was a headline in *The Sporting News*.[19] Another, in the *Chicago American*, read: "Gate Receipts Ebb, Death of Game Near."[20]

But it was difficult to worry about baseball's death throes when a harsher, more significant kind of death was dominating newspapers—casualty lists that came rolling in from Europe. (As the *Tribune* predicted, newspapers did, indeed, print casualty lists in the same editions as baseball box scores, sometimes side by side.) From April 1918, when American troops got their first real taste of the war, through July, daily casualty lists only occasionally reached the low triple digits. On May 7, American casualties for the entire war passed the 5,000 mark. On June 26, casualties passed 10,000. As of July 31, casualties were 14,331, a modest total for a nation that declared war in 1917. American troops just hadn't been doing much fighting.

In mid-July, though, the Germans began their fifth (and what would be their final) offensive—this was a continuation of the spring offensives designed to smash the Allied armies before the Americans were truly ready to fight. Those offensives had not been as successful as the Germans had hoped, however. Now, as American units were taking up positions on the front, the Germans tried one more push into France. It was their last hope—the Germans had dug deep into their reserves, drafting young boys and old men to send to the fight.

155

One French general, anticipating the coming assault, issued a statement to American and French troops, later released to the public. His message was plain. "Each man will have but one thought: Kill until they have had enough of it," the order said.[21] Thanks in large part to the Americans, the fifth German offensive was rebuffed, and the Allies soon began a counteroffensive.

"It is now a battle to the death," the *Chicago American* reported. And there was death—and casualty. On August 4, 285 American casualties were reported, the most in a single day, pushing the total past 15,000. The next day, another gruesome record was set: 716 casualties. And the next day: 965. And the next: 1,104. One soldier wrote, in a letter, "Last night, I witnessed a truly pitiful sight—the burying of our boys. The sight of our comrades being laid away for their final rest, garbed in a U.S. uniform, makes one's blood run cold."[22] From the time the United States entered the war on April 6, 1917, until August 5, 1918—a span of 486 days—a little more than 15,000 American casualties were reported. But in just one week, August 5–12, the total number of casualties swelled to 20,363. Meanwhile, the War Department pushed a bill to expand the army, making all men ages 18–45 draft eligible. Another registration was to be held September 12.

In the United States, another kind of death was lurking on the periphery. On August 14, the *New York Times* reported that officers of a Norwegian liner claimed a virulent illness that had been thriving in Europe—Spanish influenza—had killed four passengers during the ship's voyage across the Atlantic to New York. One doctor who treated other sick passengers, though, said that the immediate cause of death wasn't influenza but bronchial pneumonia.[23] They were both right.

156 THE ORIGINAL CURSE: CARL MAYS

Carl Mays wasn't particularly well liked before the Yankees settled in to play the Indians at the Polo Grounds on August 16, 1920. After that game, though, he would become one of baseball's most despised players.

In the fifth inning, Mays—pitching for the Yankees after leaving the Red Sox in a controversial 1919 trade—faced popular Cleveland shortstop Ray Chapman. Mays went into his submarine delivery and flung a fastball high and inside. Chapman, according to Mays, froze.

The ball hit Chapman near the left temple, producing a loud thud that caused spectators to gasp and turn away. Chapman's skull was fractured. He was taken, unconscious, to St. Lawrence Hospital, where doctors attempted surgery. He died early the next morning and remains the only big-league player to be killed by a pitched ball.

Mays, long considered a beanball pitcher by opponents, was immediately reviled. Players on several teams organized a boycott against him, suggesting opponents simply refuse to play when he pitched. The boycott never came to fruition, but the sentiment was clear—no one liked Mays, and the incident would forever stick with him. "The unfortunate death of Ray Chapman is a thing that I do not like to discuss," he said in the 1920 interview with *Baseball Magazine*. "It is a recollection of the most unpleasant kind which I shall carry with me as long as I live. It is an episode which I shall always regret more than anything that has ever happened to me, and yet I can look into my own conscience and feel absolved from all personal guilt in this affair. The most amazing thing about it was the fact that some people seem to think I did this thing deliberately. If you wish to believe that a man is a premeditated murderer, there is nothing to prevent it. Every man is the master of his own thoughts. I cannot prevent it, however much I may regret it, if people entertain any such idea of me."[24]

There would be more controversy for Mays. According to writer Fred Lieb, Mays may have been involved in a scheme to fix the 1921 World Series. During that series, Lieb was told that Mays had been paid a hefty sum to throw a game to the Giants. Lieb took the story to Commissioner Kenesaw Mountain Landis, who investigated but could find no evidence against Mays. Still, suspicion lingered, and Yankees owner T. L. Huston later confirmed to Lieb that Mays—and others—had thrown the World Series in '21 and '22. This probably helps explain why Miller Huggins, manager of those Yankees teams, said he'd kick Mays if he found him in the gutter.

Despite five 20-win seasons, a 207–126 record, and a career ERA of 2.92, Carl Mays is not in baseball's Hall of Fame.

157

FOURTEEN

World Series, Game 1, Chicago

SEPTEMBER 4, 1918

It was just after 3:00 P.M., and the Federal Building in Chicago's downtown Loop was bustling. As he had for the past 26 years, Edwin Kolkow, a 76-year-old veteran of the Civil War, was working in the general delivery room. Outside, by the building's Adams Street entryway, two mail clerks, William O'Meara and William Wheeler, were just leaving after finishing their shifts—O'Meara was a few steps ahead of Wheeler, who had taken extra time to tidy up before he punched out. Up the steps, toward O'Meara and Wheeler, bounded J. B. Ladd, a 22-year-old jackie who served as a messenger for the navy intelligence department in the Edison Building across the street. Down on Adams Street, Ella Miehlke, who had celebrated her 21st birthday the previous night, was stepping off a streetcar with her sister, Emma, heading toward the steps. Just in front of them was the Reverend Joseph E. Phelan of Holy Name Cathedral. Across the street, a horse was hitched to an express wagon, awaiting its driver. Big Bill Haywood, convicted IWW secretary, was on the eighth floor of the Federal Building, dictating to his secretary, while his lawyers were discussing a heated meeting they'd just had with federal attorney Frank Nebeker, who was blocking the appeal of Haywood's guilty verdict.[1]

Just a few blocks away, suite 1136 of the Congress Hotel was well appointed, thanks to *Chicago American* writer Bill Bailey (that was a stock pen name—Bailey was actually Bill Veeck, future president of the Chicago Cubs). Bailey had been named host for the mass of press expected in town to cover the World Series, but rail restrictions, plus a general lack of interest, kept the flow of visitors to the press suite down to a trickle. To look busy, Bailey would occasionally rush out of the suite, take a walk around the block, and return, breathing heavily. Most reporters were done for the day—Game 1, scheduled for September 4, had been postponed till the next day because of a steady rain. Other media members were killing time at the hotel bar or were hanging out in the room of National Commission head Garry Herrmann. It was a World Series tradition that Herrmann would bring along a trunkload of fine deli meats. This time, he also brought some rare Patagonia tripe and, of course, liquid refreshment.[2]

Down at 23rd Street and Michigan Avenue, about two miles south of the Congress, the Red Sox were lingering around the Metropole Hotel. Some had gone to the movies. Some were catching up on war news. Some were playing poker—including pitcher Sam Jones, who cleaned up $44 and declared he was all for another rainout the following day.[3] A little farther south of that, at 35th and Shields, a canvas tarp covered the infield at the White Sox park on the South Side. This was to have been the site of the Game 1, but instead there was only a flock of sheep,[4] which White Sox owner Charles Comiskey kept at the park to keep the grass well trimmed, lazily grazing in the outfield.

Up in the Loop, the clock in the Federal Building read 3:10 when an agitated man in a tan raincoat holding a cigar box with a string dangling from the side began pacing inside the rotunda. He slid over to the radiator near the Adams Street entry. He dropped the cigar box with a thud and, looking around, kicked it under the radiator. Then he hurried out.

And then. Boom.

The cigar box exploded, filling the rotunda with flames and thick black smoke, ripping an enormous hole in the Federal Building wall. The blast was so powerful that, across the street, workers in the Marquette Building and the Edison Building were thrown from their chairs. The windows of both buildings shattered, and chunks of plate glass rained onto the street below. The wall separating the rotunda from the general delivery room buckled under the force of the blast and came crashing down onto Edwin Kolkow, killing him almost instantly. William O'Meara leapt forward, but just behind him the force of the explosion shattered the bones of William Wheeler, whose

159

body fell to the ground, lifeless. A chunk of the wall tore into J. B. Ladd, sending him hard to the pavement, as pieces of his blue naval uniform scattered over Adams Street. Father Phelan rushed to his side and asked his name, but Ladd—whose mother was on her way to visit him from Kansas—could not breathe and only mouthed the words. Phelan, kneeling, administered last rites as Ladd died. Ella Miehlke was crushed so badly under a pile of debris that she could be identified only by her watch, which contained a picture of her and the young sailor to whom she was engaged. Across Adams Street, the horse, its flank cut open by a shard of glass, lay dead on its side, still hitched to its post.

Flames and screams filled the rotunda. Outside, broken glass from surrounding buildings continued to fall. Piles of debris and pools of blood littered Adams Street. The wail of fire engines echoed off the buildings. One pedestrian looked at the damage and said flatly, "Someone did a good job." The crowd outside the building grabbed the man and beat him.

Interest in the 1918 World Series was lacking. The previous year, when the White Sox played the Giants at Comiskey Park, the Series had garnered unprecedented attention—the White Sox had turned away 300,000 requests for reserved tickets, despite the fact that the commission always jacked up ticket prices for the World Series. To get a box seat in Chicago for the 1917 World Series, a fan had to buy tickets to all three games, at $15 total. The Series was so highly anticipated, though, that scalpers were getting $50 for box seats, and fans descending on Chicago from all over the Midwest—and as far away as Florida, Nevada, and California—paid willingly. Bleacher tickets sold on the day of the game were in such demand that hundreds of fans braved cold and rain to stand in line overnight. The three games in Chicago drew more than 90,000 fans, and the receipts for the entire Series topped $425,000.

In the closing days of August 1918, and into September, Cubs business manager Walter Craighead, harboring dreams of a 1917-type rush, reported a steady stream of ticket requests. When it looked like all 17,000 reserved seats would be claimed, Craighead announced that 15,000 tickets would be sold on game day, and he estimated that 30,000 fans would be in attendance for the first game. On the afternoon of September 4, Herrmann predicted the World Series would generate $25,000 for war charities (the commission had decreed that 10 percent of the receipts would go to charities), which meant Herrmann foresaw the Series bringing in $250,000. But to the veteran writers covering the Series, that seemed like a stretch. Hugh Fullerton noted that "interest is lukewarm in all parts of the city."[5] Sherman Duffy of the *Chicago Daily Journal* reported that, far from being the all-consuming affair that the '17 Series had been, he'd been given a taste of the general apathy toward this year's Series when he sat down at a bar with a Cleveland reporter. "The barkeeper . . . was moved to ask when it started."[6] The mildness of the interest was confirmed on the rainy morning of Game 1. Not only was there no overnight line, but at 6:00 A.M. just 50 people were waiting for bleacher seats.

Even if fans turned out in good numbers, it was difficult to see how the Series would turn out the $250,000 that Herrmann predicted. Hoping to do a bit of public good, the National Commission decided to give fans a break and charge only regular-season prices. Three-game box seat packages that had gone for $15 in '17 were sold at $9 in '18. Grandstand seats were just $1.50, and bleacher tickets could be had for $.50. This would, obviously, cut into the Series gate receipts. That wasn't too much of a concern for the players, though, because— as they understood it—the new rule governing the division of World Series money, passed the previous winter, set the player shares at $2,000 for the winners and $1,400 for the losers, with the rest of the players' portion of the income to be divided by the second-, third-, and fourth-place teams in each league. Players did not give a second thought to the notices slid under their hotel room doors before Game 1, reminding them that, per National Commission rules, they were entitled to split 55.5 percent (which included a 10 percent war charity donation) of the gate receipts for the first four games of the Series.

The lack of enthusiasm in Chicago was predictable. Few saw the Red Sox and Cubs as legitimate champions—instead, they were viewed as the two teams fortunate enough to have survived the attrition caused by the draft, enlistments, and shipyard dodgers. The defending champs of each league, the White Sox and Giants, at full strength, would have been likely to repeat in 1918, even if the Red Sox and Cubs had been at full strength too. In New York, gamblers felt strongly enough that the Cubs were illegitimate that many of those who had bet on the Giants to win the pennant "don't want to pay, have instructed the stakeholders not to pay and there is a merry row ahead."[7] Paul Shannon of the *Boston Post* wrote, "While never before, since the American League entered Boston, has so weak a team won the league pennant . . . it must be remembered that this is baseball's leanest year, that ever-changing conditions forced the adoption of continual experiments in an effort to recruit the waning strength."[8]

Though 1918 marked the beginning of the end of Ban Johnson's dictatorial grip on the American League, he should be credited for foreseeing what a mess the season would become. He was right in suggesting that unless a limited number of players could be granted exemptions (a statement that drew anti-Johnson outrage), the game ought to shut down. In the *Tribune*, I. E. Sanborn wrote, "[Johnson] counseled all winter a shorter season, to end by Labor day at latest, and a general curtailment to meet the coming storm. He was overruled by his narrow visioned club owners. If they had listened the present fiasco would have been avoided."[9] An article in *The Sporting News* echoed that sentiment: "Johnson's statement at that time—November last—now shows he was far ahead of most of the people connected with baseball in his estimates of what would happen to the game and even his suggestions that the gates not be opened in 1918 do not now seem to have been so far from good judgment."[10] There are many worthy criticisms when it comes to Johnson, but his handling of the war is not one of them.

The prevalence of gambling around baseball, though, was something for which Johnson could be criticized—he'd abandoned his brief antigambling crusade, and, as usual, betting odds were a much-discussed aspect of the 1918 World Series. In newspapers across the country, the gambling scene was a prominent, matter-of-fact feature of Series coverage. The Cubs were favorites, though by a slim margin. Reported odds were 10 to 8, 10 to 9, and 6 to 5. After the Game 1 postponement, some Cubs backers were a bit nervous to find that odds tightened and word spread that now the Red Sox were favored. "For my part," the *Herald*'s Burt Whitman wrote, "I know the Series is inveigling the gambling element and, much money from the Hub having appeared, the odds just naturally shifted."[11] But Hub money was countered with more Chicago money, and the favorite's mantle shifted back and forth, depending on which gambler a given reporter knew. As the *Herald Examiner*'s Matt Foley wrote, "The announcement that Pat Moran, the Philly manager, had wagered $500 on the [Cubs] helped bring about this reversal of opinion. Pat is one of those fellows who would ask odds before betting a nickel that there is war and the alacrity with which he risked half a grand on Fred Mitchell's candidates made a deep impression."[12] (Evidently, there was no problem with a manager announcing a large wager on one of the teams.)

Moran's bet must have opened some eyes, because the *Boston Post* reported this oddity: "The Cubs are favorites now and there is so much money in sight at odds of 10 to 8 that supporters of the Boston cause have become exceedingly wary. One story has it that of a pool of $43,000 raised by Chicago sports to bet on their club, less than $5,000 has been covered by those who like the Red Sox chances."[13] According to the bookmaker from whom the *Post* was getting information, then, the odds were nearly even, but *eight* times as much money had been bet on the Cubs than on the Red Sox. That may have been an aberration, but the fact was this was an odd World Series, and odd betting patterns were a notable feature.

Still, the 1918 World Series was going forward, despite reduced fan interest, despite limited projected revenue, and despite the fact that, on the day of the postponement of the first game of the Series, a vicious bomb ripped a hole in Chicago's Federal Building, killing four people (and a horse), putting all of the downtown Loop on alert, and setting off a manhunt for IWW members suspected of planting the bomb. The city was shocked and outraged. In this one moment, in this one explosion, Chicagoans saw the actualization of all those fears they had been carrying since the start of the war—fear of festering radicalism, fear of deteriorating morality, fear of violence, fear of terrorism, fear of death, fear of dissension, fear of disloyalty. Is it any wonder that, when umpire Hank O'Day called *"Play ball!"* on September 5, no one seemed to care?

The Red Sox may have been the underdog heading into the World Series, but they had some things going for them. They were mostly healthy. Harry Hooper was battling hay fever, and second baseman Dave Shean suffered a minor finger injury in practice, but both would play. The Red Sox were delighted when they arrived in Chicago to find Fred Thomas awaiting them at the Metropole, in full naval regalia. Thomas had gotten the OK to don his other uniform—that of the Red Sox—for the next two weeks, having been granted a furlough from the Great Lakes Naval Station. This was great news for Barrow. After the departure of Thomas, Barrow said, "By the time we had

163

trained Thomas so that he was an effective third baseman, the draft took him. . . . Third base has been the position where we have been hit harder than anywhere else."[14] With the venue moved to the AL's Comiskey Park, the Red Sox had an advantage in their familiarity with the grounds, which was important—baseball's pitching mounds were not set as uniformly as they are now, giving Red Sox pitchers an advantage, and with games starting in late afternoon it helped to know how the sun would affect outfielders. The Red Sox also had far more experience, having won championships in 1912, '15, and '16, while Cubs players were thin on World Series appearances.

And Boston had Babe Ruth, who had just wrapped up one of the great offensive seasons in memory. He batted .300, led the league with 11 home runs, was third with 66 RBIs, and finished second in on-base percentage—despite playing just 95 games. Ruth had done pretty well as a pitcher too. He had some tough-luck losses but was 13–7, second in the AL in winning percentage, and posted an ERA of just 2.22. Ruth wasn't necessarily Barrow's best pitcher, but he was the most consistent and the only left-hander. Whether on the mound or at bat, it was certain that Ruth would have an impact on this World Series. Mitchell was blunt in assessing Ruth's importance. "The Sox are a one-man team," he said, "and his name is Ruth."[15]

Ruth, for his part, seemed more excited for baseball than at any other time in 1918. Long forgotten were the hand injuries he concocted to keep himself off the mound, as well as the early July mutiny and shipyard dickering. In part greased by Frazee's checkbook, the Ruth-Barrow relationship had been going smoothly, and Ruth was ready to do whatever Barrow needed. "Why, I'd pitch the whole series, every game if they'd let me," Ruth said. "I hope I don't have to sit on the bench a single inning of the series."[16]

Of course, that did not stop Ruth from his usual slate of evening pursuits. Gene Fowler was a cub reporter for the *New York American* in 1918. In his book *Skyline*, Fowler recalled looking for his friend and fellow sports reporter Harry Hochstadter on the evening before Game 1. Fowler found Hochstadter, drunk, with wine agent "Doc" Krone, whose room was populated by "sports writers, gamblers and other students of human nature." Ruth was there and lifted Hochstadter to a couch, telling him he should switch to beer. Fowler remarked that Ruth seemed "fresh as a cornflower, although he had taken aboard many helpings of the sauce." Fowler asked Ruth if, given his condi-

Most thought the Cubs had the Red Sox overmatched in the World Series, but one figure loomed large for Boston: Babe Ruth. (SPORTING NEWS)

tion, he would be ready to pitch the following afternoon: "The hale young man gave me a bone-rattling slap on the back. 'I'll pitch 'em all if they say the word!' The Babe then announced that he was leaving us to keep a date with someone who wore skirts. On his way out he urged that Mr. Hochstadter be given a Christian burial."[17]

The morning of September 5 seemed to blow in from the north— cold wind and gray skies had some wondering whether Game 1 would be postponed again. This would not have been taken as bad news, because it would force the first three games to be played on Friday, Saturday, and Sunday, and the weekend dates figured to fatten up the coffers. But though the weather threatened, it never broke. When the gates of Comiskey Park opened at 10:30 A.M., hundreds of fans rushed into the bleachers and pavilion to claim the best seats, a World Series custom. But this was not a customary World Series. As the hours leading up to the 2:30 start time neared, with the sky darkening, thousands of seats remained vacant. There was one benefit to arriving early, though—batting practice. After limbering up some, Babe Ruth stepped to the plate, facing batting practice pitcher Walt Kinney, and smacked the first pitch he saw into the right-field bleachers, drawing a big ovation. As would be the case throughout Ruth's career, neither sauce nor skirts affected him. Fowler wrote, "The all-night escapade at Doc Krone's left me somewhat less effective than the Babe the next afternoon."

Though those who mingled at Krone's might have known that Ruth would be the starting pitcher, for most it was still a mystery. Barrow was devious. He announced his starting lineup—which was printed in several papers on the day of the game—with Ruth in left field, batting fourth, and either Joe Bush or Carl Mays as his Game 1 starter. Mitchell, too, was coy about his pitching selection, but the consensus was that the Cubs were going with Hippo Vaughn. Just before game time, Barrow had both Ruth and Bush warming up and pulled a surprise by tabbing Ruth for the start. And another surprise: he took pressure off Ruth as a hitter by batting him ninth against Vaughn. This freed Ruth to focus on pitching. Barrow gambled by inserting light-hitting 35-year-old George Whiteman in the cleanup spot.

Barrow, it turned out, played his hand perfectly. On the mound, Ruth was shaky in the first inning, getting two outs before allowing singles to Les Mann and Dode Paskert. He walked Fred Merkle to load the bases, but Charley Pick lifted a harmless fly ball to Whiteman in left field, and the Cubs were stifled. In the third inning, Ruth got some help from the Red Sox's defense, which was the best in baseball with a .971 fielding mark. After Max Flack singled, Charley Hollocher poked a bunt toward third, and Thomas was late to react. He hurried his throw to Stuffy McInnis, who reached around Hollocher to grab the throw for the out. It was a great play, which was no surprise—McInnis was the best first baseman in the AL and was a pioneer of using the oversize "claw" glove that all first basemen now wear. "Two out of three first basemen would have let that ball go and chased it to the stands," Hugh Fullerton wrote. "But McInnis made the play perfectly and upset the game."[18]

Fullerton noticed something else about Game 1: Chicago short-stop Hollocher "was in the wrong position for almost every batter; allowed three balls to skim past him, which a shortstop who knew the habits of the batters probably would have grabbed."[19] That would prove costly in the fourth inning, with the game still scoreless. Dave Shean walked, and, with one out, Whiteman lined a single to left field. That put Shean on second, and to make matters worse, Hollocher and Charley Pick failed to keep Shean from taking a large lead at second base. McInnis hit a hard, one-hop single to Mann in left field, and Shean broke for home without stopping, sliding in just ahead of Mann's throw. "Without his lead," I. E. Sanborn reported in the *Tribune*, "Dave could not have counted."[20]

Ruth tottered on occasion, but he was able to focus in key situations—no matter how the Cubs tried to rattle him. Every time the Cubs were at bat, first-base coach Otto Knabe bombarded Ruth with insults and epithets (Red Sox coach Heinie Wagner did the same to Vaughn). Ruth seemed impervious to Knabe's verbal jousts, though not because he was mentally tough, but because his hearing was fuzzy. According to the *Boston Post*, "Knabe picked Babe Ruth as his mark. In Game 1, he 'rode' the Boston southpaw through the full nine innings. Babe could not hear him. Teammates told him after the game, so Babe got dressed and went looking for Knabe, who had left."[21]

The Red Sox led, 1–0, though Ruth was having an awful day at the plate, going 0-for-3 with two mighty strikeouts. Still, the Cubs were very cautious with Ruth's power. In the outfield, "The first time Ruth came to bat Max Flack simply turned about and marched about forty paces toward the right wall."[22] (Note Flack's willingness to move

167

far back with Ruth at the plate—that willingness would later change, with significant consequences.) On the mound, Ruth sailed through the rest of the game, allowing just six hits and holding on for the 1–0 win. Some reporters counted the tight pitching duel as the pinnacle of baseball excellence, but most noticed that the crowd seemed, overall, bored. Biplanes from the nearby war expo circled overhead, distracting attention from the game. The loudest cheer came during the traditional stretch in the seventh inning, when the band began to play "The Star-Spangled Banner." "The yawn was checked and heads were bared as the ball players turned quickly about and faced the music," the *New York Times* reported. "First the song was taken up by a few, then others joined, and when the final notes came, a great volume of melody rolled across the field. It was at the very end that the onlookers exploded into thunderous applause and rent the air with a cheer that marked the highest point of the day's enthusiasm."[23]

If the crowd was mostly quiet, it might have been because it was so sparse. Far from the hoped-for sellout crowd of 32,000 fans, the official attendance was just 19,274. Combined with the reduction in ticket prices, gate receipts were just $30,349, and the players' share was $16,387.92—the gate had been $73,152 for the first game of the 1917 World Series, and the players' share $39,502.08. There was no way this Series would reach Herrmann's predicted $250,000 intake. No one quite noticed yet, but the checks for the players were shaping up to be much thinner than expected.

FIFTEEN

World Series,
Games 2 and 3, Chicago

SEPTEMBER 6–7, 1918

Just across Michigan Avenue from the Congress Hotel, headquarters
for press covering the World Series, the expansive fields of Chicago's
Grant Park had been transformed into replicas of the battlefields in
Flanders, Verdun, and Cambrai. The previous month, a crew of soldiers back from the war had helped re-create battle sites as they would
actually look at the front—complete with no-man's-land, barbed wire,
war planes, and miles of trenches. There was a display of war relics
brought back from the Americans' big victory at Chateau Thierry.
There were concerts, parades, and speakers—ex–secretary of state
William Jennings Bryan was among those who dropped in to give
a speech. The big attraction, put on daily, was a battle reenactment
done in a large amphitheater, showing soldiers going "over the top,"
behind heavy fire; showing an advancing tank wiping out Germans;
showing hand-to-hand combat and bayoneting; and showing the Red
Cross picking up the bodies afterward. Thousands gathered in the
amphitheater grandstand two hours before the shows started to watch
the horrors of war play out by the lakefront.[1] On Friday, September 6,
the show drew 96,000 visitors.

On that same afternoon, at Weeghman Park on the North Side,
Medill McCormick—an Illinois congressman whose family owned
the *Tribune*—was giving a speech. Five days later he would face Chi-

cago mayor William Hale Thompson in the Illinois Republican Party's senatorial primary election. Unlike Thompson, McCormick was decidedly pro war. "Like the other democracies engaged in the battle for freedom, we face a foreign foe," he said in his speech, "and like them . . . we face at home the faint-hearted, the pacifists, the defeatists, the I.W.W. and the Copperheads, the American Bolshevik, who, if they had their own way, would make of America what they have made of Russia."[2] McCormick's speech packed the stadium, drawing 20,000 loyal GOPers. (He would win the Senate seat but committed suicide when he wasn't renominated in 1924.)

As if the paltry gate receipts for Game 1 of the World Series weren't bad enough, the large crowds that were gathering around Chicago provided yet another round of insult-and-injury for the Cubs and baseball in general. While the teams took batting practice before Game 2, it was clear that, despite pleasant 65-degree temperatures, the crowd was shaping up to be virtually the same as it had been the previous day—and, indeed, it would be 20,040. Baseball's peak event, its big national showcase, was being outdrawn nearly five to one by a war reenactment. The Cubs had abandoned Weeghman Park for Comiskey's bigger seating capacity, but, ironically, the North Side field was packed and raucous for a political speech, while the stands for the World Series remained more than one-third empty.

Those who did show up at Comiskey were, at least, livelier from the outset of Game 2. There was no question who would be taking the mound for the Cubs: Lefty Tyler, who figured to be tough on the Red Sox. Boston had struggled with left-handers all season, but it was the crafty, soft-tossing type that really seemed to puzzle them. Vaughn was a left-hander with a great curveball, but he leaned on his fastball, and the Red Sox were better at handling fastballs (though there could be no complaints about how Vaughn pitched in the 1–0 Game 1 loss). Tyler, too, had a pretty good fastball, but his other pitches were his strengths. "Tyler has the 'soft stuff,' by that is meant the slow ball, the tantalizing curves, the change of pace," Bill Bailey wrote. "He has speed, but isn't compelled to rely on it. . . . The Red Sox are murder on speed, but they certainly do have their troubles with soft stuff."[3] Tyler had some extra incentive to cop a World Series victory. Though he had been a member of the 1914 champion Boston Braves, he had not gotten a win in the Series, having come out in the 11th inning of Game 3, which the Braves won in the 12th.

170

Opposing Tyler, fittingly, was "Bullet Joe" Bush, who also had some 1914 World Series demons to exorcise. Bush was with the Philadelphia A's in '14 and actually started Game 3 against Tyler in that Series. It was Bush's own error on a throw to first that lost the game in the 12th inning—Cubs outfielder Les Mann, then with the Braves, scored the winning run from second base. The 1918 season was the best of Bush's career, as he greatly improved his control and cut down on his walks after the trade out of Philadelphia. He struggled late in the season and finished 15–15. Still, some felt that, with six years of experience behind him (the most on the Red Sox's young staff), Bush was Barrow's ace, and he got the Game 2 call. One player who did not get such a call, though, was Ruth. With Tyler on the mound, and with the right-handed Whiteman having fared well in Game 1, Barrow opted to give Whiteman another crack in left field.

Tyler looked nervous in the game's early going. Harry Hooper led off, and Tyler missed the corner of the plate on three straight pitches before throwing a strike. But Hooper took the next pitch for a ball and went to first base with a walk. Tyler got two strikes on the next batter, Dave Shean, and Hooper called for a hit-and-run. Shean struck out, though, leaving Hooper scurrying toward second base with the strong arm of Cubs catcher Bill Killefer ready to throw him out. So Shean leaned out over the plate after his strikeout to block Killefer. Shean and Killefer tussled, and Killefer's throw sailed over second base. Hooper was called out because of interference, while Shean and Killefer had some dirty looks for each other. The tone of the game was set. It was going to get physical.

That incident, combined with the goat getting of coaches Heinie Wagner and Otto Knabe that marked Game 1, had everyone agitated. The Red Sox, though, were further aggravated by the events of the second inning. Boston got the first two runners on against Tyler but failed to score. The Cubs, though, got a walk from Fred Merkle, a bunt hit from Charley Pick, and a double from Killefer to score Merkle and give the Cubs a 1–0 lead. Tyler followed Killefer and rocketed a single over second base, scoring Pick and Killefer and staking the Cubs to a three-run lead.

When Wagner trotted to the third-base coaching box between the second and third innings, Knabe apparently let fly with a zinger that finally did get Wagner's goat. Wagner approached the Cubs dugout, where Knabe suggested they could go under the grandstand to settle

171

the matter. "Wagner not only went," the *Chicago Herald Examiner*'s Charles Dryden reported. "He grabbed Otto by the arm and dragged him along through the dugout." This was an unwise decision for Wagner. Knabe had not played at all that season and, out of shape, was thicker than usual. "A guy might as well try to wrestle a depth bomb," Dryden cracked.[4] The fight took place out of public view, and the details are contested (Wagner would later claim that he was punched by multiple Cubs, who said they merely tried to break up the scuffle), but some of the Red Sox charged across the field to the Cubs dugout. By the time they got there, though, the umpires had taken notice and the fracas had been defused. "Report has it that it was a Cubs' day all around and that Wagner got only second money in the scrap," according to *The Sporting News*. "At any rate, he emerged from the dugout with his uniform torn and plastered with mud, indicating he had been the under dog in a rough and tumble."[5] Thereafter, a policeman was stationed outside the dugouts.

Given a lead, Tyler settled in. He allowed a walk to start the third but gave up just one hit in the next four innings. He got into a jam in the eighth after Wally Schang singled off Hollocher's glove. With one out, Hooper hit a line drive to right field, and Schang took the turn at second base, heading for third. But Flack got there quickly, and, "throwing on a line with deadly accuracy, caught [Schang] far away from the base. It was a disheartening out for Boston."[6] It was typical of Flack, though, who was one of the better right fielders in the National League. The Red Sox rallied anyway, starting the ninth inning by rattling Tyler with back-to-back triples from Amos Strunk and Whiteman (yes, him again). But Tyler got Stuffy McInnis to hit a harmless grounder back to the mound, and Barrow followed with an odd choice—rather than Ruth, he sent pitcher Jean Dubuc, who was one for six at bat all season, to pinch-hit. Barrow was waiting to use Ruth in the pitcher's spot, but that was two batters away. Sure enough, Dubuc worked Tyler with a series of foul balls but struck out on a very wide curveball. Schang then popped out, while Ruth stood watching from the on-deck circle. The Cubs won, 3–1, and evened the Series.

The Cubs and Red Sox put up just five runs in the first two games of the World Series, and if the trend toward low scoring kept up, managerial decisions were going to be important. Two decisions by Barrow had already played a big role—his decision to use Whiteman in the

Cubs manager Fred Mitchell's diligent adherence to "percentage" baseball put him well ahead of his time. (CHICAGO HISTORY MUSEUM)

cleanup spot helped win Game 1, and his decision to hold off on using Ruth as pinch hitter helped lose Game 2. Mitchell, for his part, also had made a big decision, though it had nothing to do with the World Series. He was 40 years old, owned an apple orchard in Stow, Massachusetts, and had a three-year-old daughter with his young wife, Mabel. In less than a week, on September 12, the War Department would expand the draft registration requirement to ages 18 to 45, but given his status as a father and a farmer, Mitchell was virtually assured of being exempt from war service. Still, he announced after Game 2 that he'd signed up to join the army's quartermaster corps in Chicago and would take the exam immediately after the World Series.

But before then, Mitchell had another big decision to make. He had to pick a pitcher for Game 3, and though he played his choice close to the vest, it's likely he knew what he'd do all along. Most of the "dope artists"—that class of reporter, led by Hugh Fullerton, who analyzed players and statistics scientifically to predict the Series—pegged 20-game winner Claude Hendrix as the Game 3 starter. But Mitchell was different, ahead of his time. Of course, Mitchell could not know this back in September 1918, but, in 2003, a book called *Moneyball* would revolutionize the way fans, media, and executives saw baseball. *Moneyball* described the strict adherence of one team, the Oakland A's, to well-defined statistical principles applied to all aspects of the game, big and small. Baseball decisions—from scouting and drafting players to deciding when to steal and how to arrange the defense for a specific batter—had mostly been left to the gut feelings and biases of old-timers. But the A's analyzed all decisions mathematically. This, too, was Mitchell's approach. His methods were more rudimentary, but still, he was the *Moneyball* manager of his era.

"[Mitchell] has employed a system of percentages in his attack and defense, and indications are he has installed the system well into the mind of each one of his players," James Crusinberry wrote in the *Tribune*. "There are managers in baseball who play 'hunches' and there are others who yield to sentiment and some who play favorites and perhaps some who simply trust to luck or main force, but Fred Mitchell sticks to the system of percentages, no matter what happens. . . . Mitchell will always know whether the percentages favor success in doing a thing one way or whether they favor his doing it some other way."[7]

The percentages were undoubtedly in favor of surprising everyone and bringing back Hippo Vaughn for Game 3, even on one day's rest, rather than using either of his right-handers. Spitballer Phil Douglas had a good ERA (2.13), but after an 8–2 start, he had lost seven of his most recent nine decisions. Hendrix, at 20–7, had a very good season, leading the league in winning percentage, but Mitchell could see Hendrix's numbers for what they were: the product of luck. Hendrix's

2.78 ERA was slightly higher than the league average. He allowed 229 hits in 233 innings, an average of 0.98 hits per inning. The league average was 0.93. Hendrix was just an average pitcher who was lucky enough to play for the team that led the league in runs and won him some games he should have lost. There also was a report that "Claude complained of a sore arm yesterday, and unless the wing had entirely recovered in the just-before-the-battle warmup, Shuffling Phil Douglas was to hurl."[8]

Even if his arm was strong, putting Hendrix on the mound meant Barrow would insert the left-handed Ruth in left field, and Mitchell did not need to look at the percentages to know that Boston was much more difficult to handle with Ruth in the batting order. A fatigued ace left-hander—like Vaughn—with no Ruth was a better choice than a well-rested, average right-hander like Hendrix facing a lineup anchored by Ruth. Mitchell might have been overly cautious with Ruth, who had not homered since July and hit just .259 over the last five weeks of the season. But Mitchell had seen batting practice. He was not afraid to announce that he had no intention of messing with the Babe. "A right hander would have had Ruth coming up to hit," Mitchell said, "and if he got hold of one, good night. He is a wonderful natural ballplayer, and nobody I've seen takes the cut at a ball he does. He is liable to knock any kind of pitch anywhere."[9]

As the 2:30 start time for Game 3 approached on September 7, temperatures were comfortable, but the sky was overcast. Still, things at Comiskey Park were looking generally brighter. A flock of "dipper girls" strolled the stands collecting donations for the soldiers' tobacco fund, "to keep our boys in smokes over there."[10] The girls likely took in a good amount, because for the first time in the Series the ticket business was brisk. It helped that it was a Saturday, the only weekend game on the World Series schedule—and it was on the schedule only because of the Game 1 postponement. Many questioned why the National Commission did not juggle the schedule to ensure that both a Saturday and a Sunday game, always the biggest draws, could be played in Chicago. (Boston's blue laws did not permit baseball on Sundays.) It also helped that the Cubs had shown some life and evened the Series, bolstering the enthusiasm of the locals. The 20,040 fans at Game 2 had been a slight improvement on Game 1, but the pool of money generated by that crowd actually *decreased* (the players' pool was $16,198.38), as fans passed on the more expensive boxes to sit in the cheap seats. But the crowd filing in for Game 3 looked more like a World Series crowd, with 27,054 fans showing up.

Carl Mays was penciled in as the Boston starter, and there had been enough rumors suggesting Vaughn would start Game 3 for the Cubs that, as the Red Sox took outfield practice, both Ruth and Whiteman manned left field. When Vaughn was announced as the starter, Whiteman remained and Ruth—who had, earlier in the week, stated that he hoped he would not have to sit out an inning—again went back to the bench, dejected. Vaughn was given a loud ovation by the home fans as he loped to the mound.

Vaughn didn't disappoint. He allowed a cheap hit to Hooper in the first inning and a single to Whiteman in the second but in both cases was able to pitch out of trouble with ease. After a three-up, three-out third inning, the Red Sox got to Vaughn in the fourth. Vaughn tossed a curveball inside to Whiteman, who leaned in and was hit by the pitch. Stuffy McInnis and Wally Schang followed with singles, scoring Whiteman and setting up a first-and-third situation with one out. Everett Scott attempted a suicide squeeze, and when Vaughn reached the ball, all he could do was hold it—Merkle had charged the bunt too, and no one was covering first base. McInnis scored on the play, and the Red Sox had a 2–0 lead.

Fred Mitchell's percentage system hadn't figured on two things, starting with Whiteman. His run scored in the fourth inning meant that he now had figured in the scoring for three consecutive games. There was no way Mitchell could have guessed that Whiteman, a 35-year-old journeyman who had 86 games of big-league experience and had been purchased from the minors for just $750, would hit .400 in the first three games of the World Series off the best one-two punch in the National League. Nor could the percentages have possibly shown that the Cubs would have such bum luck against Carl Mays. Certainly Mays was well rested—he had not pitched since tossing the back-to-back games of the doubleheader against Philadelphia on August 30—and it hurt the Cubs that no one in the National League pitched submarine style like Mays. But Mays managed to hold the Cubs to just one run, coming on an RBI single in the fifth by Killefer. The Cubs had chances, moving a man into scoring position against Mays in five of the last six innings, but were consistently frustrated in clutch situations.

The frustration climaxed in the ninth inning, when, with two out, Charley Pick beat out a ground ball to Shean and stole second. Pick broke for third when one of Mays's pitches got away from Schang and, as Pick slid, he raised his spikes, ready to inflict some pain should third baseman Fred Thomas try to tag him. Pick got tangled up with Thomas as the throw from Schang arrived, and the ball trickled away from Thomas's glove. Immediately, Mitchell—coaching third—yelled to Pick, telling him to score. Pick got up, hesitated, and emerged from the cloud of dirt toward home. But the ball had not gotten very far into foul territory. Thomas recovered and zipped a perfect throw to Schang. Pick, again with his cleats up, "slid home with a running broad jump."[11] Schang grabbed the throw from Thomas and slapped a tag on Pick, whose spikes did not find Schang's calf as planned but, rather, tore into the right shin of Bill Klem, the umpire. Klem called Pick out, sealing one of the most thrilling game-winning outs in World Series history.

Pick's failed dash put the Red Sox up, two games to one, with the rest of the Series to be played in Boston. The game ended at 4:30, giving the teams three and a half hours to clean up, have a bite to eat, and board the Michigan Central at the LaSalle Street Station in Chicago's Loop. The train was scheduled to leave at 8:00 P.M. on Saturday and arrive in Boston at 10:50 P.M. on Sunday. The usual frills of World Series travel were gone. The Red Sox booked two cars, while the Cubs, the newspaper writers, and the National Commission booked one each. Through the night, players, writers, and team officials stayed up playing whist, poker, and craps, smoking all the while. Between the noise and the smoke, sleep was impossible. Charles Dryden wrote of the train, "Our combination World's Series and Monte Carlo special . . . entered the home stretch for Boston, leaving a pale blue haze of cigarette and cigar smoke along the right of way."[12]

177

It wasn't all gambling and tobacco. There still was the lingering possibility of fisticuffs. After bad blood developed over the thrashing that Wagner took under the stands in Game 2, concern was raised about putting ticked-off players together on a train for 27 hours. "There was an unconfirmed rumor last night that F. Otto Knabe was to be blasted apart or something in revenge for spilling Heinie Wagner on his back during the second game," the *Herald Examiner* noted. "President Weeghman said he heard threats to that effect, but could not state who uttered them."[13] Aboard the train, though, a more important topic of conversation spread. A group of players from both teams put aside on-field antagonism and poker games to discuss the jarring reality that was settling in with the players after the first three games in Chicago: the gate receipts were terrible.

This was especially troubling when taken in combination with the action of the National Commission the previous January. At the time, Ban Johnson, Garry Herrmann, and John Tener (replaced by John Heydler after Tener's August resignation) altered the rules for the division of money generated not only by the World Series but by all postseason series—in cities with two clubs, like Chicago, Boston, St. Louis, New York, and Philadelphia, the American League team would play the National League team in a postseason, crosstown series that usually drew healthy crowds and good payouts for the teams and players. In changing the split, the Commission's goal was to allow more players to share in postseason money. The players' World Series pool was to remain the same, 60 percent of the gate receipts for the first four games. But the payouts would be capped at $2,000 for each player on the World Series winner and $1,400 for the losers. At 25 players per team, that figured to be $78,000 total for the two teams—$50,000 for the winners and $28,000 for the losers. Whatever money was left in the players' pool beyond $78,000 would be divided by the teams finishing in second, third, and fourth place in each league. That way, half the league shared in the big World Series payouts.

But there was some fine print to consider. For one thing, the new rules had been based on the receipts of the incredibly expensive and well-attended 1917 World Series. The players hadn't stopped to consider what would happen if the receipts didn't match those of '17. There was also the provision in the new rule that allocated a share of the gate receipts from all crosstown postseason series to the World Series pool. When the A's played the Phillies in Philadelphia, for example, half the player money was to be added to the World Series money, bolstering the payout World Series players would get. With the work-or-fight order in effect, though, there were no crosstown postseason series. Players participating in the World Series were giving up part of their winnings to teams that had finished second through fourth, but they weren't getting anything in return.

Aboard the train, players figured out what was happening. The gate receipts for the three Chicago games were terrible. It wasn't so much the sparse crowds that were draining the pool. It was the reduced ticket prices. Even the sizable crowd at the third game had generated total receipts of only $40,118. But 10 percent of the pool had been promised to war charities, lowering the Game 3 receipts to $36,106.20. The players would get 60 percent of that, or $21,663.72. The three-game players' pool total was just $54,230.02. Even if Game 4 in Boston was a sellout, it was obvious that this Series would not come close to matching 1917's $152,000 player pool. With the commission still planning on giving payouts to teams that finished second, third, and fourth, stark reality sank in for the Cubs and the Red Sox: the winners were not going to get $2,000, and the losers would not get $1,400. On the train, the players were told that the winners' share would be just $1,200 and the loser's share $800. Even those numbers, it turned out, were optimistic.

The players were angry. Some wanted to abandon the Series then and there—hollow chatter, because that would ensure no one got any money. But not long before, the Red Sox had used a strike threat successfully, demanding that Harry Frazee pay their usual salaries for the first two weeks of September. "It is pitiful to read that the Boston Red Sox, preliminary to entering the World's Series, organized a strike for their salaries through September 15," *The Sporting News* reported. "They told Owner Harry Frazee that if they did not get the half a month's salary they would not play the series. It is to be regretted that Frazee was not in a position to take them at their words and call off the whole show."[14] Frazee had given in. Now the Red Sox were threatening to strike again.

It was decided that a committee of players would approach the National Commission with a demand for full shares, and if that did not work, a willingness to compromise at $1,500 for the winners and $1,000 for the losers. Hooper, along with Shean, would represent the Red Sox. Mann and Killefer would represent the Cubs. When Hooper told Herrmann the players wanted to meet Sunday afternoon, he was told that Ban Johnson had taken a later train and the players would have to come back and meet with the commission at the Copley Plaza Hotel in downtown Boston on Monday morning, before Game 4.

Not everyone was worked up about the payout fuss. Ruth, for one, didn't much seem to care. Not that he didn't like money; he just didn't worry about it—money, it seemed, was always there when he wanted it. As Fred Thomas would later explain, "Babe was an irresponsible

179

guy. I'd never go out with him. He'd spend money all right, but he'd spend your money. He made more money than anybody but he never had any."[15] Instead, Ruth spent the afternoon moving up and down the aisles, plucking straw hats off passengers and punching out the tops. It was past Labor Day, after all, and a straw hat after Labor Day was a fashion faux pas. As part of his horseplay, Babe got tangled up in some roughhousing with pitcher Walt Kinney and wound up smacking the middle finger of his left hand. It swelled up and would need to be treated with iodine. Barrow was not pleased, because Ruth was his Game 4 starter.

But now there was some doubt as to whether there would be a Game 4 at all.

THE ORIGINAL CURSE: HIPPO VAUGHN

Luck was not smiling on Hippo Vaughn in his first two appearances in the 1918 World Series—he'd allowed three runs in 18 innings and had two losses to show for it. Three years later, more bad luck would end his career prematurely.

From 1914 to 1920, Vaughn was among the best starters in the National League, posting 143 wins in seven seasons. But in 1921, at age 33, things went sour. On July 9, Vaughn had a terrible outing in New York, dropping his record to 3–11. He'd given up the first career home run to his old teammate, pitcher Phil Douglas, walked off the mound, and, according to the *Tribune*, "Big Jim hasn't been seen since. . . . He failed to come to the hotel where the Cubs are stopping and hadn't been located tonight."[16] Vaughn, it turns out, was as unhappy with Johnny Evers (then the Cubs manager) in 1921 as Red Sox players had been in the spring of '18. "I could have hung on for a few more years, I guess, but my arm was hurting and Manager Johnny Evers told the newspapers the trouble was, 'in my head,'" Vaughn later explained. "Kind of made me mad."[17] Vaughn was suspended by Evers and turned up back in Chicago with a semipro outfit. Evers was fired shortly thereafter and replaced by Bill Killefer, prompting Vaughn to report back to the team. The Cubs attempted to reinstate him.

Not so fast. In the view of Commissioner Kenesaw Mountain Landis, Vaughn had jumped his contract by signing with the semipro team. Landis ruled that Vaughn could not play for the remainder of the season. Even after the season, the *Tribune* reported that Vaughn's semipro team, the Beloit Fairies, agreed to tear up Vaughn's contract to allow him to return to the Cubs, but, "semi-pro men, however, claim Vaughn's case was taken before Landis and turned down. 'Hippo' then went back to Beloit and signed another contract."[18] Vaughn may have had a sore arm, but it certainly got better. He pitched semipro ball around Chicago until he quit at 47 years old—and even then, he insisted, it was his legs that gave out, not his arm. Landis's excessively tough ruling brought a premature and ignominious end to what had been a brilliant career.

SIXTEEN

World Series,
Games 4 and 5, Boston

SEPTEMBER 9–10, 1918

As the Red Sox and Cubs were speeding across the Midwest toward Boston aboard the Michigan Central on Sunday afternoon, a Hamburg-American liner pulled into the city's navy yard. On the ship were 195 soldiers who had been "invalided" by the war. Among that group were 52 stretcher cases, those who were so badly wounded that they could not get out of bed. They were sent to Boston City Hospital. There were 13 cases of shell shock taken to the Boston Psychopathic Hospital. The other soldiers went to various naval hospitals around the area. Their arrival was heralded by newspapers across the country. Even in Chicago, a picture of one of the wounded—a forlorn, one-armed young soldier sitting with a smiling nurse—appeared in the *Herald Examiner*. In Boston, executives at the *Globe* contacted the hospitals and offered to buy tickets to the upcoming World Series games for all the injured men who were fit enough to attend.

At the same time, it was decided that another group of debilitated soldiers—200 sailors at Commonwealth Pier in East Boston—had to be transported too. But they had not yet been to war. They were sick, far too sick to be put into a hospital. They had contracted Spanish influenza, a particularly virulent form of the flu that led to lethal pneumonia. It had been passed around on the battlefields of the front, but between the usual high death tolls of the war and military censors who did not want the enemy to know about the illness, the flu had not been reported widely. (Spain had remained neutral in the war, and because the press there reported on the epidemic, it became known as "Spanish flu.") It had shown up in pockets around the United States in 1918, but not until men began returning from the front were concerns raised about an outbreak here. When the illness of the sailors on Commonwealth Pier became known, they were quickly quarantined. While preparations were being made for Game 4 at Fenway, state guardsmen went to the top of Corey Hill in Brookline, one of the highest points around Boston, and built a tent camp. By that evening, the 200 flu-stricken soldiers were transported into the tents.

Where World Series talk in Chicago had been trumped by talk of the war and the Federal Building bomb, World Series talk in Boston was overshadowed by news of the invalided battlefield heroes and simmering rumors of a fast-spreading fatal flu virus. For ballplayers, as the end of the season—and, quite possibly, the end of baseball and the good living the game provided—drew near, there was an increased need to squeeze out every dollar before the shutdown hit. Many of the players figured to be inducted into the army themselves soon. Helping to hammer home that reality was the presence of erstwhile Red Sox lefty Dutch Leonard, who joined the team in the Fenway dugout for Game 4. Leonard and several other players who dodged the draft by joining the shipyard league had been nabbed by the War Department and forced into the army. Now Leonard was simply waiting for his draft call. The sight of Leonard was a stark reminder for ballplayers that, from now on, there would be no more collecting a good salary while hiding from the war. It wasn't a stretch for them to look at pictures of the invalided soldiers, to hear stories about the sailors sick with Spanish flu, to see someone like Leonard being kicked into the army, and to imagine their future selves. How were they supposed to provide for themselves and their families? What about mortgages and car payments and kids? What if *they* were invalided?

183

Little wonder that money remained first on the minds of the players and that, just a few miles from the site of the tent camp at Corey Hill, Garry Herrmann received a phone call from Cubs outfielder Les Mann. The player representatives wanted to talk about World Series shares. They were not about to let this issue go. They felt they'd been promised $2,000 for the winners and $1,400 for the losers, and "their

Les Mann was a speedy, reliable outfielder for the Cubs, but he was also a key figure in the players' battle for a better share of the World Series receipts. (CHICAGO HISTORY MUSEUM)

stand is that the other clubs should be left out of the proposition until the stipulated sums are paid, or that the commission should come up with the deficit."[1] If they could not be guaranteed that money, they would not play Game 4. Herrmann informed Mann, however, that Ban Johnson still had not arrived—his train would get him into Boston shortly before game time. If the players wanted to meet, Mann was told, they would have to wait until after Game 4. Not that it would matter. The commission, Herrmann claimed, did not have the authority to change the rule without a vote from all 16 team owners. Otherwise, some owners could sue on behalf of their players. "We could end the series at this point," Herrmann threatened, "and divide the money that's coming to the players equally among the club owners."[2]

No one really wanted to end the Series, and what neither side wanted to acknowledge was that their arguments had gaping flaws.

The players had not really been promised $2,000 and $1,400—if they had read the new rule for World Series shares closely, they would have seen that the commission was merely giving the players what had already been agreed on. They were entitled, after the war charities donation, to 55.5 percent of the receipts for the first four games, minus the money that would go to the second-, third-, and fourth-place teams. That was what the commission was authorized to pay them. On the other hand, the commission was leaning on the notion that it could do nothing to change the rule without a full vote of both leagues. This was utter bunk. When the rule changes originally were passed the previous winter, there had been no league-wide vote. In fact, the rule explicitly said that the commission was using "plenary power to revise the rules and regulations governing contests for the World's Series . . . pertaining to the players' share of the receipts."[3] That is, the change was enacted on the authority of the National Commission alone. The National Commission had every right to change the rule further as it saw fit.

What's unclear, though, is why the commission wouldn't do the logical thing and at least eliminate the shares slated to go to other teams. It wasn't a matter of greed. This issue was one of dividing the players' shares, but the owners' shares and the National Commission's share would not be affected. The commission was not being stubborn because it was trying to keep more money for itself or the teams. Why not just allocate all the money in the player pool to the World Series participants? The answer, most likely, was hubris. To change the rule at the behest of the players would make the commission look weak. In hindsight, it had been a mistake to change the Series ticket pricing without making a corresponding change in how the player pool was handled. But look at how the commission handled other issues in baseball, like the use of freak pitching deliveries or the growing gambling problem. Over the brief course of the game's history, baseball's overseers *never* admitted mistakes. They were not about to start now.

Still, Mann and the players agreed to go forward with Game 4 only with the understanding that they would meet with the commission later (some reports had the meeting scheduled for that night, while others put it at 10:00 A.M. the following day). This was a happy turn of events for Boston fans—around the city, interest in the World Series had slowly perked up. "A revival of some of the oldtime World Series enthusiasm was seen in Boston in the increased crowds that gathered

185

about the bulletin boards in newspaper row to cheer the news of the Red Sox's victory in Chicago," the *Tribune* reported.[4] They figured to have quality entertainment. The World Series games had been very well played, if not well attended. The pitching was brilliant, the strategy decisive, the fielding consistent, and the baserunning heads-up. When there were mistakes, such as Charley Pick's attempt to take home at the end of Game 3, they were mistakes of overaggressiveness, not nonchalance or failure of focus.

But after the long train ride from Chicago, after the players figured out they were going to be paid only half the money they thought they'd get, the level of play sank. The final games of the Series were defined by strange and crucial blunders. This, quite possibly, was not a coincidence. The players knew they were coming up short on money and had plenty of time and opportunity to consort with each other on the issue. They were in Boston, the capital of baseball betting, where less than two months earlier two Reds players had sauntered into a poolroom and easily arranged to fix a game. They were playing in a Series in which the betting had been unusual, and stories began to appear about the players' anger over the revised player pool split. The setting was perfect for the enterprising bettor. There was no easier target for gamblers hoping to fix ball games than a group of players dissatisfied with their pay.

At about 2:00 P.M. on Monday, 30 minutes before Game 4, 54 wounded soldiers gathered at Boston City Hospital and piled into automobiles provided by the Red Cross. They got to Fenway Park just before game time and, as they slowly made their way to grandstand seats—some with heads wrapped to cover skull wounds, some hobbling with badly mangled, or even missing, limbs—the other soldiers in attendance stood and saluted. The crowd cheered, and throughout the game lines of people approached the soldiers to shake their hands. The soldiers, of course, just wanted to watch the game and cheer on the Red Sox. (Well, not Private Harry Hansen, who had lost his arm at Chateau Thierry. He hailed from Percy, Illinois, and backed the Cubs.)[5]

There was excitement around the soldiers, and Boston was expecting the return of old-time World Series enthusiasm, but again the weather did not cooperate. A drenching rain the previous day kept attendance low, as only 22,183 showed for Game 4, well below the packed-house crowd of 34,000 the Red Sox were predicting. Boston

held a 2–1 lead in the Series, but still, the betting lines were tight—
the Red Sox were only five-to-four favorites. Babe Ruth, his swollen
finger stained yellow with iodine, was able to take the mound for the
Red Sox. For the Cubs, rumors spread that Mitchell would start one
of his right-handed spitballers, Claude Hendrix or Phil Douglas. But
in the end Mitchell did not stray from his strategy. Lefty Tyler again
would be his starting pitcher.

When Ruth took the mound, fans finally diverted their attention
away from the injured soldiers and gave Babe a big ovation. Max Flack
stepped in against Ruth and stroked a single to right field, and almost
immediately Game 4 began to look funny. Charley Hollocher lined
out to shortstop, and, with Les Mann at the plate, Flack took a big
lead at first and just seemed to stop paying attention. Red Sox catcher
Sam Agnew took a pitch from Ruth and threw down to McInnis at
first base, picking off Flack for the second out and stopping any notion
of a Cubs rally. Considering the circumstances, and how tight the first
three games had been, this had to be maddening for Mitchell to witness. It would get more maddening, though. In the third inning, Flack
reached on a force out and was sacrificed to second base by Hollocher.
With two out, Flack again took a big lead and *again* seemed to fall
asleep on the bases, idly kicking the dirt and "giving the brown study
stuff a play around the sacks."[6] Ruth turned and threw to second base,
and, for the second time in the game, Flack was picked off. It's difficult to get picked off during a game at all, but to be picked off twice
in the most important game of the season is a head scratcher. There
have been 104 World Series in baseball history, but Flack remains the
only player to be picked off twice in the same Series game.

Shoddy play from the Cubs—from Flack, specifically—continued
in the fourth inning, with Tyler facing Ruth and two men on base.
Tyler was careful with his first three offerings, throwing three consecutive balls. With a full count, Tyler stepped off the mound, looked
out to right field, and wondered why Flack was playing so shallow
against the best left-handed batter in the game, especially after, in
Game 1, Flack had just automatically moved into deep right field.
"Flack was in too close," the *Herald Examiner* reported. "Tyler waved
him back. Flack did not pay attention to the command. Once again
Tyler motioned him, but Max was obstinate."[7] The result was predictable. Tyler gave Ruth a strike, and Ruth crushed it into right. Flack,
already playing shallow, inexplicably took a step in before turning to

187

chase after Ruth's hit. The ball landed well over Flack's head and rolled easily to the fence. Ruth had a triple. Two runs scored.

For the first seven innings, the Cubs failed to score. Ruth was wild—his finger was sore, and he walked six batters in the game—but it wasn't until the eighth inning that the Cubs finally rallied, almost in spite of themselves. Ruth walked Bill Killefer to start the inning, and Mitchell sent up Hendrix (a very good hitter) in place of Tyler. Hendrix singled, bringing up Flack. Ruth started by unleashing a wild pitch, allowing Killefer and Hendrix to move up. But Hendrix took such a wide lead at second base that he was nearly picked off, and Mitchell, having seen enough bad Cubs baserunning on that afternoon, pulled Hendrix and inserted pinch runner Bill McCabe. With two men on, no outs, and Ruth clearly tiring, "Here was a fine chance for Max Flack to redeem himself," the *New York Times* commented. However, "Flack again fell down, sending an easy grounder right into the hands of [first baseman] Stuffy McInnis."[8] Hollocher grounded out, scoring Killefer, and Mann followed with a single that scored McCabe, tying the game.

After pinch-hitting for Tyler and having to pinch-run for Hendrix because of his knuckleheaded baserunning, Mitchell had only one choice for the bottom of the eighth inning—Phil Douglas, who had warmed up in the bullpen every game but was finally making his first World Series appearance. It did not go well. Douglas was a big guy and a spitballer, to boot, but throughout his career he had never been particularly error-prone or wild. Still, he started the inning by allowing a single to Wally Schang. He then threw wildly past Killefer (the pitch was counted as a passed ball), allowing Schang to move to second base. When Hooper attempted a sacrifice bunt, Douglas came shufflin' off the mound, picked up the ball, and threw it well over Merkle's head into right field, allowing Schang to score and giving the Red Sox a 3–2 win. Boston now held a three-games-to-one lead.

This was not at all a typical performance for the 1918 Cubs. One player, Flack, was picked off twice. The same player ignored the explicit command of his pitcher, who implored him to play deeper with the heaviest hitter in the game at bat, and followed that by failing miserably in a clutch situation. There also was the pitcher, Hendrix, who ran the bases so badly the manager had to pull him, though he was scheduled to take the mound the next inning. Another pitcher, Douglas, let up a hit and a passed ball and threw the game away with

188

a wild heave to first base on a bunt. In the *Globe*, Ed Martin summed it up best: "The Cubs did not look like a whale of a team."[9]

The Cubs did not dwell long on their Game 4 misfortune. Almost as the game ended, the attention of the players turned back to money. They still wanted $2,000 and $1,400 but would be willing to compromise at $1,500 and $1,000. "In the wake of this third and what amounts to the decisive defeat of the World Series, the Chicago Cubs were not only a disconsolate but a highly disgruntled force last evening," the *Boston Post* reported. "The subject of a much-depleted monetary reward for engaging in the classic disturbs them mightily. Threats to strike and refuse to play today's game were uttered, and were uttered freely. This, unless the National Commission guarantees at least $1,000 to each player of the losing club."[10] The players wanted to meet with the commission immediately. But the players were, again, put off, and, according to the *Post*, a player-commission meeting was scheduled for 10:00 A.M.—four and a half hours before Game 5—at the Copley Plaza Hotel.

Finally, the players got their meeting with the commission. It was brief. Johnson, Heydler, and Herrmann again hid behind their inability to change the rule on payouts without a full vote of team owners. Even as the players presented different options for compromise, the commission would not budge. The matter would be considered, the players were told, but there would be no final answer until after Game 5 was played. The players could see they were being stalled—and that if the Red Sox won Game 5, it would not matter. The Series would be over, the game would be shut down for the duration of the war, and the players would be without contracts and without leverage. The player representatives returned to Fenway, angry. The commission, pleased at having defused the situation, celebrated. And when Ban Johnson and Garry Herrmann celebrated, there was almost always some libation 80 proof or stronger involved.

At the park, the teams gathered in the Red Sox locker room underneath the Fenway Park stands. They reached a consensus. If the commission wanted to stall, that was fine. The players would stall too. They would not play until the commission gave them a guarantee on money. If the commission refused, the players would ask that their shares be donated to the Red Cross and go home. But while this revolt was brewing beneath the grandstand, up in the park itself, glorious late-summer weather combined with the possibility of a Red Sox championship attracted a sizable crowd. By 2:00 P.M., nearly 25,000 fans had settled in. But with the game set to start in 30 minutes, something wasn't right. There was no batting practice. There were no players. Mann, in street clothes, had quickly popped onto the field for a word with Walter Craighead. But that was it. Both teams had remained in their locker rooms. They were on strike.

Just after 1:00 P.M., Johnson, Heydler, and Herrmann got word of trouble. They were not well equipped for trouble at the moment. They were drunk. They likely continued to drink, even after hearing about the player strike—they did not show up at Fenway until 2:35 P.M., according to the *Boston American*'s Nick Flatley. Upon arriving, Johnson's speech, according to the *Herald Examiner*, was "replete with repetitions, bubbles and strange Oriental spices."[11] The commissioners gathered in the tight umpires' quarters. They were joined by Hooper and Mann, while a horde of writers and fans tried to see what was happening. The players, again, made their cases. But after sizing up the condition that Johnson, Heydler, and Herrmann were in, they could see it was no use. Herrmann spoke first, rambling about how much he'd done for baseball. Johnson began to sob and pushed Herrmann aside. Flatley marked down his speech: "I went to Washington," he said, grandly thumping his own chest for emphasis and directing his speech to Hooper, "and had the stamp of approval put on this World's Series. I made it possible. I did. I made it possible, Harry. I had the stamp of approval put on the World's Series, Harry. I did it, Harry. I did it."[12]

Herrmann then spoke up again. "Let's arbitrary this matter, Mister Johnson," he said. According to Flatley, "Then [Herrmann] launched forth into a brilliant exposition of the history of baseball's governing board. Expert reporters took notes for a while, then quit, befuddled." Hooper later recalled that Johnson, "came over to me [and said], 'Harry, you know I love you. Go out and play the game.' He put his arm around my neck and wept on my shoulder, repeating, 'I love you. For the honor and glory of the American League, go out and play.' Heydler never opened his mouth. It was apparent we had no one to talk to."[13] The Cubs and Red Sox had little choice. They'd have to play and hope that the commission would give them another hearing when they sobered up. Before agreeing to take the field, though, Hooper said he insisted that the commission assure the players they would not be punished for the strike. Johnson agreed.

Outside, fans were restless. The Fenway band was ripping off numbers as quickly as possible, and several mounted policemen positioned themselves around the perimeter of the field to quell any thoughts of riotous demonstrations. Fans again began to cheer when the contingent of wounded soldiers entered, this time even more dramatically— three of the wounded, unable to navigate the Fenway stairs, were carried to their seats by their brethren. "The crowd outside burst into an immense roar of approval as the wounded soldiers and sailors came into the ball park," the *Herald* reported. "These mighty heroes of the real game must have made everyone within hearing of that tribute think a mite."[14] Finally, ex-mayor John Fitzgerald, who had witnessed the negotiations in the umpires' room, took hold of a megaphone and announced to the crowd that the strike had been settled and the players would go forward with Game 5 "for the good of the game and the public."[15] At 3:30, an hour late, the Cubs and Red Sox took the field.

When Game 5 finally got under way, play was snappy. Sam Jones took the mound for the Red Sox, and Mitchell trotted out Vaughn again. The Cubs whacked Jones freely, collecting seven hits and five walks, scoring three runs. They threatened constantly throughout the game, putting runners in scoring position in five of the nine innings. Boston's hitters, meanwhile, barely touched Vaughn, and when they did, the rally was quickly scotched with a double play. Only twice did the Red Sox move a runner to second base. Three times a Red Sox rally was cut short by a double play. The Cubs won easily, 3–0.

But, remember, the Cubs had to win. The teams were still trying to gain some concession on players' shares, and if the Red Sox had won, the commission would have no reason to give up anything.

THE ORIGINAL CURSE: SHUFFLIN' PHIL DOUGLAS

Phil Douglas, the pitcher who threw away Game 4 for the Cubs, was an alcoholic. He had grown up in the South, and his youth was marked by three prominent features—day labor, baseball, and corn whiskey. By the time he came to the Cubs as a 25-year-old in 1915, three organizations (the White Sox, Reds, and Dodgers) had been enticed enough by Douglas's talent to sign him, but repulsed enough by his personal habits to let him go. Douglas was prone to taking what he called "vacations," a euphemism for benders. Even as a big-leaguer, he tended to drink away his earnings. Before the 1918 season, it was written that Douglas "lives down in Tennessee on a farm so poor that a rabbit passing through has to carry his rations."[16] Though he was a solid pitcher for the Cubs, his drinking was a problem. Manager Fred Mitchell would later say of Douglas, "There was no harm in that fellow. He didn't fight with the boys, or burn down houses. It was just that I never knew where the hell he was, or if he was fit to work."[17] Mitchell and the Cubs finally gave up on Douglas in 1919, sending him to the master of the reclamation project, John McGraw.

McGraw treated Douglas harshly, keeping him under near-constant surveillance. But he got the most out of Douglas, who went 14–10 in 1920 and 15–10 in 1921. Douglas was 11–4 in 1922 and having his best year when he slipped away from McGraw's operatives and went on a drinking binge. When Douglas was found, he was tossed in the West End Sanitarium, where he was forced to stay for five days. He was released in early August and, shortly thereafter—perhaps still in a posttreatment haze—Douglas wrote a letter to ex-Cubs teammate Les Mann, who had moved on to the Cardinals.

In the letter, Douglas told Mann he could not stand to pitch for McGraw anymore. If he stayed with the Giants, Douglas feared, he would help McGraw win the pennant. He didn't want that. "So you see the fellows," Douglas wrote to Mann, "and if you want to send a man over here with the goods, and I will leave for home on the next train, send him to my house so nobody will know, and send him at night." At the time, the Cardinals and Giants were tied for the National League lead, and Douglas presumed that, without him, the Giants would lose the race to the Cardinals (he was, in the end, wrong on that count). Mann immediately gave the letter to his manager, Branch Rickey, who turned over the letter to Commissioner Kenesaw Mountain Landis.

Landis went to the Giants' team hotel, met with McGraw, and decided to ban Douglas from baseball. The *New York Times* called Douglas a "pitiful figure as he said good-bye to the other Giant players."[18] On seeing Landis, Douglas asked, plaintively, "Is this all true, Judge, that I am through with baseball?"

"Yes, Douglas, it is," Landis said, visibly saddened.

"Do you mean that I can never play baseball again?" Douglas asked again.

"Yes, Phil, I am afraid that that is just what it means."

Douglas is usually portrayed as a sympathetic figure who had no real intention of getting involved in a payoff scheme with Mann and the Cardinals. Rather, he is usually seen as a victim of McGraw's tyranny and the disease of alcoholism. But McGraw certainly did not see him that way and indicated that Douglas's crookedness went beyond the Mann letter. "We have the absolute goods on Douglas," McGraw said. "We have the letter written in his own handwriting. We have overheard some of his telephone conversations. He admits the charge, and now he is a disgraced ball player, just as crooked as the players who threw the 1919 World's Series. . . . It will be a fine thing for the sport—this exposure of another 'shady' player."[19]

In 1952, Douglas, 30 years out of baseball and wheelchair-bound, died at age 62, after his third stroke.

SEVENTEEN

World Series, Game 6, Boston

SEPTEMBER 11, 1918

One thing that's clear about baseball from the years up to and including the 1919 Black Sox scandal is this: it was not difficult to throw a game. Perhaps Ban Johnson could sell the public on the notion that pulling off a fix of a baseball game would be harder than drawing water from an empty well, but those in the game knew better—and, in retrospect, so do we. The actions of Hal Chase and Lee Magee show that, in 1918, setting up a fixed game was as simple as walking into a pool hall and filling out a check. It wasn't necessary to have the whole team on board. Chase, apparently, tried to fix games on his own. And, if John McGraw was right in what he told Fred Lieb about the 1917 World Series—McGraw said that second baseman Buck Herzog "sold him out" by playing out of position—then something as simple as an infielder intentionally shading too far one way could have been enough to throw a whole World Series. A fix did not require the unified action of an entire team. One reason the Black Sox were exposed was that their attempt at a fix was audacious, indiscreet, and widely known among players throughout the league and gamblers throughout the country, so that it was only a matter of time before *someone* started spilling the conspiracy's secrets. Fixes did not have to be that way.

As for the mechanics of fixing a game, they weren't very difficult. "It's easy," Cicotte said in his Black Sox testimony. "Just a slight hesitation on the player's part will let a man get on base or make a run.

I did it by not putting a thing on the ball. You could have read the trade mark on it by the way I lobbed it over the plate. A baby could have hit 'em. . . . Then, in one of the games, the first, I think, there was a man on first and the Reds batter hit a slow grounder to me. I could have made a double play out of it without any trouble at all. But I was slow—slow enough to prevent the double play, period. It did not necessarily look crooked on my part. It is hard to tell when a game is on the square and when it is not. A player can make a crooked error that will look on the square as easy as he can make a square one. Sometimes the square ones look crooked."[1]

When he was testifying about Chase in 1918, Reds manager Christy Mathewson described the methods he'd seen Chase use to throw games: "I mean such plays as momentary hesitation in handling bunts and then throwing too late to get any runner; getting his feet crossed and catching balls thrown slightly wide, thereby having to try for his catch with one hand and resulting in a muff; playing ground hits, that he could have easily got in front of with one hand, so that the opposing batter got credit for a base hit; going after balls hit almost directly at the second baseman, which compelled our pitcher to make running catches at first base of long, hard throws, frequently thrown by Chase wide of the bag, or starting in for bunts that the pitcher could easily handle, then stopping, leaving first base uncovered. In some of these games, his failure, while at bat, to either hit or bunt the ball in attempting the squeeze play or the hit-and-run play, caused me to order the discontinuance of these plays."[2]

Reds outfielder Edd Roush commented that, even when Chase was trying to lose, he made it look good—when Chase was suspended for indifferent playing, his batting average didn't look very indifferent. He was hitting .301, 12th best in the National League. (Magee, too, was batting .301.) A player could put up very good individual numbers while intentionally kicking away games. "If he wanted to win, you couldn't throw that ball where he couldn't come up with it," Roush told interviewer Lawrence Ritter. "But if he didn't want to win, he would get over to that bag, he'd always cover that bag late. . . . Course, he was slick at it. Now, I hit ahead of Chase in the batting order, I hit third, he hit fourth. In a ball game he'd lose, he might have three base hits in it."[3]

Chase, remember, was throwing games right under the noses of his teammates and manager. Reporters covering the Reds that year, who

195

watched every game, sometimes expressed frustration with the team's performance, but no accusations of crookedness were lodged until Mathewson finally suspended Chase. If Chase and the Reds could fool their beat reporters, average fans would be fooled, too. In *Eight Men Out*, Asinof explained that a fix could come from anywhere on the diamond: "Exploiting their own talents, bribed players learned to become adept at throwing games. A shortstop might twist his body to make a simple stop seem like a brilliant one, then make his throw a bare split second too late to get the runner. An outfielder might 'short-leg' a chase for a fly ball, then desperately dive for it, only to see it skid by him for extra bases. Such maneuvers were almost impossible for the baseball fan—even for the most sophisticated sportswriter—to detect."[4]

None of the games in the 1918 World Series were blowouts. None featured the horrible pitching performances and long strings of flubs by fielders that would be features of the blatantly crooked 1919 World Series. A much subtler fix was possible, one that fans, sportswriters, managers, or even teammates might not recognize as it was happening—indeed, one that might not be figured out, ever.

September 11, 1918, opened with an early frost in New England and disturbing news for Bostonians—or maybe disturbing, maybe not. The city's Board of Health announced fears of a Spanish flu epidemic by direly warning that citizens should restrict such routine behaviors as spitting, riding in elevators, or sharing a drinking cup. Up on Corey Hill, the tent camp housing the sick was growing. But while acknowledgment of the presence of a serious and spreading sickness should have been cause for alarm, there was a nothing-to-see-here feel to the way that authorities were handling the Spanish flu reports. A doctor at Massachusetts General Hospital said there had not been an unusual number of cases of flu combined with suffocating pneumonia, the hallmark of the Spanish flu. The head of the local naval district said there were only about 160 cases, and "He is of the opinion that it's just plain grippe, without any fancy Spanish influenza trimmings."[5] He was wrong.

For the members of baseball's National Commission the day opened in Boston with nasty hangovers, but, in a happy change for Johnson, Heydler, and Herrmann, it did not open with further harassment from the committee of players seeking to wring more money out of their

World Series shares. The players had given up on the commission. Instead, the player committee (now represented by Harry Hooper and Carl Mays for the Red Sox, Bill Killefer and Les Mann for the Cubs) met with more reasonable power brokers—their team owners. Both Charley Weeghman and Harry Frazee assured the players that the teams would try to find a way to increase their compensation, either by petitioning the other owners or by having the teams themselves fill in the monetary shortfall as much as possible. It's likely that the players took these vague promises with due grains of salt. But it was, at least, something.

It was still chilly by 2:00 P.M., 30 minutes before the start of Game 6. The crowd, anxious about whether the game would start or be called off by another player strike, was relieved to see both teams on the field in uniform. Not that there were many present. The cold, combined with the general disenchantment over the ugliness that had delayed Game 5, further depressed attendance. Only 15,238 showed for Game 6, the smallest World Series crowd since 1909. The public wanted to hurry the 1918 baseball season to its end, and, it seemed, so did the players. During warm-ups, according to the *Chicago Herald Examiner*, "The Red Sox took a horrible chance. They posed for a picture as champions of the world half an hour before play started. . . . Money worries and strike problems have escaped athletes to forget their natural superstitions. It must be due to the war."[6] Thus the Red Sox virtually declared themselves champions while the World Series was still in play. The gambling fraternity was not so sure—the *Boston American* claimed that, even with a lead in the Series, odds of only ten to eight or ten to nine were being given on Boston.[7]

The Red Sox had Carl Mays, whose underhanded pitches had been so baffling for the Cubs in Game 3, on the mound for Game 6. Chicago countered, of course, with a left-hander—Lefty Tyler, going on one day's rest. Mays appeared to be in good form from the beginning. He usually had trouble only when his submarine shoots got too high in the strike zone, and on this day he was keeping his pitches low. Mays set down the first five Cubs hitters in order when, with two out in the second inning, Charley Pick looped a single off the inner part of his bat handle. Before Mays threw another pitch, though, he looked over at Pick at first, wheeled around, and flung the ball to McInnis. Pick was picked off easily.

Tyler was shaky to start. He retired Hooper and Dave Shean, but when Amos Strunk floated a fly ball to shallow left field, Charley Hollocher ran out from shortstop, bobbled the ball, and dropped it. Strunk was awarded a hit. But Tyler escaped damage when George Whiteman followed with a long fly to Dode Paskert. In the second, Tyler again retired the first two batters but walked Fred Thomas. Wally Schang hit a grounder to Hollocher, who fielded it and paused before flipping the ball to Pick at second base. Thomas was safe, and Hollocher would have been charged an error, except that Thomas overslid the bag, and Pick tagged him out. Tyler had gotten by without giving up a run, but the defense behind him was not inspiring much confidence.

That defense finally broke down in the third inning. Tyler walked Mays on four pitches, and Hooper moved Mays to second base with a sacrifice. Tyler walked Shean, and both Shean and Mays moved up on Strunk's ground out. With two outs and runners on second and third, Whiteman came to bat. He sent a line drive to right field, and Tyler, sure he had escaped the jam, began walking to the dugout. But, as the *New York Times* reported: "Flack came running in to make an easy catch. He caught up to the rapidly descending ball and had it entirely surrounded by his hands. Tyler was offering thanksgiving for crawling out of a bad hole when the ball squeezed its way through Flack's buttered digits. As the ball spilled in a puddle at Flack's feet, both Mays and Shean were well along their way home before Flack's alarm clock went off and woke him up."[8] In the *Tribune*, I. E. Sanborn thought, perhaps, Flack had an excuse: "Max muffed it squarely, with only the fact that he was on the run and the sun was in his eyes to excuse him."[9] To the *Boston American*, Flack seemed distraught: "It was a fearful muff and broke Flack's stout heart, but it just naturally happened."[10]

198

The Red Sox led, 2–0, but in the top of the fourth inning Flack almost single-handedly cut the lead in half. He drove a single to right field and moved up on a ground out by Hollocher. Mann was hit by a pitch but was picked off by catcher Wally Schang. As Mays was walking Paskert, Flack broke for third and stole the base safely. Fred Merkle followed with a single, scoring Flack and putting the score at 2–1, Red Sox. Tyler continued to struggle with wildness, and the Cubs defense continued to look unsteady. In the fourth, the Red Sox beat out two infield hits, and Tyler walked another batter, but again, Tyler avoided damage thanks to nice plays from his infielders. At the plate the Cubs did not even dent Mays. He did not allow a hit in the fifth, sixth, or seventh innings. In fact, as Mays zipped through the entire Chicago lineup, not one Cub knocked a ball out of the infield in any of those three innings—of the nine outs made, five came on harmless taps back to Mays.

That changed in the eighth, when Fred Mitchell made a last desperate attempt to salvage the Series. He pulled Deal for pinch hitter Turner Barber. Mays swooped into his delivery and sent a pitch down around Barber's knees. Barber reached down and clubbed the pitch into left field. "Whiteman," the *Hartford Courant* reported, "before the series hardly known to baseball fame, rushed in with the ball dropping faster and faster, grabbed the sphere below his ankles and took a clean somersault, the great momentum rolling him up on his feet again. He staggered dizzily, but with great elation, slammed the ball to Scott and the ball went flying around the infield as an expression of the joy of the Sox in such a remarkable catch."[11] The fans roared. Whiteman's teammates went out to see if he was hurt. He waved them off at first, but after the next out was made Whiteman came off the field with an injured neck. Ruth took his place in left field. Yes, that's right—Babe Ruth was a pinch fielder for George Whiteman.

The catch capped the brief brush with glory for Whiteman, the slightly paunchy, 35-year-old Barrow purchasee. Whiteman hadn't done much of note during the season. He hadn't done much of note throughout his career, spent mostly in the minors. He had been called up to the Red Sox in 1907 with Tris Speaker, but while Speaker went on to become a Hall of Famer, Whiteman played just four games and went back to the minors. He resurfaced in 1913, at age 30, when he played 13 games with the Yankees. Now the catch on Barber's liner sealed Whiteman's status as World Series hero. He hit .250, with a .348 on-base percentage, scored two runs, knocked in another, and, in Game 6, hit the liner that was muffed by Flack for two Red Sox runs. "He was the active principal in all four of the Red Sox victories," Hugh Fullerton wrote, "got on base more times and in more ways than any other player; made the decisive plays and [in Game 6] he capped the climax."[12] All of this was fitting. Not only did Whiteman's performance shred Mitchell's plan to limit Ruth's impact on the Series, but, as one Cub said, "[Whiteman] wouldn't even be in the league but for the war."[13] The baseball season had been dominated by war, and here

199

the star of the World Series was a player whose very presence in the big leagues was owed entirely to the fact that the war had drained the Red Sox of all other options.

Any notion of a Cubs comeback ended with Whiteman's catch. Mays got two pop outs to finish the eighth and two more pop flies to start the ninth. With two out in the final inning, Mann sent a roller to Shean, who flipped the ball to McInnis at first base. The game, the Series, and the 1918 season were over. The Red Sox were World Series champions for the fifth time—the most of any team. But the players, uncertain of the proper reaction, simply headed for the locker room. The fans filed out. "Baseball's valedictory this afternoon should have been played to the weary strains of Chopin's Funeral March," the *Times* commented. "The smallest gathering that ever saw the national game's most imposing event sat silently about, and watched Boston win and Chicago lose. There was no wild demonstration of joy when the last man went out, and Stuffy McInnis, with the ball in his hand, led the scramble of the players to the clubhouse. No hero was proclaimed, no player got a ride on anyone's shoulders, no star was patted on the back or madly cheered to a niche in baseball's temple of fame. The finish was as uneventful as the last moment of a double-header in Brooklyn."[14]

Indeed, the funeral theme was widely reiterated in reports about the '18 World Series. "This World Series is probably the last which will be played in some time," wrote Sherman Duffy in the *Chicago Daily Journal*. "It seems certain that baseball as it now exists is gone. It has been losing its hold because of intense commercialism into which it had fallen. Its shameful deathbed display was the finishing touch."[15] As the *Courant* noted, "Taps for professional baseball for the duration of the war sounded at Fenway Park today."[16] Wrote Sanborn: "Professional baseball is dead."[17]

200

That night, the Cubs met at Boston's South Station and boarded the train that would take them back to Chicago. Team president Charley Weeghman had to rush, after the game, to a Boston board to register for the draft, which would expand to include ages 18 to 45 the next day. Weeghman still made the train. Some Cubs stayed east. Otto Knabe went back home to Philadelphia. Lefty Tyler went to his Massachusetts farm. Reserve catcher Tommy Clarke, who had appeared in one game all season, went off to his home in New York.

For those going to Chicago, it was a long ride. No one, apart from Hippo Vaughn and Lefty Tyler, had performed particularly well. As a team, the Cubs hit .210, after batting .265 during the season. Pick was the top hitter, at .389, followed by Merkle (.278) and Flack (.263). Hollocher, after amassing the most hits in the National League, batted just .190. Paskert, too, hit .190. Killefer hit .118. The pitchers had been brilliant, holding the Red Sox to a .189 average and just nine runs in the six games, but the defense cracked at all the wrong times, and the baserunning mistakes were devastating. The Cubs were second in the league in stolen bases in the regular season, but in the Series they stole just three—they were picked off four times and caught stealing five times. "In the wake of the scrappy [Red Sox], there is a trail of Chicago's shattered hopes, sleepy base running, silly errors and sillier bases on balls," the *New York Times* wrote.[18]

Aboard the train, Killefer and Mitchell went into a private conference to decide how to divide the losers' share of the gate receipts. The pool was a shallow one, just $13,641.64. Killefer and Mitchell set aside $1,000—$300 to be given to the team trainer and $700 to be divided among Grover Cleveland Alexander, Rowdy Elliott, Pete Kilduff, Tom Daly, and Vic Aldridge, the Cubs players who were in the service. The rest of the money was divided into 22 shares, with Speed Martin and Tommy Clarke splitting a share. Each share was $574.62. The Red Sox did better—$1,108.45 each—but considering that players opened the Series expecting $2,000 and $1,400, there was sharp disappointment when the totals were officially settled.

The Cubs got back to Chicago late on the night of September 12, which meant that when they got up the next morning they had just three days to find essential employment or else be subject to immediate induction into the army. Some were already in Class 1A and were simply awaiting the draft call—Killefer, Hollocher, catcher Bob O'Farrell, and utility man Bill McCabe. Killefer, in fact, had been planning a five-day fishing trip after the Series, but when he arrived at Cubs park his draft notice was waiting for him. He would be expected to show up at Camp Custer in Michigan by September 17. Les Mann would return to his job with the YMCA. Merkle and Rollie Zeider claimed they were retiring from baseball and heading to their farms. Hippo Vaughn, too, had a farm in Texas. Chuck Wortman, Nick Carter, Charley Deal, and Charley Pick were slated to work and play ball for steel or shipyard companies. Two players who were scrambling at the last moment to find essential employment were Max Flack and Phil Douglas. Flack eventually got a job working on road construction, and Douglas found work with Alabama Power in Birmingham.

The Red Sox, too, scattered. Hooper returned to his ranch in California, announcing that he would retire. Fred Thomas returned to the navy. Babe Ruth signed up with a shipyard, while Amos Strunk, Joe Bush, Heinie Wagner, Sam Agnew, and Walt Kinney weighed offers to do likewise. Mays was awaiting his draft call. Sam Jones went to work in an oil field out West. Whiteman found ground aviation work and would never play in the majors again. Wally Schang, Stuffy McInnis, and Everett Scott scrambled for jobs, and according to the *Boston American*, it was likely that Scott, McInnis, and Dave Shean would follow Hooper into retirement.[19] No one really knew what it was that they were retiring from anyway. "The players went their respective ways firmly convinced that baseball as a trade was a thing of the past," the *Chicago Daily Journal* reported. "It is a difficult problem, for many of the ball players never have learned any trade or profession save that of ball playing and it leaves them in a rather helpless condition."[20]

In the *Globe*, 34-year-old Eddie Martin—the wittiest of Boston's beat reporters, successor to sportswriting legend Tim Murnane—wrote an article for the September 13 edition, detailing the post–World Series plans of the Red Sox. It was the last piece of work Martin would publish. He had taken some time off, but his vacation was interrupted when, on October 3, his wife, Delia, became ill with the flu. Then pneumonia. By the next morning, she was coughing violently as her lungs filled with fluid and she struggled to breathe. Martin did not leave her side, though, even as he began to cough and struggle to breathe himself. Delia died that morning, and Ed was taken to a hospital in the afternoon. He responded well to treatment at first but the next day was overwhelmed by pneumonia and died. Ed and Delia Martin were buried together at Holyhood Cemetery in Brookline, less than two miles from the Spanish flu tent camp on Corey Hill.

By the end of September, Spanish flu outbreaks had been reported in 26 states. One Massachusetts doctor, in late September, described the viciousness of the illness: "It is only a matter of a few hours then until death comes, and it is simply a struggle for air until they suffocate. It is horrible. One can stand it to see one, two or twenty men die, but to see these poor devils dropping like flies sort of gets on your nerves. We have been averaging about 100 deaths per day, and still keeping it up."[21]

On October 1, estimates had the number of Spanish flu cases in Massachusetts at 75,000, with 800 dead in Boston alone. In Europe, the Allies, reinforced by the Americans, were pushing the Germans farther and farther back. By October 5, Kaiser Wilhelm was sending telegrams to President Wilson asking for peace. Allied victory was finally declared on November 11, but across the country and across the world the Spanish flu continued to ravage whole populations. By the time the pandemic passed in 1919, about 500,000 had died in the United States—10 times the number of Americans killed on the war's battlefields. Worldwide, the total dead has been estimated at 20 million to 30 million people, making it the single worst pandemic killer in recorded history.[22]

THE ORIGINAL CURSE: LEFTY TYLER

It seemed 1918 would be a breakthrough year for Lefty Tyler. He was only 28, had gone 19–8 in 33 starts, and finished with an ERA of 2.00, a career best and second in the National League behind Hippo Vaughn. But when Tyler reported to spring training the following year, he had developed soreness in his shoulder. He tried to pitch through it, but every time he took the mound his arm suffered. He made his last appearance of the season on June 24, amid fears that Tyler was suffering from neuritis. The Cubs sent him to the Mayo Clinic, where Tyler was "given as thorough an examination as man was ever given. The institute doctors were advised not to spare any expense in diagnosing his case. They did not. They took every test used and known in the establishment, and when they finished they pronounced Tyler a perfect specimen in everything except his teeth, and to them they attributed his trouble."[23]

The Mayo diagnosis: Tyler's bum choppers were causing a poisoning of his blood, and he needed to have all his teeth removed except two. Alas, it was no help. His arm trouble continued, and he posted an 11–12 record in 1920. In July 1921, Tyler was 3–2 when—at just 31 years old—the Cubs released him, citing the failure of his shoulder to respond to treatment. Tyler played with the Rochester Red Wings in 1922, after which, he retired.

203

EIGHTEEN

History: Throwing the World Series

"What the war, the war department, the players, and the club owners did to professional baseball in this A.D. 1918 was plenty," wrote I. E. Sanborn on December 29 in the *Tribune*. "For a time it looked as if the sport would be listed officially on the casualty record of the year as, 'died of wounds,' but the present verdict seemed to be, 'wounded, degree undetermined.'"[1]

Baseball was wounded. But not dead. With the armistice in Europe ending the war in November 1918, baseball did return in 1919. So did Harry Hooper and Fred Merkle and Stuffy McInnis—of all the Cubs and Red Sox World Series players who claimed they were retiring, only Rollie Zeider did not come back. Predictions of professional baseball's demise proved premature. Even with a shortened, 140-game schedule, attendance skyrocketed in 1919, as a record 6.53 million fans went out to see ball games. That off-season, stinging from the losses of 1918, owners conspired to keep the salaries of returning players low, but still, after an entire year of being slammed as slackers and a World Series marred by an ugly haggle over money, 1919 marked the restoration of the big-league ballplayer's status as a hero in America.

In the eyes of baseball's overseers, though, the status of players involved in the 1918 World Series remained low. Ban Johnson had, before Game 5, promised Hooper that the National Commission would not retaliate against the players for their World Series strike, but just before Christmas of 1918 members of the Red Sox received letters from John Heydler—the players would not be given the traditional emblems that were awarded to World Series champions because of, as Heydler wrote, "the disgraceful actions of the ball players during the series."[2] Heydler was apparently acting without Johnson's knowledge. In December 1920, George Whiteman wrote to Johnson about the emblems. The following February, Johnson wrote to Herrmann: "It is still my firm conviction that [Whiteman] should be awarded an emblem. . . . He is entitled to an emblem and will treasure it because of his only identification with a World's championship contest."[3] But Whiteman never would get his emblem. For more than seven decades, Red Sox players petitioned baseball's commissioners for the emblems, with no luck. It wasn't until 1993 that major-league baseball finally acknowledged the mistake and gave out 1918 World Series emblems to the heirs of Red Sox players.

But emblems were not going to do Harry Frazee much good either way. The 1918 season had not paid off the way he expected, and it's likely that the 1919 boom in attendance came too late to help his bottom line. In the summer of '19, he began what would become a long selling-off of talent to the Yankees, sending Carl Mays (who was boycotting the team) to New York for two players and $40,000. From there the descent of the Red Sox came quickly and hit its nadir with the sale of Babe Ruth. Frazee finally sold the team in 1923.

That made Frazee a bit luckier than Lucky Charley Weeghman. His paltry finances couldn't even keep him in baseball through the end of the 1918 calendar year. Having sold out his stock to William Wrigley, Weeghman left the team in December. Fred Mitchell took over as president, keeping his role as manager too. Throughout 1918, it had looked like the Cubs and Red Sox—once the war was over— had bright futures, with pennant-winning teams expected to be bolstered by the return of players like Grover Cleveland Alexander for the Cubs and Duffy Lewis and Dutch Leonard for the Red Sox. But those futures were not so bright after all. The Cubs finished third in 1919 and would not win another pennant for 11 years. The Red Sox finished sixth and would not win a pennant until 1946.

And neither team would win a championship until the Red Sox finally broke through in 2004. The Cubs, of course, still had not won a World Series through 2008, which means that after the 1918 World Series the teams combined to play 186 seasons (that's 86 years for the

Red Sox and 100-and-counting years for the Cubs) without winning it all. This almost impossible reality, as baseball fans know, caused backers of both teams to indulge in the notion that their teams were cursed—that because Frazee sold Babe Ruth to the Yankees, Boston was doomed to failure for 86 years and that, because the Cubs booted a goat from a 1945 World Series game, the North Siders have been wandering in baseball infamy for all these decades.

But doesn't the assignment of these disparate curses to the Cubs and Red Sox overlook the obvious? *The two teams played each other in a World Series and fell into inexplicable funks immediately after.* The Red Sox sold Ruth after the 1919 season. But take a look at their '19 record, with Ruth still in the fold: 66–71, which landed them in sixth place. The Red Sox went from World Series champs to near the bottom of the league in one season. If the franchise was cursed, that curse settled in immediately after the 1918 season, even before the Ruth sale. Heck, baseball even refused to recognize the Red Sox's win with World Series emblems—the curse, it seems, had settled in by Christmas of '18. And if it's the billy goat curse that has kept the Cubs down all these years, how can we explain their failure to win a championship in the years before 1945? The Cubs played 37 championship-free seasons before the billy goat curse was allegedly uttered. There is something unsatisfactory about the timing of both curses. There must be a different curse, an original curse, one that began when the Red Sox and Cubs played against each other for the only time in the 20th century, a curse spawned when the two franchises bought their way to pennants during the worst complete baseball season in history, a curse that not only crippled the two teams on the field but seeped into the lives of the players off the field.

Perhaps the 1918 World Series—which probably should not have been played in the first place—was fixed; perhaps everyone around baseball, including Eddie Cicotte and Harry Grabiner, knew it; and perhaps the 1919 Black Sox were inspired by it. Now *that* would be cause for a curse.

There is an interesting letter, dated May 13, 1924, in the Hall of Fame file of outfielder Les Mann. At the time, Mann was having a contract dispute with Reds owner Garry Herrmann. In the letter, Mann writes, "I have protected your game and my game on three occasions. The last episode, the 'Douglas case' was my last and one that proved to me

After 1918, Cubs pitchers (from left) Lefty Tyler, Hippo Vaughn, Phil Douglas, and Claude Hendrix would all take strange downward turns. Tyler injured his shoulder, and Vaughn was forced out of baseball, while Douglas and Hendrix got caught up in separate gambling scandals. (CHICAGO HISTORY MUSEUM)

that my mind, being diseased towards base ball professionally was not unwarranted. I have never gambled on the club in cards or other wise. I always was against it and that placed me in wrong on every club. The 'Douglas case' was a frame to get me, I really believed."[4]

Oh, to have Mann explain what he meant!

It was Mann who turned over the letter that Phil Douglas sent in 1922, the letter in which Douglas promised to quit playing for John McGraw in exchange for "the goods." That letter got Douglas banned from baseball. History portrays Douglas as a tragic figure, a patsy done in by the evil of alcohol and the even bigger evil of McGraw. This view is pervasive thanks in large part to a sympathetic article that appeared in the *New Yorker* four years after Douglas's death and an even more sympathetic book, *One Last Round for the Shuffler*, that appeared in 1979. But it doesn't sound like Mann thought too highly of Douglas—he seems to think Douglas was trying to frame him. But for what? For something involving Mann's opposition to gambling, which, "placed me in wrong on every club"? And what did Mann

207

mean by protecting baseball "on three occasions"? One, and what he called the last, was the Douglas situation. What about the other two, which apparently came earlier?

Might Mann have known something about the 1918 World Series and spoken up about it? Might he have implicated Douglas? Could that be why Mann thought Douglas was framing him?

In the span of one week in the summer of 1919, the Cubs traded away Douglas to Brooklyn and then traded Mann and Charley Pick to the Braves for Buck Herzog, a known gambler. We know how teams at the time handled gamblers—they shuffled them around to other teams. Perhaps, at some point in the 1919 season, Mann had gone to team officials about the 1918 World Series, perhaps he pointed at Douglas, and perhaps that put him "in wrong" with his Cubs teammates. Thus the Cubs would have had to trade away Mann and Douglas under duress, agreeing to take problem players from the Braves and Dodgers in return. That, at least, would explain what Mann meant when he wrote to Herrmann.

This is all theory, of course, but that's precisely the challenge. Baseball was so secretive about its gambling problem that, nearly a century later, we are left only with theories and best guesses. The truth was buried very effectively. But, given all the evidence—the uncertain circumstances of the players in general, the drastic and unexpected reduction in World Series shares, the rumors that have popped up in a diary and a deposition—the best guess is that, yes, something was not right about the 1918 World Series.

It is unlikely that the Series, though, was fixed from the beginning. There was some question about the Cubs' play in Game 1—Charley Hollocher was often out of position, according to writer Hugh Fullerton, and the Cubs allowed Dave Shean to get a questionably large lead off second base to set up the winning run—but, mostly, the performance of the two teams was sharp in the first three games at Comiskey Park. It was not until the train ride from Chicago to Boston, when players were finally hit with the reality of the poor payouts the World Series would bring, that the games turned suspiciously sloppy. At that point players would have been low-hanging fruit for would-be fixers.

Considering the prevalence of gamblers around the Series, and the ease with which they mixed with players (Gene Fowler, for one, saw

208

gamblers hanging out in Doc Krone's room, drinking with Babe Ruth), it's likely that bribe offers were made to players even before the Series. If those offers were resisted over the course of the first three games, the National Commission's stubborn unwillingness to beef up the teams' very slim payouts probably eroded that resistance. Why should players not accept some money to play some crooked games? Why should the players protect the honor of a sport that was not, as they saw it, being honorable to the players? The Cubs may have intended to play an honest Series. But the actions of the National Commission would have made it easy to shove aside honest intentions.

Game 4 smells very foul. Max Flack's performance was not just bad. It was historically bad. He was picked off twice, he tapped a harmless grounder back to the pitcher in a key situation, and he committed an obvious misplay on Ruth's triple. Flack also made the fatal error in Game 6, and though he did score the Cubs' only run in that game, he was excessively aggressive in scoring that run—he stole third with two outs, and if he had been caught, he would have broken the time-honored baseball maxim that states baserunners should never make the third out at third base. Flack certainly had incentives. He had a young child at home outside St. Louis and, unlike many of the players, did not have a farm to which to return. As the Series ended, Flack was one of the few Cubs who had not lined up essential employment. He would have needed money.

Claude Hendrix, too, comes into question for his awkward Game 4 baserunning, which was bad enough to force Mitchell to pull him out of the game. Hendrix, it was reported, was lucky not to have been caught while taking an unnecessarily big lead after reaching second base, which would have killed a Cubs rally had he been thrown out. And Hendrix has a questionable reputation working against him. In 1920, he would be pulled from a scheduled start because gamblers contacted the Cubs and claimed he was crooked. Hendrix was not officially banned because of that, but he was released the next year, and suspicion about his connection with gambling lingers.

Douglas's performance in Game 4, too, is suspicious. He probably was rusty, and that could very well explain his struggles. But Douglas found a way to make mistakes at every turn. He pitched a terrible eighth inning, allowing a hit and a passed ball, which he followed with his wild toss to Merkle on a bunt attempt. That throw lost the game. Because of the letter that he sent to Mann in 1922, Douglas, too, has a reputation working against him. Douglas also was notoriously bad with money and, like Flack, did not have essential employment lined up as the World Series was progressing.

If there was a Cubs fix, it probably involved these three, and perhaps others. Remember how Cicotte had phrased the fix rumor: "Well anyway there was some talk about them offering $10,000 or something to throw the Cubs in the Boston Series. There was talk that somebody offered this player $10,000 or anyway the bunch of players were offered $10,000." Perhaps Flack was "this player." Or, perhaps Flack, Hendrix, and Douglas were "the bunch of players."

Of course, Hendrix and Douglas were not starting pitchers at all during the World Series, so their impact was limited. But, remember, Mitchell's decision to use only Vaughn and Tyler in the Series was unexpected and controversial—most thought that either Douglas or Hendrix, if not both, would get starts in the Series. It would make perfect sense for gamblers to target them. Considering how awfully they performed when they finally did appear on the World Series field in Game 4, if gamblers had bribed Hendrix and Douglas, it would have been money well spent. And there's another possibility. Maybe Mitchell knew something. Maybe he'd heard that gamblers had gotten to Hendrix and Douglas, and he decided to use only Tyler and Vaughn not because of his percentage system but because he didn't trust that his two right-handers were on the level.

The Chase-Magee affair in Boston shows how easy it was for players looking to throw a game to find gamblers to back them in 1918. If the Cubs threw the Series, they could have found ways to make money from it on their own. But if, as Grabiner's diary indicates, pitcher Gene Packard was involved with fixing the Series, he would have been well connected on the Cubs side. Packard had been with Chicago in 1916, as well as for spring training and part of the 1917 season. He had been a teammate of Hendrix, Flack, and Douglas and was an ex–Federal League comrade of Flack and Hendrix (though Packard played for Kansas City). Packard had spent the season in St. Louis, a town well stocked with gambling characters. A year later, St. Louis would be one of the epicenters of the Black Sox scandal—gambler Carl Zork, of St. Louis, was among those indicted with White Sox players for the fix. During the Black Sox trial, theater owner Harry Redmon testified that Zork bragged about fixing the 1919 World Series with "a red-headed fellow from St. Louis." St. Louis was also home to Kid Becker, the gambler rumored to have set up a 1918 Series fix that he called off because of a lack of funds.

The Cubs had the motive and the means to fix the last half of the World Series, and Games 4 and 6 have the crucial errors and bizarre baserunning mistakes that are indicative of fixed games. But, if there was a fix, one question looms: what about Game 5, a 3–0 Cubs win? Why didn't the Cubs throw that one? There are two possible explanations. It may be that Vaughn, not in on the fix, was simply having a dominant day and, even if his teammates behind him wanted to throw the game, they would not get the opportunity. The Red Sox got just three hits after all. But if we really want to expand the conspiracy possibilities, there is the chance that it was the *Red Sox* who played indifferently in Game 5. They would have had plenty of incentive not to win that game. Boston held a 3–1 lead at that point, as players for the Red Sox and Cubs were still trying to get either their club owners or the National Commission to give them better payouts for the World Series. The only leverage the players had in the fight was playing or not playing—their power was derived from the threat of another strike. If the Red Sox had won, the Series would have been over and the players' leverage would have been gone. It may have been that the Red Sox did not get many hits off Vaughn because they were not trying to get many hits off Vaughn.

Ambrose Bierce wrote, "History is an account, mostly false, of events, mostly unimportant, which are brought about by rulers, mostly knaves, and soldiers, mostly fools." This notion fits neatly around the days of gambling scandals in baseball. The game's history was easily manipulated by its knave rulers (the magnates) and its fool soldiers (the players). There was, obviously, one great scandal in that era of baseball—the fixing of the 1919 World Series—and once word of that conspiracy reached the public, the challenge for baseball's leaders became to limit the damage such a massive hoax could cause to the image of the game. After much political struggle among league power brokers, and after the embarrassing criminal trial that ended in 1921 with eight accused White Sox players granted an acquittal, major-league baseball did precisely the right thing from a public-relations standpoint: it shaped history as favorably as possible.

211

Already, tough, well-respected federal judge Kenesaw Mountain Landis had been brought in as the commissioner, the white knight who would, in the eyes of the public, single-handedly clean up base-ball's gambling problem and return honesty to the game. Landis immediately went to work, banning the eight Black Sox players despite the acquittal and famously declaring, "Regardless of the verdict of juries, no player that throws a ball game; no player that undertakes or promises to throw a ball game; no player that sits in a conference with a bunch of crooked players and gamblers where the ways and means of throwing games are planned and discussed and does not promptly tell his club about it, will ever play professional baseball."

Landis's message was clear: the Black Sox were guilty, they were banned, the gambling problem was solved. Landis would continue to deal with game-fixing allegations throughout the early part of his ten-ure as commissioner, but never did he act as decisively as he did with the Black Sox. Nor did he delve into the questions that surrounded the scandal. He did not investigate teams (the 1919 Giants, for example) that were known to be riddled with gamblers and problem players. He did not seek answers to obvious questions, like why Cubs official John O. Seys had been a stakeholder for Abe Attell's 1919 bets or why former Cubs president Charley Weeghman was so friendly with Mont Tennes, a gambling kingpin whom Landis himself had investigated. He did not seek to find out whether other teams might have thrown past World Series. He did not even look into the initial scandal that started the courtroom revelation of the Black Sox—the fixing of the August 31, 1920, game between the Cubs and the Phillies.

To do so only would have deepened baseball's wounds and further shaken the public's faith in the honesty of the game. Landis did not deal with gambling in baseball by getting down to the roots of the problem. He dealt with it by containing it, by funneling as much as he could into the Black Sox file, punishing those involved and ignor-ing the rest. He was successful—history says little about the allegedly fixed 1920 Cubs game, the 1919 Giants, or the possibility of other fixed World Series. Now fans who look back on the early days of baseball see eight men suspended from the White Sox for fixing the 1919 World Series and leave it at that. History does not tell us about World Series fixes in 1912 or 1914 or 1921, because, if those Series were crooked, baseball's knave rulers did not want anyone to know. So, we can look back on that era of baseball and accept the official history, which says that big-time game fixing started and ended with the Black Sox (with a Hal Chase or a Lee Magee sprinkled in for those who happen

212

to look closely). Or we can examine history's fringes for clues about what's been omitted intentionally from the official story.

Skeptics will, no doubt, wonder how baseball's magnates could pull off such an extended hoax, how officials and players of the game could allow such a problem to blossom without exposing it or cutting it off altogether. The answer is simple: they were making money. Dragging the game down with gambling scandals made no sense for owners. Prosperity tends to provide a pretty big blind spot. We see that in today's game. Baseball is currently in the midst of a two-decade Steroid Era, and there is no question that the higher-ups of the game have known about and ignored deadly drug abuse over the past 20 years. One of the hallmarks of the Steroid Era, though, was that players were hitting tremendous home runs and fans were flocking to ballparks in record numbers. The game's drug problem was known, but owners were making so much money that it was better to simply ignore it.

We can put baseball's gambling problem in the early 20th century in the same context as the current performance-enhancing drug problem. Only in recent years have revelations about PEDs become widespread, and though we now have public accusations and evidence against players such as Barry Bonds, Alex Rodriguez, and Roger Clemens, there are likely dozens of players—especially those who played in the 1990s, before the drug problem became widely known—who used performance enhancers but, effectively, got away with it. So it was with gambling in the 1910s. Many simply got away with it. Yes, the 1919 Black Sox got caught, and, yes, Landis made examples of the eight Chicago players and a handful of others. But he did not poke through every game-fixing rumor from the previous 20 years, fearing that he would do too much harm.

Similarly, in December 2007, former senator George Mitchell, appointed by commissioner Bud Selig to look into the doping problem in baseball, released his report, naming 89 players accused of using performance enhancers. Far more than 89 players used PEDs, of course, and more names have come out as a result of other investigations. But the Mitchell Report was designed to do exactly what Landis and baseball had done 86 years earlier with the gambling problem: to contain it and to shape history favorably.

To believe that the 1919 World Series was the first and only one to be fixed by gamblers is to believe the official history. It would almost be like believing that the 89 players named in the Mitchell Report are the only ones to have used PEDs.

So, we can wonder about the 1918 World Series. We can wonder why a private detective would tell White Sox secretary Harry Grabiner that Gene Packard was a "1918 Series fixer" and wonder why Grabiner kept that filed in his journal. We can wonder why Eddie Cicotte would say that the Black Sox figured they could throw the World Series because they'd heard the Cubs did it the year before. We can wonder whether Kid Becker had plans to fix the 1918 World Series and whether he really did abandon those plans. We can wonder what Les Mann meant when he wrote that he "protected your game and my game on three occasions" and why he felt he'd been framed by an ex-teammate.

Most important, though, is that we can picture it. If we really look at the lives of ballplayers in 1918, if we really picture what it was like to walk a mile in their ball caps, then we can see that a fix not only is a possibility but is even understandable and excusable. We can put together long strands of circumstances that would lead good, level-headed men to at least consider throwing the '18 World Series—or part of the Series—to get a decent payday before the death of their sport arrived. We know that players felt they had been deceived about the amount of money they'd receive for their participation in the Series. We know that players were not feeling particularly loyal to the game or to their teams. We know that baseball was not expected to return in 1919 and that whenever the game was taken up again it was not expected to provide the living it previously had. We know that, because of the war, players were soon to be forced into low-paying jobs or sent to the army. We know that players and gamblers mixed freely, that few towns had gambling scenes as active as those in Boston and Chicago, and that fixing a game was an easy task. We know that inflation was ruining the economy, that Americans seemed to be surrounded by an odd mix of violence and repressive morality, that the country was at war and on edge.

An extraordinary set of societal circumstances. A 1918 World Series fix. A pair of decades-long curses descending on two of baseball's best-loved franchises. It's really not difficult to picture it at all.

214

NOTES

Chapter 1

1. *Chicago Tribune*, May 10, 1914.
2. John McGraw, manager of the Giants, stated as much in an interview reprinted in the November 11, 1920, issue of *The Sporting News*.
3. *Sports Illustrated*, September 17, 1956.
4. Dewey and Acocella, *The Black Prince of Baseball*, p. 248.
5. *Sports Illustrated*, September 17, 1956.
6. Stout and Johnson, *Red Sox Century*, p. 89.
7. Pietrusza, *Rothstein*, p. 151.
8. Lieb, *Baseball as I Have Known It*, p. 105.
9. *New York Times*, October 2, 1920.
10. Lieb, *Baseball as I Have Known It*, p. 131.
11. Pietrusza, *Rothstein*, p. 159.
12. Veeck, *The Hustler's Handbook*, p. 296.

Chapter 2

1. On his draft registration card, Weeghman listed his residence as the Edgewater Hotel, built in 1916 by John T. Connery and designed by architect Ben Marshall, who also did the Blackstone and the Drake hotels in Chicago.
2. *Chicago Tribune*, December 10, 1917. On December 9 the paper reported that "a mysterious telegram arrived" for Weeghman,

causing his early departure. Weeghman, "accompanied by Walter Craighead, his private secretary, caught the Twentieth Century."

3. If not for Charley Weeghman and the Federal League Whales, the Cubs would likely still be playing on Chicago's West Side, and what we now know as Wrigleyville would be just another North Side neighborhood.

4. Personal interview with Reverend Sonny Smith, Weeghman's great-nephew.

5. *Chicago Tribune*, April 26, 1914.

6. *Chicago Tribune*, January 23, 1916.

7. *Baseball Magazine*, May 1916.

8. *Chicago Tribune*, March 6, 1916.

9. *The Sporting News*, January 14, 1918.

10. Simon, *Deadball Stars of the National League*, p. 216.

11. *Chicago Daily News*, December 11, 1917.

12. *Chicago Tribune*, December 12, 1917.

13. *Chicago Daily News*, December 11, 1917.

14. *Philadelphia Inquirer*, December 12, 1917.

15. Veeck, *The Hustler's Handbook*, p. 264.

16. *Philadelphia Inquirer*, December 12, 1917.

17. *Chicago Daily News*, December 3, 1917.

18. *Chicago Tribune*, December 6, 1917.

19. *Chicago Daily News*, December, 21, 1917.

20. *Chicago Tribune*, January 8, 1918.

21. *The Sporting News*, January 14, 1918.

22. *The Sporting News*, January 14, 1918.

23. *Chicago Tribune*, August 12, 1920.

CHAPTER 3

1. Levitt, *Ed Barrow*, p. 165.

2. *New York Times*, September 17, 1925.

3. Levitt, *Ed Barrow*, p. 126.

4. Lieb, *Baseball as I Have Known It*, p. 269.

5. *Sports Today*, August 1971.

6. Ritter, *The Glory of Their Times*, p. 151.

7. Lynch, *Harry Frazee, Ban Johnson and the Feud That Nearly Destroyed the American League*, p. 42.

8. *Baseball Magazine,* March 1919.
9. *The Sporting News,* February 21, 1918.
10. *The Sporting News,* March 14, 1918.
11. *Chicago Daily News,* December 21, 1917.
12. *Chicago Daily News,* December 21, 1917.
13. *New York Times,* January 6, 1918.
14. *Chicago Tribune,* May 17, 1917.
15. *Chicago Daily News,* November 23, 1917.
16. *Chicago Tribune,* November 22, 1917.
17. *Chicago Tribune,* November 23, 1917.
18. *Chicago Tribune,* November 25, 1917.
19. *Chicago Tribune,* March 13, 1918.
20. *Chicago Tribune,* March 24, 1918.
21. *Chicago Tribune,* March 13, 1918.
22. *New York Times,* June 5, 1929.

CHAPTER 4

1. *Boston Globe,* March 23, 1918.
2. This section is a tribute to *Boston Globe* reporter Ed Martin, one of the funnier writers on any baseball beat, whose spring training stories were especially witty. Many of the Barrow stories here come from Martin's coverage of the spring of 1918. He wrote on March 23 that "Leonard had his first workout today. He wore a rubber shirt, as he has some poundage to leave here." The March 21 edition of *The Sporting News* commented, "A rubber shirt is said to induce perspiration. Some knocker who has studied physics and physiology may contend that the rubber shirt merely prevents evaporation, but a ball player who wears one knows a whole lot better. . . . For the information of the young and uninformed, it may be explained here that a red flannel undershirt keeps away rheumatism. There is something in the color that does it. A white flannel undershirt doesn't do the work."
3. According to the March 24 edition of the *Boston Globe,* Ruth, "gave a party" on the train and sang that song.
4. *Boston Post,* March 25, 1918.
5. *Boston Globe,* March 25, 1918: "Every ball player in the park said [the homer] was the longest drive they had ever seen."

217

6. *Boston Globe*, March 25, 1918. Barrow told Mays not to throw hooks, "but Carl declared he could not resist the desire to bend a few."
7. *Boston Globe*, March 26, 1918. Leonard's exact words, though not spoken to Barrow.
8. *Boston Post*, March 13, 1918.
9. *Boston Globe*, March 27, 1918. "As manager Barrow was walking in," Martin wrote, "a car full of athletes passed him and shouted, 'You are good for a couple more blocks.'"
10. *The Sporting News*, February 21, 1918.
11. *Boston Globe*, March 20, 1918.
12. *Boston Post*, March 14, 1918.
13. Ritter, *The Glory of Their Times*, p. 243.
14. Ritter, *The Glory of Their Times*, p. 144.
15. *Boston Globe*, March 25, 1918.
16. *Chicago Daily News*, April 11, 1918.
17. *The Sporting News*, March 7, 1918.
18. *Chicago Tribune*, April 11, 1918.
19. *Chicago Daily News*, April 5, 1918.
20. *Chicago Daily News*, April 6, 1918.
21. The interview is part of the Asinof papers, held by the Chicago History Museum.
22. Maharg's links to the Phillies are explored at philadelphiaathletics .org/history/linktocubs.htm.
23. Veeck, *The Hustler's Handbook*, p. 263.
24. *Chicago Tribune*, July 22, 1921.

CHAPTER 5

1. Alexander would later call Hornsby the greatest batter he ever faced.
2. *Chicago Tribune*, April 27, 1918.
3. This was standard soldier's pay during the war. A photograph of Alexander ran in the May 9, 1918, edition of the *St. Louis Post-Dispatch*, showing him in his uniform looking over his cot and blankets, under the headline "Private Alexander Taking First Slant at 'Props' of New $30 Job."
4. *Chicago Tribune*, March 21, 1918. Alexander and Wrigley "went to the home of Douglas Fairbanks to appear with the movie star in some pictures for the benefit of the submarine base at San Pedro."

5. This was an actual Red Cross poster, one of many wartime posters that hung on posts around the country.
6. *Chicago Tribune*, April 17, 1918.
7. *New York Times*, April 14, 1918.
8. *Lincoln [Nebraska] Daily Star*, April 6, 1917.
9. *New York Times*, April 6, 1917.
10. *Chicago Daily News*, April 6, 1918.
11. Willmott, *World War I*, p. 161.
12. *Chicago Daily News*, April 6, 1918.
13. *New York Times*, August 23, 1918.
14. Farwell, *Over There*, p. 134.
15. *Boston Globe*, April 7, 1918.
16. *Chicago Daily News*, April 12, 1918.
17. *Los Angeles Times*, March 20, 1918.
18. *Chicago Daily News*, April 23, 1918.
19. *Chicago Tribune*, April 25, 1918.
20. *The Sporting News*, May 2, 1918.
21. *Chicago Tribune*, April 18, 1918.
22. *New York World*, June 10, 1930.
23. *New York World*, June 10, 1930.
24. Letter from Frick to Landis, in Alexander's Hall of Fame file.
25. *The Sporting News*, November 15, 1950.
26. *New York Herald Tribune*, January 20, 1939.
27. *The Sporting News*, February 22, 1934.

CHAPTER 6

1. The *Chicago Tribune* reported on April 19, 1918, that Flack was ailing. According to the *Daily News*, he had a fever and the flu.
2. After returning from the war, John Flach also moved to Chicago and got a job with McCarthy and Fisher music publishers. When the publishers would come up with a new song, John would test it out as an opening act at the Thalia Theater.
3. According to the May 22, 1918, edition of the *Belleville News-Democrat*, Jack Flach left for Jefferson Barracks, and before he departed, he was given a farewell gift watch by the courthouse employees. Judge George A. Crow made the presentation, and Jack, the silver-toned tenor of the courthouse, sang "Joan of Arc" to express his thanks.

4. *Belleville News-Democrat*, April 13, 1914.
5. *Chicago Tribune*, May 12, 1918. Writer James Crusinberry noted that the Cubs would have won the game had Max Flack, who was as sure on a fly ball as any of them, not dropped one in a most critical spot.
6. *Chicago Daily News*, June 5, 1918.
7. *Chicago Tribune*, May 10, 1918.
8. *Chicago American*, July 31, 1918.
9. *Chicago Tribune*, June 19, 1918.
10. *Chicago Tribune*, June 19, 1918.
11. *Chicago Daily News*, June 14, 1918. The bill did not pass, but the committee that slipped it in obviously saw alcohol as a matter of conserving agricultural resources.
12. *Chicago Tribune*, March 10, 1918.
13. *Chicago Daily News*, April 6, 1918.
14. Farwell, *Over There*, p. 131.
15. *Chicago Tribune*, October 4, 1916.
16. Chicago History Museum website: encyclopedia.chicagohistory.org/pages/352.html.
17. *New York Times*, October 16, 1916.
18. Kennedy, *Over Here*, p. 186.
19. Alcott quote is from PBS's online version of *Murder at Harvard*. It can be found at pbs.org/wgbh/amex/murder/peopleevents/p_immigrants.html.
20. *Boston Globe*, April 21, 1918.
21. *Boston Post*, August 15, 1918.
22. Ellis, *Echoes of a Distant Thunder*, p. 363.
23. *Boston Globe*, April 21, 1918.
24. *New York Times*, April 23, 1918.

CHAPTER 7

1. The February 5, 1918, edition of the *Boston Globe* reported, "The California papers say that when 'Dutch' left there a week ago yesterday, he made the announcement that he was going East to enlist as a yeoman at Charlestown Navy Yard. It is known that before the close of the baseball season he made tentative plans for enlisting, but put them aside because of the illness of his wife."
2. Leonard's World War I draft card can be seen on ancestry.com.

3. Ritter, *The Glory of Their Times*, p. 301.
4. *The Sporting News*, June 27, 1918.
5. *Boston Globe*, May 22, 1918.
6. *Boston American*, May 11, 1918.
7. Letter from Harry Hooper to writer Lee Allen, dated May 10, 1963. Located in Hooper's file at the Hall of Fame.
8. *Boston American*, May 11, 1918.
9. *The Sporting News*, May 23, 1918.
10. *American Journal of Clinical Medicine*, 1914, p. 435.
11. *Boston Globe*, May, 24, 1918.
12. Montville, *The Big Bam*, p. 72.
13. *Boston American*, July 20, 1918.
14. *Boston American*, May 29, 1918.
15. *Chicago Tribune*, June 12, 1918.
16. *Baseball Magazine*, August 1918.
17. Jones, *Deadball Stars of the American League*, p. 456.
18. *Boston Globe*, June 17, 1917.
19. *Chicago Tribune*, June 18, 1917.
20. *Boston Globe*, August 31, 1915.
21. *Chicago Daily News*, May 29, 1918.
22. *Chicago Tribune*, July 30, 1918.
23. *The Sporting News*, December 26, 1918.
24. *The Sporting News*, June 6, 1918.
25. *The Sporting News*, December 26, 1918.
26. Asinof, *Eight Men Out*, p. 14.
27. Nowlin, *When Boston Still Had the Babe*, p. 76.

CHAPTER 8

1. Baker won plaudits for his visit to the front and his willingness to see the war firsthand. His travels were detailed everywhere he went, and he did, indeed, visit trenches and see a bomb explode yards away from his transport. When he returned, in a speech called, "At the Front," he described the story of the Frenchwoman.
2. *Chicago Tribune*, May 24, 1918. With the rainout, the Giants reportedly stayed at their hotel and collected news about the work-or-fight edict.
3. *Washington Post*, May 24, 1918.
4. *Chicago Tribune*, May 24, 1918.

5. *Chicago Tribune*, May 27, 1918.
6. Douglas was a well-known alcoholic. Mann, meanwhile, was something of a health nut, and nuxated iron was a common blood-enhancing supplement. The Mann-Douglas relationship would prove to be fateful, as we'll later see.
7. *The Sporting News*, November 20, 1919. Tyler would go to the Mayo Clinic in 1919 and be found to be "in perfect health except for very bad teeth."
8. *New York Times*, May 24, 1918.
9. *Chicago Daily News*, May 23, 1918.
10. *Chicago Tribune*, May 26, 1918.
11. *Chicago Tribune*, May 27, 1918.
12. *Chicago Herald Examiner*, May 27, 1918.
13. *Chicago Tribune*, May 28, 1918.
14. *Chicago American*, July 31, 1918.
15. *Chicago Tribune*, June 1, 1918.
16. *Chicago Daily News*, June 10, 1918.

CHAPTER 9

1. *New York Times*, June 4, 1918.
2. *New York Times*, June 5, 1918.
3. *New York Times*, May 23, 1918.
4. *New York Times*, June 6, 1918.
5. The text, and an audio recording, of Gerard's speech can be found at firstworldwar.com/audio/loyalty.htm.
6. *New York Times*, June 2, 1918.
7. *Boston American*, June 7, 1918.
8. *Chicago Daily News*, June 8, 1918.
9. Farwell, *Over There*, p. 127.
10. Holli and Jones, *Ethnic Chicago*, p. 102.
11. *Chicago Daily News*, June 1, 1918.
12. *Boston Globe*, June 6, 1918.
13. *The Sporting News*, June 13, 1918.
14. *Boston Globe*, June 7, 1918.
15. *Boston American*, May 5, 1918.
16. *Boston Globe*, June 14, 1918.
17. *Boston American*, June 23, 1918.

18. *New York Times,* June 12, 1918.
19. *Boston American,* June 16, 1918.
20. *Chicago Tribune,* June 19, 1918.
21. *Chicago Tribune,* June 28, 1918.
22. *Boston American,* June 29, 1918.
23. *Chicago Tribune,* February 8, 1921.
24. *New York Times,* September 27, 1920.

CHAPTER 10

1. Duffey wrote in the *Post,* "Several of the players are following the movements of the Allies by means of maps clipped from various newspapers and every evening a Board of Strategy including Hooper, Walter Mayer, Strunk and a few more gather after dinner to just see what improvements the day's doings have produced in the situation over there." He joked about the players' mispronunciations.
2. The *New York Times* reported that the capture of Vaux Village on July 2, was, for the Americans, "the most important military operation they have so far executed."
3. Zingg, *Harry Hooper,* p. 39.
4. Ritter, *The Glory of Their Times,* p. 139. Hooper worked for Western Pacific railroad while playing for Sacramento and explained, "I played with the Sacramento club mainly because they promised to get me a surveying job."
5. Jennings did say this—and more—about Hooper in 1913. The quotes are in Hooper's file at the Hall of Fame.
6. *Sports Today,* August 1971.
7. Letter from Harry Hooper to writer Lee Allen, dated May 10, 1963. Located in Hooper's file at the Hall of Fame.
8. *Boston Globe,* July 4, 1918.
9. Letter from Harry Hooper to writer Lee Allen, dated May 10, 1963. Located in Hooper's file at the Hall of Fame.
10. *The Sporting News,* July 11, 1918.
11. *Boston Globe,* July 5, 1918.
12. *Boston Globe,* July 5, 1918.
13. *Sports Collector's Digest,* November 3, 2000. Thomas acknowledged that joining the navy with diabetes wasn't the smartest thing. "I shouldn't have done that," he said, "but I did."

14. *Boston American*, July 13, 1918.
15. *Boston Globe*, July 10, 1918. Mrs. High was typical. Baseball wives frequently pressured their husbands to join the shipyard so they could make money and avoid the war.
16. Ritter, *The Glory of Their Times*, p. 145.
17. *Chicago Tribune*, July 12, 1918.
18. *Boston American*, July 9, 1918.
19. *Washington Post*, July 20, 1918.
20. *Washington Post*, July 21, 1918.
21. *Boston Globe*, July 21, 1918.
22. *Washington Post*, July 23, 1918.
23. *Chicago Tribune*, July 23, 1918.
24. Zingg, *Harry Hooper*, p. 154.
25. *Boston Globe*, July 27, 1918.
26. *The Sporting News.* November 11, 1920.

Chapter 11

1. Allen, *The National League Story*, p. 160.
2. *Chicago Tribune*, June 24, 1920.
3. *Boston American*, July 28, 1918.
4. *Chicago Tribune*, July 29, 1918.
5. *Chicago Tribune*, July 31, 1918.
6. *Chicago Tribune*, July 28, 1918.
7. Ruether's letter is part of the Chicago History Museum's Asinof papers collection.
8. The Department of Labor features an "inflation calculator" at bls .gov/data/inflation_calculator.htm.
9. Evenden, E. S. *Teachers' Salaries and Schedules in the United States, 1918–1919*, p. 109.
10. *New York Times*, August 28, 1918.
11. *Boston Globe*, July 26, 1918.
12. *The Sporting News*, August 13, 1942.
13. *New York Times*, September 22, 1910.
14. Lieb, *Baseball as I Have Known It*, p. 98.
15. *The Sporting News*, June 6, 1918.
16. From writer Lawrence Ritter's interview with Roush, available on compact disc at the Baseball Hall of Fame.

17. *The Sporting News*, August 15, 1918.
18. *The Sporting News*, April 23, 1947.
19. Dewey and Acocella, *The Black Prince of Baseball*, p. XII.

CHAPTER 12

1. The East Coast experienced a brutal heat and humidity wave in early August, and the *New York Times* reported on August 6, 1918, "that some 400,000 persons were at Coney Island and the nearby resorts."
2. The details of Jacob Hollocher's early life can be found in census data on ancestry.com. He did grow up on a farm, began working for his brother (who was 24 years older than he was), and settled into life insurance thereafter. When Charley was young, Jacob pushed him into baseball.
3. Charley's brother, Louis Milton Hollocher, did have a middling minor-league career as a second baseman, batting .217 in a brief stint with Spokane in 1918 and then returning to the game after the war from 1920 to 1926, primarily for Terre Haute in the Three-I League. In the October 1918 edition of *Baseball Magazine*, Hollocher told of his brother's enlistment and the letter he'd sent from Parris Island. According to census data, Milton also got married before joining the marines.
4. On August 3, 1918, the *Chicago Daily News* reported, "Hollocher was given a box of cigars for getting the first hit of the game. The smokes were presented by a naval officer. Hollocher said, 'Thank you,' for the gift, but, as he did not use tobacco, passed them to the sailors in the stands."
5. *Chicago Tribune*, June 10, 1918.
6. *Chicago Tribune*, August 6, 1918.
7. *Chicago Daily News*, August 23, 1918.
8. *Chicago Tribune*, August 3, 1918.
9. *Boston Globe*, August 4, 1918.
10. *Boston Globe*, August 11, 1918.
11. *Chicago Tribune*, August 5, 1918.
12. *Chicago Tribune*, April 3, 1918.
13. *Chicago Tribune*, May 10, 1918.
14. *Chicago Tribune*, April 14, 1918.
15. *Chicago Tribune*, January 20, 1918.

16. *Chicago Daily News*, August 10, 1918.
17. *Chicago Tribune*, August 18, 1918.
18. *St. Louis Post-Dispatch*, January 26, 1933.
19. *Chicago Tribune*, August 5, 1923.
20. *St. Louis Post-Dispatch*, August 15, 1940.

CHAPTER 13

1. In November 1920, Carl Mays opened up to *Baseball Magazine* about his history of unpopularity, which followed him wherever he went in the game. Notes 1–3 are taken almost verbatim from quotes of Mays's in the *Baseball Magazine* interview. This exact quote went: "There is such a thing as popularity. We all know people who are popular without being able to explain why they should be. We also know people who are not popular, and yet they may be even more deserving of respect. Popularity does not necessarily rest on merit. Nor is unpopularity necessarily deserved."
2. *Baseball Magazine*, November 1920.
3. *Baseball Magazine*, November 1920.
4. *Boston Globe*, August 11, 1918.
5. Nowlin, *When Boston Still Had the Babe*, p. 81. Mays is described as having "the disposition of a man with a permanent toothache."
6. *Baseball Magazine*, November 1920.
7. *Baseball Magazine*, June 1918.
8. *The Sporting News*, August 22, 1918.
9. *Baseball Magazine*, October 1918.
10. *Chicago Daily News*, August 29, 1918.
11. *The Sporting News*, August 22, 1918.
12. *Chicago American*, August 16, 1918.
13. From the diary of 89th Division soldier Andrew Oleson, at olesons.com/diary.htm.
14. *The Sporting News*, September 12, 1918.
15. *Boston Globe*, August 30, 1918.
16. *Boston Herald*, August 31, 1918.
17. *Chicago Tribune*, August 31, 1918.
18. *Chicago Tribune*, September 2, 1918.
19. *The Sporting News*, August 22, 1918.
20. *Chicago American*, August 1, 1918.

21. *Chicago American*, July 19, 1918.
22. Farwell, *Over There*, p. 185.
23. *New York Times*, August 14, 1918.
24. *Baseball Magazine*, November 1920.

CHAPTER 14

1. Description of the scene at the Federal Building is taken from September 5, 1918, editions of the *Chicago Tribune, Chicago Herald Examiner*, and *Chicago Daily News*.
2. *Chicago Tribune*, September 5, 1918.
3. *Boston Globe*, September 5, 1918.
4. *Chicago Daily Journal*, September 5, 1918.
5. *Boston American*, September 5, 1918.
6. *Chicago Daily Journal*, September 5, 1918.
7. *Chicago American*, August 21, 1918.
8. *Boston Post*, September 1, 1918.
9. *Chicago Tribune*, August 18, 1918.
10. *The Sporting News*, August 29, 1918.
11. *Boston Herald*, September 5, 1918.
12. *Chicago Herald Examiner*, September 5, 1918.
13. *Boston Post*, September 5, 1918.
14. *Baseball Magazine*, October 1918.
15. *Boston Herald*, September 5, 1918.
16. *Boston Herald*, September 4, 1918.
17. Fowler, *Skyline*, p. 109.
18. *Boston American*, September 6, 1918.
19. *Boston American*, September 6, 1918.
20. *Chicago Tribune*, September 6, 1918.
21. *Boston Post*, September 7, 1918.
22. *Chicago Tribune*, September 6, 1918.
23. *New York Times*, September 6, 1918.

CHAPTER 15

1. *Chicago Tribune*, September 8, 1918.
2. *Chicago Tribune*, September 7, 1918.
3. *Chicago American*, September 4, 1918.

4. *Chicago Herald Examiner*, September 7, 1918.
5. *The Sporting News*, September 12, 1918.
6. *The Sporting News*, September 12, 1918.
7. *Chicago Tribune*, September 4, 1918.
8. *Boston American*, September 7, 1918.
9. *Boston American*, September 7, 1918.
10. *Boston American*, September 8, 1918.
11. *New York Times*, September 8, 1918.
12. *Chicago Herald Examiner*, September 9, 1918.
13. *Chicago Herald Examiner*, September 8, 1918.
14. *The Sporting News*, September 12, 1918.
15. *Sports Collectors Digest*, November 3, 2000.
16. *Chicago Tribune*, July 11, 1921.
17. *Chicago Tribune*, May 30, 1966.
18. *Chicago Tribune*, December 28, 1921.

CHAPTER 16

1. *Boston Post*, September 9, 1918.
2. *Boston Post*, September 11, 1918.
3. *The Sporting News*, February 21, 1918.
4. *Chicago Tribune*, September 8, 1918.
5. *Boston Globe*, September 10, 1918.
6. *Boston Globe*, September 10, 1918.
7. *Chicago Herald Examiner*, September 10, 1918.
8. *New York Times*, September 10, 1918.
9. *Boston Globe*, September 10, 1918.
10. *Boston Post*, September 10, 1918.
11. *Chicago Herald Examiner*, September 11, 1918.
12. *Boston American*, September 10, 1918.
13. *Pawtucket Times*, August 24, 1975.
14. *Boston Herald*, September 11, 1918.
15. *Boston Globe*, September 11, 1918.
16. *The Sporting News*, January 31, 1918.
17. *New Yorker*, May 12, 1956.
18. *New York Times*, August 17, 1922.
19. *New York Times*, August 17, 1922.

Chapter 17

1. Asinof, *Eight Men Out*, p. 172.
2. Dewey and Acocella, *The Black Prince of Baseball*, p. 277.
3. From Ritter's interview with Roush, available on CD at the Baseball Hall of Fame.
4. Asinof, *Eight Men Out*, p. 13.
5. *Boston Globe*, September 11, 1918.
6. *Chicago Herald Examiner*, September 12, 1918.
7. *Boston American*, September 11, 1918.
8. *New York Times*, September 12, 1918.
9. *Chicago Tribune*, September 12, 1918.
10. *Boston American*, September 12, 1918.
11. *Hartford Courant*, September 12, 1918.
12. *Boston American*, September 12, 1918.
13. *Chicago Daily Journal*, September 12, 1918.
14. *New York Times*, September 12, 1918.
15. *Chicago Daily Journal*, September 12, 1918.
16. *Hartford Courant*, September 12, 1918.
17. *Chicago Tribune*, September 12, 1918.
18. *New York Times*, September 12, 1918.
19. *Boston American*, September 12, 1918.
20. *Chicago Daily Journal*, September 14, 1918.
21. The doctor's quote can be found at http://1918.pandemicflu.gov/your_state/massachusetts.htm.
22. Venson, *The United States in the First World War*, p. 577.
23. *The Sporting News*, November 20, 1919.

Chapter 18

1. *Chicago Tribune*, December 29, 1918.
2. *Pawtucket Times*, August 24, 1975.
3. The letter is in George Whiteman's file at the Baseball Hall of Fame.
4. The letter is in Les Mann's file at the Baseball Hall of Fame.

BIBLIOGRAPHY

Abbott, Dr. W. C.; Burdick, Dr. A. S.; Waugh, Dr. W. F.; Slee, Dr. Richard; Achard, Dr. H. J. *The American Journal of Clinical Medicine.* Chicago: The American Journal of Clinical Medicine, 1914.

Ahrens, Art, and Gold, Eddie. *Day by Day in Chicago Cubs History.* West Point, N.Y.: Leisure Press, 1982.

Alexander, Charles C. *John McGraw.* Lincoln, Neb.: University of Nebraska Press, 1995.

Allen, Lee. *The National League Story.* New York: Hill and Wang, 1961.

Asbury, Herbert. *The Gangs of Chicago.* New York: Basic Books, 1940.

Asbury, Herbert. *Sucker's Progress: An Informal History of Gambling in America from the Colonies to Canfield.* New York: Dodd Mead, 1938.

Asinof, Eliot. *Eight Men Out: The Black Sox and the 1919 World Series.* New York: Henry Holt and Company, LLC, 1966.

Beaver, Daniel R. *Newton D. Baker and the American War Effort, 1917–19.* Lincoln, Neb.: University of Nebraska Press, 1966.

Carney, Gene. *Burying the Black Sox.* Washington, D.C.: Potomac Books, 2007.

Clark, Tom. *One Last Round for the Shuffler.* New York: Truck Books, 1979.

Creamer, Robert W. *Babe: The Legend Comes to Life.* New York: Simon & Schuster Paperbacks, 1974.

Dewey, Donald, and Acocella, Nicholas. *The Black Prince of Baseball: Hal Chase and the Mythology of Baseball.* Wilmington, Del.: Sport Media Publishing Inc., 2004.

Duis, Perry R. *Challenging Chicago: Coping with Everyday Life, 1837–1920.* Urbana, Ill.: The University of Illinois Press, 1998.

Ellis, Edward Robb. *Echoes of Distant Thunder: Life in the United States, 1914–1918.* New York: Kodansha, 1996.

Evenden, E.S. *Teachers' Salaries and Schedules in the United States, 1918–1919.* Washington, D.C.: National Education Association, 1919.

Farwell, Byron. *Over There: The United States in the Great War, 1917–1918.* New York: W. W. Norton & Company, Inc., 1999.

Fowler, Gene. *Skyline.* New York: The Viking Press, 1961.

Ginsburg, Daniel E. *The Fix Is In.* Jefferson, N.C.: McFarland & Company, Inc., 2003.

Holli, Melvin G, and Jones, Peter. *Ethnic Chicago: A Multicultural Portrait.* Grand Rapids, Mich.: Wm. B. Eerdmans Publishing Company, 1977.

James, Bill. *The New Bill James Historical Baseball Abstract.* New York: The Free Press, 2001.

Jones, David. *Deadball Stars of the American League.* Dulles, Va.: Potomac Books, 2006.

Katcher, Leo. *The Big Bankroll: The Life and Times of Arnold Rothstein.* New York: Da Capo Press, 1959.

Kavanagh, Jack. *Ol' Pete: The Grover Cleveland Alexander Story.* South Bend, Ind.: Diamond Communications, Inc., 1996.

Keene, Kerry, Sinibaldi, Raymond, and Hickey, David. *The Babe in Red Stockings: An In-Depth Chronicle of Babe Ruth with the Boston Red Sox, 1914–1919.* Champaign, Ill.: Sagamore Publishing, 1997.

Kennedy, David M. *Over Here: The First World War and American Society.* New York: Oxford University Press, 1980.

Kohout, Martin Donnell. *Hal Chase: The Defiant Life and Turbulent Times of Baseball's Biggest Crook.* Jefferson, N.C.: McFarland & Company, Inc., 2001.

Levitt, Daniel R. *Ed Barrow: The Bulldog Who Built the Yankees' First Dynasty.* Lincoln, Neb.: The University of Nebraska Press, 2008.

Lieb, Fred. *Baseball as I Have Known It.* Lincoln, Neb.: University of Nebraska Press, 1977.

Lynch, Michael T., Jr. *Harry Frazee, Ban Johnson, and the Feud That Nearly Destroyed the American League.* Jefferson, N.C.: McFarland & Company, Inc., Publishers, 2008.

Marshall, S.L.A., *World War I.* New York: Mariner Books, 2001.

Mayer, Harold M., and Wade, Richard C. *Chicago: Growth of a Metropolis.* Chicago: University of Chicago Press, 1969.

Montville, Leigh. *The Big Bam: The Life and Times of Babe Ruth.* New York: Doubleday, 2006.

Morgan, Anna. *My Chicago (1918)*. Chicago: Ralph Fletcher Seymour, date unknown.

Murdock, Eugene. *Ban Johnson: Czar of Baseball*. Westport, Conn.: Greenwood Press, 1982.

Murphy, Cait. *Crazy '08*. New York: HarperCollins Publishers Inc., 2007.

Nowlin, Bill. *When Boston Still Had the Babe: The 1918 World Champion Red Sox*. Burlington, Mass.: Rounder Books, 2008.

Pietrusza, David. *Judge and Jury: The Life and Times of Judge Kenesaw Mountain Landis*. South Bend, Ind.: Diamond Communications, Inc., 1998.

Pietrusza, David. *Rothstein: The Life, Times, and Murder of the Criminal Genius Who Fixed the 1919 World Series*. New York: Carroll & Graf Publishers, 2003.

Ritter, Lawrence S. *The Glory of Their Times: The Story of the Early Days of Baseball Told by the Men Who Played It*. New York: Macmillan and Company, 1966.

Russo, Frank, and Racz, Gene. *Bury My Heart at Cooperstown: Salacious, Sad, and Surreal Deaths in the History of Baseball*. Chicago: Triumph Books, 2006.

Seymour, Harold. *Baseball: The Golden Age*. New York: Oxford University Press, 1971.

Seymour, Harold. *The Early Years*. New York: Oxford University Press, 1960.

Sheard, Bradley. *Lost Voyages: Two Centuries of Shipwrecks in the Approaches to New York*. New York: Aqua Quest Publications, Inc., 1998.

Simon, Tom. *Deadball Stars of the National League*. Dulles, Va.: Brassey's, Inc, 2004.

Skipper, John C. *Wicked Curve: The Life and Troubled Times of Grover Cleveland Alexander*. Jefferson, N.C.: McFarland & Company, Inc., 2003.

Sowell, Mike. *The Pitch That Killed*. New York: Collier Books, 1989.

Spink, J. G. Taylor. *Judge Landis and Twenty-Five Years of Baseball*. New York: Thomas Y. Crowell, 1947.

Stout, Glenn, and Johnson, Richard A. *The Cubs*. New York: Houghton Mifflin Company, 2007.

Stout, Glenn, and Johnson, Richard A. *Red Sox Century*. New York: Houghton Mifflin Company, 2000.

Sullivan, Dean A. *Middle Innings: A Documentary of Baseball, 1900–1948*. Lincoln, Neb.: University of Nebraska Press, 1998.

Veeck, Bill, and Linn, Ed. *The Hustler's Handbook*. New York: Fireside, 1965.

Venson, Anne Cipriano. *The United States in the First World War*. New York and London: Garland, 1995.

Vice Commission of Chicago. *The Social Evil in Chicago*. Chicago: Gunthorp-Warren Printing Company, 1911.

Willmott, H. P. *World War I*. New York: DK Publishing, 2003.

Zingg, Paul J. *Harry Hooper*. Urbana, Ill.: The University of Illinois Press, 1993.

INDEX